REGIONAL IMPACT OF COMMUNITY POLICIES IN EUROPE

Regional Impact of Community Policies in Europe

Edited by
WILLEM MOLLE
Nederlands Economisch Instituut, Rotterdam

and
RICCARDO CAPPELLIN
Università Commerciale Luigi Bocconi, Milano

Avebury

Aldershot · Brookfield USA · Hong Kong · Singapore · Sydney

© Netherlands Economic Institute 1988

Published by
Avebury

Gower Publishing Company Limited
Gower House
Croft Road
Aldershot
Hants GU11 3HR
England

Gower Publishing Company
Old Post Road
Brookfield
Vermont 05036
USA

British Library Cataloguing in Publication Data
Regional impact of Community policies
   in Europe.——(Studies in spatial
   analysis).
   1. European Economic Community——
   Economic policy
   2. European Economic Community
   countries——Economic conditions
   I. Molle,W.T.M.   II. Cappellin, Riccardo
   III. Series
   330.94   HC241.2
Library of Congress Cataloging-in-Publication Data

Regional impact of Community policies in Europe.

   (Studies in spatial analysis)
   Includes bibliographies.
   1. European Economic Community countries--Economic
conditions--Regional disparities. 2. Regional
planning--European Economic Community countries.
3. Europe--Economic integration. I. Molle, Willem.
II. Cappellin, Riccardo. III. Series.
HC241.2.R427 1988   330.94'0558   87-26974
ISBN 0-566-05587-2

Printed and bound in Great Britain by
Athanaeum Press Limited, Newcastle-upon-Tyne

Contents

Contributors

Bernard Bourgeois	Institut Economique et Juridique de l'Energie, Grenoble (France)
Rafaele Brancati	Centro Studie di Politica Economica, Rome (Italy)
Johannes Bröcker	Institut für Regionalforschung, Universität Kiel (Federal Republic of Germany)
Riccardo Cappellin	Università Luigi Bocconi, Milano (Italy)
Brian Fullerton	Department of Geography, University of Newcastle upon Tyne (United Kingdom)
Andrew Gillespie	Centre for Urban and Regional Development Studies, University of Newcastle upon Tyne (United Kingdom)
Willem Molle	Nederlands Economisch Instituut, Rotterdam (The Netherlands)
Karin Peschel	Institut für Regionalforschung, Universität Kiel (Federal Republic of Germany)
Wolfgang Steinle	Empirica, Bonn (Federal Republic of Germany)
Dirk Strijker	Landbouw-Economisch Instituut, 's-Gravenhage (The Netherlands)
Jan de Veer	Landbouw-Economisch Instituut, 's-Gravenhage (The Netherlands)

Preface

The European Community could not have realised its integration objectives without major structural adaptations of the economies of the member states, which often had profound regional effects. As the EC developed and common policies evolved in the areas of agriculture, trade, coal and steel, and energy, it became clear that the daily functioning of the EC, too, affected the regions deeply.

Now the preamble to the Treaty of Rome had stated as one objective of integration "to reduce the differences existing between the various regions and the backwardness of the less favoured regions". Mindful of that injunction, the Commission undertook to co-ordinate its own policies, trying to estimate their probable impact before making them definitive. Because little was as yet known of it, the impact of EC policies on regions became a major object of study. Many relevant investigations have been carried out, some initiated and financed by the Commission, others on the initiative of researchers. Up till now access to the results of these studies has been rather difficult, as they had been published either not at all or only partly in widely disparate journals and series. The first objective of this book is to bring these studies together into one volume to facilitate a comprehensive study. To that end a first exchange of views among the authors took place at the 1984 European Conference of the Regional Science Association in Milan. It became clear there that the available material, once systematised and completed, would permit a 'state of the art' of the subject. Finding the missing links proved a harder job than foreseen; however, the various contributors have co-operated excellently to meet the standards and fit the structure set for this book. Many thanks are due for their friendly support.

Other persons beside the authors have been most helpful. We cannot mention them all, but want to thank in particular Dr. Wäldchen of the Commission and many of his colleagues for stimulating our thoughts during many discussion sessions on the various subjects treated in the book. Thanks also to Hein van Haselen and Michele Polo for the useful material they have contributed. A special word of thanks is due to Mrs Elderson, who has edited the English, identifying errors of

ix

presentation and failures in consistency as she went, and who typed the whole manuscript with the skill and diligence which characterise her.

Willem Molle
Riccardo Cappellin

1 The Co-ordination Problem in Theory and Policy

R. CAPPELLIN and W. MOLLE

1.1. Introduction

The regional problems facing the European Community are of long standing and have become more pronounced since Greece, Spain and Portugal joined up. Because the disparities among the regions of Europe were considered politically unacceptable, for some decades a regional policy has been pursued on the European level. However, by now we have come to understand that any improvement achieved by regional policy, may be undone by the (sometimes unforeseen) regional effects of other policies. This book sets out to analyse the type and magnitude of such effects.

Before attacking that central point, we will in this first chapter give an idea of the importance of the regional problems in Europe. Their cause has long been debated among theorists and politicians concerned with regional economic development. We will briefly review the most important theoretical explanations, thus painting the background against which the policy effects can be studied.

To remedy the effects of all sorts of policy measure, regional policy is often resorted to. A good understanding of the role of regional policy can make us appreciate the policy measures that will be discussed in detail in subsequent chapters. Therefore, a section of this chapter will be devoted to regional policy.

Finally, we will draw up a general framework for the analysis of the question with which this book is concerned, which is, how the regions of the Community are affected by its policies.

1.2. Regional problems and disparities

1.2.1. Disparities in wealth levels

Regional problems in the EC are usually assessed with the help of only a few indicators. For purposes of policy making, the EC itself (CEC 1984a) uses the so-
called synthetic indicator, which is composed of GDP per capita and unemployment. A geographical picture of the differences in GDP/P-levels is given in map
1.1; the results of statistical analyses by Molle et al. (1980) for the EC9 and by
van Haselen and Molle (1980) for the EC12 are reproduced in the table below.

Table 1.1
Theil-indices of GDP per capita in the EC, 1950-1977

	EC9				EC12			
	1950	1960	1970	1977	1950	1960	1970	1977
Total	.068	.047	.039	.068	.125	.102	.073	0.100
Country	.040	.028	.023	.052	.095	.081	.061	.083
%	59	55	59	76	76	79	78	83

Source: van Haselen and Molle (1980).

The table clearly indicates that the disparity among regions had diminished a
great deal in the period 1950-1970, but stood to increase considerably with the
extension of the EC: the index of Theil for the EC12 is about double that for the
EC9. Or, more specifically: the ratio between the income levels of the richest and
the poorest regions, only 5 for the EC9, would increase to 14 for the EC12.

Disparities reflect for the most part differences among nations; they diminished
in the years between 1950-1970 because the lower-income countries were growing
faster than the EC average. Regional factors are responsible for the remaining
part of the disparities; indeed, the flow of capital from rich to poor regions and of
labour from poor to rich regions helped to reduce the regional disparities. The development of the welfare state was a third important factor (Molle 1986).

The economic and monetary depression following upon the 1973 oil crisis has
disturbed some tendencies towards equilibrium. The table shows that in particular
the 'national' disparities have widened, while the 'regional' component has shown
itself rather stable.

In a recent study, Clausse, Girard and Rion (1986) try to shed some light on the
latest trends in the EC10. Some of their results are given in the next table. To
circumvent possible distortions due to the turbulent exchange rates of the period,
they have calculated their indices not only in ECU (on the basis of exchange
rates), but also in purchasing-power parities (PPP).

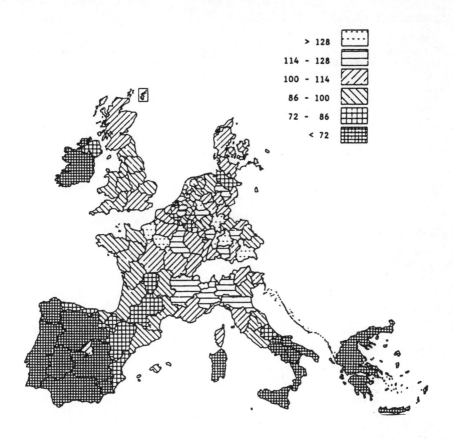

> 128	
114 - 128	
100 - 114	
86 - 100	
72 - 86	
< 72	

Map 1.1
Differences in GDP:P levels in the EC 1980;
EUR12 = 100 (purchasing-power parities)

The next table, based on their analysis, shows that after the turbulence in 1982, the index of disparity settled on approximately the 1970 level, both in ECU and in PPP. The table also reveals that the use of PPP tends to attenuate the differences in the indicators commonly used: actually, the fast change between 1970 and 1978 registered in the bottom row of percentages is not at all reflected in the upper row of percentages; moreover, in 1970 as well as in 1982, the figures of the latter are one third lower only than those of the former[2].

3

Table 1.2
Theil-indices of GNP/P disparity, EC10, 1970-1984

	1970	1974	1978	1984
GNP/P (PPP)				
Theil index, total	1.24	1.20	1.20	1.27
national component	0.45	0.41	0.44	0.45
%	37	34	37	36
GNP/P (ECU)				
Theil index, total	1.83	2.63	3.17	1.94
national component	1.04	1.85	2.43	1.15
%	57	70	77	59

Source: Clausse et al., 1986.

1.2.2. Other indicators

Other indicators often used to identify problem regions are unemployment and outmigration.

Unemployment has been growing fast all over the EC, as is evident from the following table.

Table 1.3
Unemployment as a percentage of the total labour force (EC9)
1950-1985

Country	1950	1960	1970	1980	1985
Germany	9	1	1	4	9
United Kingdom	2	2	3	8	12
Italy	9	8	5	9	13
France	1	1	1	7	11
The Netherlands	2	1	1	5	14
Belgium	5	4	3	11	14
Denmark	3	2	1	7	9
Ireland	5	5	6	10	17
EC	5	3	2	7	11

Source: Eurostat and NEI.

Region-wise, unemployment is strongly concentrated in Southern Italy, the United Kingdom and Ireland (except the South East), and to a lesser extent in South West France. Some other regions, such as Nord/Pas de Calais, and Wallonie, are also severely afflicted. For the three new entrants, comparable figures are not available.

The combination of low GDP/P and much unemployment is often due, either to a concentration of agriculture, coupled with a deficient development of modern economic activities (as in Southern Italy and Ireland), or to restructuring problems of old industrial areas (as in Nord/Pas de Calais, central England). That explains why agricultural and industrial policies are so essential to regional equilibrium. The world-wide competition with which old established industries find themselves faced once the European market is opened to external trade, also entails problems. Lack of equipment and infrastructure are further causes of underdevelopment, which warrants a closer look at energy, transport and communication aspects. Traditionally, the lack of qualified manpower is cited as a major obstacle to development, which social policies are trying to overcome[3].

1.3. Theories and policies of regional development

1.3.1. The traditional approaches

Much thought has been given by regional theorists to the factors underlying regional differentiation. Various schools of thought are reflected in their theories. The traditional ones are closely associated with more general economic thinking, in particular (neo)classical and Keynesian theories; both of them set great store by factor mobility (capital and labour) and have greatly affected the way in which regional economic policies were devised[4].

According to the neoclassical model (Borts and Stein 1964, Siebert 1970) the evolution of regional disparities depends on the availability and interregional mobility of production factors. Flexible prices and wages on regional markets guarantee the full utilisation of regional resources. Capital tends to move to regions where labour is cheap and abundant. Therefore, the neoclassical policy was to try and increase the return on investments in the less developed regions, and reduce the gap between private and social costs or benefits by credits and fiscal incentives and by improving the industrial infrastructure. Moreover, interregional mobility of the labour force (migration) may help to abate unemployment in the less developed regions and raise the welfare of both individual workers and the national economy. So, at one stage in the development, schemes to stimulate migration were drawn up.

The neoclassical growth model was criticised by many because it overlooked scale economies, large non-marginal investments and external economies. All critics moreover stressed demand factors, so we may call them Keynesians. The critics developed models such as the cumulative-growth model (Myrdall 1957, Hirschmann 1958, Kaldor 1970, Holland 1976), the export-base model (North 1953, Czamanski 1964) and the development-pole model (Perroux 1955, Paelinck 1965, Hansen 1972). The export-base model, stressing the importance of an elastic demand for regional exports and taking into account intersectoral linkages and intermediate demand, has become the most prominent. Like the neoclassical one, it attributes great importance to the mobility of capital and labour.

Agglomeration economies and indivisibilities stimulate the progressive growth of productivity and production in the most developed regions. Less developed regions, on the contrary, may suffer if workers migrate to other regions, leaving their markets depleted and their labour supply deprived of young and skilled workers, while capital is prevented from moving to the less developed ones by various obstacles. Hence the frequently heard argument that such indirect measures as incentives and infrastructure policy fail to diminish disparities; direct investments of large public and private corporations are needed, and public authorities should stimulate these by administrative constraints and contracts. On the intraregional and urban levels, the authorities should try and curb autonomous growth processes by tight zoning regulations. Central areas would then become less congested and a better spatial balance could be achieved between central and more peripheral regions.

According to Keynesian theory, macro-economic policies of demand management may fail to counterbalance the spontaneous market forces that favour regional disparity; therefore, economic efficiency should be partly sacrificed to more social equity, and redistributive policies should be introduced to help the less favoured regions by sustaining their consumption levels, improving their social services and creating employment in public administration.

The Keynesian approach to regional policy has been criticised for various reasons. Large firms located in peripheral areas have failed to achieve the hoped-for self-sustained growth of these areas. Any positive effects are indirect, and minor in respect of the resources employed. Large plants have even had a negative effect on local labour markets, jeopardising the small local industrial activities already in existence. Extensive public transfers and a growing public sector have weakened the autonomy of these regions and quelled any inclination towards new and efficient industrial enterprise. Indeed, the economy has prospered more in intermediate regions, where national regional policies have intervened far less. In intermediate regions, the growth of small firms has been more important than the establishment of branch plants of large national or international firms.

Geographically and sectorally, spatial diffusion proceeded at a gradual pace (Camagni and Cappellin 1981). In fact, following the major transportation routes, it affected first the intermediate regions contiguous to the most developed ones. Growth in these intermediate regions was intersectorally balanced, as all sectors were growing at an above-average rate. Overall productivity and per capita income rose by the gradual reconversion of labour resources from low-productivity to high-productivity sectors.

From various empirical studies (Klaassen and Molle 1982, for instance), most industrial movements appear to have been short-distance ones. The shift of industrial production to intermediate and peripheral regions has been determined by 'implicit' relocations due to the different birth and death rates of firms in the various regions (Gudgin 1978). In intermediate and peripheral regions, the creation of many small firms has increased industrial employment. Local entrepreneurial qualities have been decisive for the development of these regions. Small firms adjust more readily to changes in the economic environment, and a favourable regional environment has enabled them to keep their production costs in check.

Moreover, labour migrations have decreased. The negative migration balance of some peripheral regions has reversed owing to the decrease of industrial employment in the most developed regions and the gradual improvement of living conditions in the less developed regions.

When the economic recession hit all industrialised countries in the 1970s, inflation and balance-of-payment problems forced national governments to adopt restrictive monetary and fiscal policies. As a result, large firms became loth to invest in, and move their plants to, the less developed regions, and the resources devoted to interregional policy dried up. Actually, high inflation rates, troubled labour relations, and the increasing congestion of large metropolitan areas have reduced many large firms in metropolitan areas to severe difficulties, while small firms in intermediate and peripheral areas enjoyed a relative advantage in production costs. The need to restructure the production processes and increase productivity made firms adopt process innovations and labour-saving technologies. The changed macro-economic and sectoral evolution of European economies led to the decentralisation of industrial production and to an increasing spatial separation between service and manufacturing phases.

1.3.2. The endogenous-growth approach

The failure of interregional policy schemes on the national level and the weakening interregional mobility of firms and labour force gave rise to a new approach to regional development, which may be called the "endogenous" approach (Richardson 1978, Ciciotti and Wettmann 1981, Biehl 1980, Cappellin 1983a, Aydalot 1985).

Theories of endogenous growth are based on the assumption of a sharp contrast between the increasing mobility of goods and the stability of regional environments characterised by such factors as the skills of the labour force, technical and organisational know-how, social and institutional structures. Regional policy should, therefore, aim not so much at the mobility of production factors - as was suggested in neoclassical and Keynesian approaches -, as at the full use and productivity of local resources.

In the endogenous approach, regional development is not interpreted as the effect of the "optimum" choice of locations by interregional firms, but as the effect of local firms in individual regions taking up appropriate productions. In that view, a region's sectoral specialisation is determined by a process of natural selection: firms which fit the local environment survive and thrive while others wither and die.

As a result, adherents to the endogenous approach now focus on the analysis of regional location factors, while neoclassicists and Keynesians attributed but a minor role to spatial factors or considered only labour costs and agglomeration economies relevant.

Early comments on the endogenous-growth approach, written in the 1970s, emphasised the spatial separation of various production stages within the production processes (Crum and Gudgin 1977, Hamilton 1978), the development of local systems characterised by the flexibility of small firms and the economies of scale of large ones (Garofoli 1983, Fua' and Zacchia 1983). Other authors have stressed the role of institutions and political factors, such as the 'autonomy' (Stöhr and Todtling 1982, Aydalot 1985) with respect to non-local firms and national policies.

The evolution of the national economies during the late 1980s, the gradual recovery from the recession of the previous decade, lower inflation rates, increasing corporate profits, the progressive internationalisation of firms, the diffusion of new 'technological paradigms' which horizontally affect all sectors, have changed the external conditions of regional development.

With increased demand, product innovations became more alluring than process innovations: to make new products, to differentiate or improve them, grew more important than to reduce production costs. By the same token, entrepreneurs preferred "soft" investments in "human capital" to investments in machinery for further automation of production processes. While industrial employment is on the wane, hi-tech activities are waxing fast. In high-skill professions, the absolute level of employment has risen even within industrial activities, and employment in service sectors has grown fast. Technological ability rather than capital is becoming the crucial "barrier to entry" in new productions and new markets. So, the development of the local ecnomy depends on its capacity to transfer its resources from old activities to new ones, notably by mastering new product technologies. R&D stimulation, training, improved information and know-how were the new topics.

Unlike earlier contributions, which stressed the importance of production costs, recent contributions to the endogenous-growth approach emphasise the role of entrepreneurial factors and the diffusion of innovations (Ewers and Wettmann 1980,

Thwaites 1982, Cappellin 1983b, Molle 1983). Various theories emphasise that the development of a local economy depends on its capability continuously to reconvert its resources from old, less productive uses to new, more productive ones. According to the product-life-cycle model and the filtering-down model, traditional productions diffuse toward the less developed, more peripheral areas, following the urban hierarchy (Vernon 1966, Fred 1977, Pedersen 1970, Malecki 1983, Camagni, Diappi and Leonardi 1986, Noyelle and Stanback 1984, Nijkamp 1986). Therefore, to keep their relative development at par, central areas must attract new economic activities.

According to the incubator hypothesis, new productions grow in large urban areas because of external economies (Thompson 1968, Leone and Struyck 1976, Ciciotti 1984). The reconversion process of the various areas may also be determined by a 'crowding-out' effect similar to that occurring in the urban land market (Cappellin 1983a): more productive activities draw local, semi-fixed resources, such as labour, from the more traditional ones, which then must relocate to more peripheral areas.

The greatest contribution to the sectoral reconversion of urban areas and a major factor of recent changes in regional disparities is the growth of tertiary activities. The central, more developed regions record the highest levels and the greatest absolute increases of service occupations (Goddard 1975, Daniels and Holly 1983). Apparently, services grow fastest in the areas where industrial employment is declining. Their growth is not related to the quantitative growth of industrial activities, as the export-base model suggests, but to the technological change in industrial activities.

However, the possibility of exporting services to other areas renders the local supply of favourable inputs, such as skilled labour and access to information, more important than the local demand of services (Bailly et al. 1985, Cappellin 1986). This explains the growth of specialised and innovative services also in medium-size urban centres with a favourable local environment.

The importance of skilled labour to the growth of modern industrial and service activities may reverse the causal relationship between population growth and employment growth. In fact, according to the 'counterurbanisation' model (Fielding 1982, Van den Berg et al. 1986, Hall and Hay 1980, Klaassen et al. 1981), population grows faster in the smaller urban areas owing to the change in the residential preferences of the labour force. The quality of the natural, urban and social environment attracts to a region the most high-skilled labour, whose presence may then attract new technologically advanced economic activities to that region.

The endogenous approach, like the neoclassical approach, stresses the supply side of the regional economy but favours a more disaggregated analysis of regional endowments than the latter. From its emphasis on the qualitative evolution of local resources (human, venture capital, entrepreneurship) and smoothly operating local institutions, the endogenous approach appears to rely on active intervention; in that respect it is similar to the Keynesian aproach, which had more confidence in the role of the government and in entrepreneurs' "autonomous" investment decisions rather than in automatic market mechanisms.

The endogenous approach attributes more importance to local authorities than to national regional policies. Its adherents have advocated more generous administrative autonomy for regional communities, regional and subregional development programmes for all regions - not only those favoured by national governments and European Community - and the participation of all relevant economic subjects of individual regions.

Indeed, to promote technological change, in particular by disaggregating national schemes, was the crucial objective of regional policies in the 1980s. The successful conversion of regional economies requires new, technically advanced, infrastructure to improve the external environment, and local entrepreneurship to create new activities. To that end, the active collaboration between private and public institutions is indispensable.

1.3.3. Conclusions

This short survey of the theories of regional growth emphasises the close relationship between these theories and the changes in regional policy in the last few decades (Figure 1.1). Policy makers have turned from policies based on the mobility of production factors to policies mobilising the endogenous develpment and from policies aiming to contain production costs to policies aiming to mobilise entrepreneurship and innovations. These new theories and policies have sprung naturally from changes in the macroeconomic, sectoral, technological and spatial trends that mark the phases of economic development in European countries. Regional economic theories and policies have gradually absorbed such elements as cost factors of labour and capital, the provision of infrastructure, industrial and technology change, and many objects of national and Community policies.

Unfortunately, regional policies have often been less effective than had been hoped, because they tend to adjust but slowly to changes in the economic environment. For economic policies to be successful, the changes in the factors underlying regional disparities at different stages of economic development need to be carefully analysed. Indeed, regional policies which try to curb natural trends rather than affect the underlying factors, have rarely been successful.

1.4. Regional policy on the European level

1.4.1. Foundations of a European regional policy

Having briefly discussed the nature of European regional problems and the interface of theory and policy, let us now try to get an idea of the regional policy of the European Community[5]. The first question that arises is how European policy is distinct from national policy. A first difference lies in the executive agency. In the member states the policy maker is always the central government, the most complete incorporation of government authority and the umpire deciding about the equilibrium among the parts of its territory. These states themselves are regions of a larger territory, however. In the previous sections we have seen that within that larger territory there are 'balance' problems at least as serious as those within each EC member state. The question then arises who is responsible for the equilibrium among these "macro" regions. Until recently the answer to that question was univocal: the states themselves. In an effort to keep their prosperity at least at par with that of other countries, states availed themselves of all possible kinds of instruments, such as monetary policy, trade policy, national growth policy, policies with respect to capital and knowledge, and sometimes even military intervention. Indeed some of these instruments were sometimes applied not only to maintain the balance among states, but also to promote the equilibrium among regions of one state; a case in point is the use of tariffs to support the textile industry, which is strongly concentrated in a few regions.

9

PERIOD	THEORIES	POLICIES

A. FACTOR-MOBILITY APPROACH

1950

a. neoclassical approach

- neoclassical growth model
- welfare economics and
  cost/benefit analysis

a. neoclassical approach

- infrastructure policy

- capital-incentives policy

1960

b. Keynesian approach

- cumulative-development model

- export-base model
- polarised-development model

b. Keynesian approach

- investment incentives,
  administrative constraints
- location of public firms
- planning agreements with large
  private corporations
- public transfers to households
- growth of public-sector
  employment

B. ENDOGENOUS-GROWTH APPROACH

1970

a. production-cost approach

- functional-division-of-labour

- local-small-firms-system model
- autonomous-development model

a. production-cost approach

- administrative decentralisation
  and regional autonomy
- regional and subregional planning
- public-private co-operation
- incentives to industrial
  restructuring
- fiscal incentives to employment
  creation
- unemployment subsidies
- job-creation and small-firms
  policies

1980

b. innovation-diffusion approach

- incubator model

- product-life-cycle model
- urban filtering-down model

- service-location model
- counter-urbanisation model

b. innovation-diffusion approach

- R&D and business-service
  incentives
- export-development incentives
- professional and managerial
  education
- sectoral labour mobility
- venture capital
- environmental policies
- technological infrastructures
- metropolitan-system policies

Figure 1.1
Theories of regional development and regional policies
1950-1980

As Europe became united, and notably with the venue of the EC, the picture has changed. That the fathers of the EEC were quite aware of the regional problems is evident from the preamble of the Treaty of Rome, where it says that the member states are "anxious to reduce the differences existing between the various regions and the backwardness of the less favoured regions". Nevertheless, no proper European regional was provided for in the treaty of the European Economic Community, in spite of repeated warnings by academics (e.g. Giersch 1949) that European integration would spell problems for certain regions. Indeed, the creation of the Common Market and the development of a collective foreign-trade policy deprived member states of some instruments they had been using to further national and also regional growth if the supported industries were regionally concentrated. Moreover, through the harmonisation achieved especially on the industrial and social planes, national instruments in those fields have lost much of their implicit power to control regional developments. The realisation of an Economic and Monetary Union (EMU) (which for the time being is improbable) would curtail even more the instruments available to national states (Williamson 1976); for example, individual states could then no longer pursue a national exchange-rate policy.

So, measures of regional policy are necessary to cope with the possible effects of the initial (Customs Union) and progressive further (EMU) integration. Besides, the day-to-day functioning of the European Community needs the constant accompaniment of adequate measures of regional policy. Structural changes due to economic, technological, environmental and social developments continue to occur, demanding progressive adaptation. Unless by measures of regional policy compensation is given to regions suffering from these developments, the very functioning of the Community may be in jeopardy. A clear example is what has happened to the steel industry. The lack of alternative activities in "steel regions", where subsantial cutbacks in employment were necessary during the latest crisis, has induced certain member states to give heavy support to the established industry, to which other member states have responded by threatening to close the frontiers. Now that would mean a direct violation of the foundations of the Community (free market and international specialisation), jeopardising the whole European structure, on which the prosperity of Europe has meanwhile largely come to depend.

Obviously there is more than enough reason, not only on the national, but also on the European level, to put forward the traditional "economic-efficiency" argument in favour of a European regional policy. But the equity argument for regional policy also has a European dimension, insofar as a regional transfer of resources would be an act of solidarity between prosperous and less prosperous regions in Europe. The recent tendency of the European Community to emphasise social and human aspects as well as purely economic ones also favours efforts to improve regional equilibrium on the European level measures of regional policy.

1.4.2. Objectives and instruments

The objectives of European regional policy have been formulated at many places in different ways. One of the most representative official statements (CEC, 1977) defines the following two objectives:
-    to diminish current regional problems as they occur both in the traditionally less developed regions and in regions involved in a process of industrial or agrarian transformation;
-    to prevent new regional disparities that could result from structural changes in world economy, etc.
The obvious question is now what the EC has undertaken to attain these objectives. Little enough at first, mainly because it was poorly equipped for it. As a matter of fact, in 1958 nobody had an idea of the size and nature of regional problems on the European level. As we have seen, the Community took up its work

without receiving sufficient authority in regional matters from the Rome Treaty[6]. To obtain that authority turned out to be a long procedure. However, by dint of constant diligence the Commission has gradually acquired the necessary instruments, and the regional element has become more and more prominent among the policy areas of the EC.

The regional policy of the European Community is conducted in co-operation with the member states. Indeed, the Community's regional policy does not replace but complements the regional policies carried out by the member countries [7].

Four main tasks can usefully be distinguished.

1.   An activity taken on by the Commission at an early stage was that of <u>learning about the regional situation and regional developments</u> in the Community. On that subject the Commission has carried out or commissioned several studies (EC 1961, 1964, 1969, 1971, 1973, 1981, 1984a). The main purpose of the reports is to keep knowledge of the old problems up-to-date and to recognise new problems as soon as they present themselves. These reports also serve as a foundation for discussions with member states about priorities in regional policy and the changes to be carried through in this policy.

2.   A second task which the Commission had given itself was to <u>co-ordinate its own policies in a number of areas,</u> such as those of agriculture, social affairs, coal and steel, energy, industry, transport, foreign trade. Many policy measures taken in these fields affect regional development. To know how great their impact is in respect of total policy would help to consider the regional element when formulating policy measures.

3.   A third task of the Commission in the setting of regional policy is the <u>co-ordination of activities of member states.</u> As early as 1965 this was recognised as necessary, and a proposal was submitted to draw up regional programmes for the EC's problem regions. It took almost 10 years to get that proposal accepted, but at the moment a large number of policy programmes have already been published [8]. Their purpose is to establish clearly what measures the competent organisations in these regions are taking with respect to infrastructure, schooling, housing, etc., so that the EC can co-ordinate them, identify any gaps, and check the progress.

4.   A fourth and last task could finally be undertaken after years of negociations (in 1975)[9] , when with the creation of the <u>European Regional Development Fund</u> (ERDF) the European Commission acquired the financial means to intervene directly in the development of certain regions [10]. The Fund 3[9] ECU grants subsidies to stimulate investments in economic activities and to develop the infrastructure. To be eligible for investment support, activities must already be receiving aid from the member state in question or one of its agencies. The financial means of the Regional Fund are distributed by a flexible key that strongly favours low-income countries. Part of the Funds is destined to regions adversely affected by Community policy other than regional policy.

1.4.3. New regional developments; a new Fund regulation

To adapt the working of the ERDF to the exigencies of the new situation, three types of changes have recently been carried out.

The first relates to regional innovation. Indeed, the previous sections have described certain changes that have occurred in the general economic and regional development of Europe since the crisis of the early 1970s with important implications for regional policy. As a matter of fact, regional policy used to rely very much on mobile industry, and now that the sources for that type of activity have dried up, every region falls back on its own indigenous potential. Moreover, regions have to be innovative, for no more standard solutions from outside can be hoped for. The consequences of these changes were recently evaluated by the European Commission, and on the basis of its proposal to reorient EC policy the Council of Ministers has adopted a new regulation of the Fund, introducing three new types of measures (Reg EEC 1787/84 0.7.20.L 169,28.6.1984). Measures of the first type are those meant to help companies to advice on management and organisation questions, allowances for the development of new products, etc. To improve the infrastructure, the ERDF may also stimulate the creation of agencies compiling and distributing information on product innovation and technological innovation, as well as evaluating the prospects of markets and the technical feasibility of production processes. The first object is to provide services to small and medium-sized companies that otherwise would have no access to such information, so essential for operating efficiently.

The second category of measures relate to the spatial distribution of funds. To make regional policy more effective, the amounts from the Regional Fund channelled to long-standing problem areas have been stepped up. Such areas are found in countries with a structural GDP per head far below the EG average. Indeed, some 68 per cent of the Fund (after enlargement, see Reg EEC 3641/85; 0.7. no. L.27.12.85), is now reserved to the four Mediterranean countries Greece, Italy, Spain and Portugal, which accommodate 36 per cent of total population but contribute only 22 per cent of GDP to the EC12.

Finally, the regulation stipulates the elaboration of programme aid rather than project aid, and some improvements to the administration of aid measures.

The conclusion of this short description of European regional policy may be that it is growing fast in scope and constantly adapting itself to new needs. We will come back to it in the concluding chapter.

1.4.4. Co-ordination with other policies

The obligation to co-ordinate EC policies to improve their regional impact is already indicated in the treaty of Rome. Art. 39.2.a instructs the EC to take account, in working out the Common Agricultural Policy, of "structural and natural disparities between the various agricultural regions"; art. 80 stipulates that the Commission in examining rates and conditions of transport shall take account of the "requirements of an appropriate regional economic policy, the needs of underdeveloped areas and the problems of areas seriously affected by political circumstances", and art. 92.3 stipulates that aids granted by States may as an exception to the general rule be considered compatible with the common market if they are intended to "promote the economic development of areas where the standard of living is abnormally low or where there is serious underemployment".

The second task of EC regional policy, the co-ordination of other EC policies, has been given increasing attention once it had become overtly known that some of the richer regions of the Community benefited far more from the common agricultural policy than the poorer ones (Henry 1981). The Commission responded to that development by monitoring closer than before the regional impact of its policies - which is the very subject of the present book. Co-ordinating efforts are made by three different approaches:
(1)   by analysis. Analyses have been or are being made of the regional effects of the most important policy measures taken in the past by the European Community with respect to agriculture, industry, energy, infrastructure, etc.;
(2)   by administrative consultation. Representatives of DG XVI, Regional Policy, of the Commission are present at the meetings where policy plans of other Directorates General are elaborated, to be able to judge at an early stage their possible negative impacts on the regional equilibrium in Europe. In the

final appreciation of such plans, the regional aspect can then also be considered:

(3)   by taking specific regional compensation measures whenever the objectives of other policies cannot be reconciled with regional-policy objectives.

The changes in certain policies (for instance price policies in agriculture, regional distribution of EIB-investments, etc.), brought about by action as mentioned under heading 2, are difficult to evaluate, but some of them will be taken up in the next chapters, although the analysis there will be rather of the type meant under heading 1. Quite concrete action has already been taken with respect to compensation measures. In the framework of the ERDF, specific measures have been taken to compensate mediterranean regions in France, Italy and Greece for the losses they will incur through the recent enlargement of the EC with Spain and Portugal. Other ERDF measures apply to regions affected by industrial decline in the steel, shipbuilding and textile sectors. Yet other specific ERDF actions are taken with respect to energy (VALOREN).

A second type of action, wider in scope, tries to adapt the situation in the less favoured regions to the requirements of modern economic activities. The STAR programme for telecommunication infrastructure, and STRIDE for R&D services will be described in subsequent chapters.

1.5.   Regional policies and regional impact of non-regional policies; a framework for analysis

1.5.1. The co-ordination issue

In the previous section we have seen that EC regional policy has taken upon itself the co-ordination of other Community policies and the prevention or compensation of their negative regional effects. To that end, the tool kit of regional policy has been enlarged. However, that decision may have cut a few administrative knots, but leaves quite a few scientific co-ordination problems unsolved. Indeed, economic problems often seem clear enough to be solved by a straightforward measure. However, the frequent failure of economic policies to arrive at such a solution, and the occurrence of negative unplanned side effects, demonstrate that the necessity of taking the complexities of the economic system into account when designing policies. Moreover, a conflict may arise or a trade-off suggest itself between such objectives of regional policy, for instance improved employment opportunities, standard of living, etc., in the less favoured regions, may clash, or demand a trade-off, with the objectives of other economic policies, such as lower inflation, balance-of-trade surplus, national growth and sectoral restructuring.

The figure below illustrates some of the issues associated with the relation between regional policy and other national and Community policies.

In agreement with the traditional theory of economic policy, first a clear distinction must be drawn between the objectives and the instruments of policies (rows and columns). Next, a division can be made into, on the one hand, regional policies, undertaken on the Community as well as the national and regional levels, and on the other all other policies, whether pursued on the Community or the national levels, dealing with specific sectors or other domains (monetary policy, industrial policy, international trade policy, etc.).

The interdependence between regional and national policies is illustrated by the four cells of figure 1.2. To keep matters simple, we will leave aside the internal co-ordination of all national policies grouped in A (for instance between trade and monetary policies or between industrial and employment policies). The usual assumption is for national instruments to aim at national objectives (cell A) and regional instruments at regional objectives (cell D).

| | | OBJECTIVES | |
		All other policies	Regional policies
INSTRUMENTS	All other policies	A	B
	Regional policies	C	D

Figure 1.2
Interdependence of Community, national and regional policies

Actually, the situation of cell A is more involved, because national objectives concerned with employment, inflation, exports, balance of trade, sectoral outputs, and others, are in fact the aggregates of the corresponding regional variables. Indeed, national policies tend to be ineffective or, more often, inefficient because they may have different, even contradictory effects in different regions. In a more effective and efficient national policy, measures should be regionally differentiated, allowing the efforts to be concentrated on those regions where they are apt to be most successful, and preventing the positive effects in some regions from being contradicted by negative effects in others. Even the effects of national policies on national objectives may depend on the different regional structures found within a country; therefore, national policies should be articulated to account for different regional reactions to policy instruments.

Moreover, national policies may have direct and indirect effects on the specific objectives of regional policy (cell B), such as the decrease of regional disparities and the promotion of regional development potential. In some cases, a conflict may arise or a trade-off negociated between the objectives of different policies; in such cases a compromise should be reached. If the regional effects of national policies are neglected, even stronger measures of regional policy may become necessary to compensate for the negative impact of specific national policies on regional disparities. Waste of resources and unnecessary public intervention may thus be provoked, which could have been avoided if the national policies had been designed to achieve national objectives without damaging regional ones in the first place.

Regional policy is obviously aimed at regional objectives (cell D), but the gradual evolution of regional-policy strategies of the last three decades shows how much their effectiveness depends on the changing general economic structure and on the strategies of other national policies. To give an example: while a restrictive monetary policy is pursued, a constraint on location may have little effect.

Finally, regional policies may have important effects on national objectives (cell C). Regional income subsidies, for instance, have an effect on the public deficit and on inflation; regional investment incentives may lead to overcapacity on the national level and affect the objectives of industrial and international-trade policies. On the other hand, regional policies may eliminate sectoral bottlenecks and have a positive effect on inflation and the balance of trade.

1.5.2. Methods of analysis

The complex relations of regional and other policies briefly described in the pre-vious section point to the need for complex tools of analysis, tools that can ac-count for the mechanisms transmitting the various national and Community policy instruments to the regions, and the feedbacks of regional growth to the growth of the national or Community economy. Ideally this would call for the construction of complex multi-national, multi-regional models.

A few attempts have been made to make such models operational (see, for a review, Albegov et al. 1980; Issaev et al. 1982), including one on the European lev-el (Courbis 1981). Two approaches can be distinguished, the top-down one and the bottom-up one.

Multiregional econometric models built according to a 'top-down' approach con-sist of a national macro-econometric model explaining the behaviour of national variables, and a set of regional 'satellite' econometric models disaggregating the national variables to the regional level. These models may be useful to evaluate the regional impact of national policies (cell B) and the changing effectiveness of regional policies on regional objectives (cell D) according to the changing macro-economic framework. They are inadequate, however, to evaluate the effects of national instruments on national objectives (cell A), what with the limits imposed by the high aggregation of the variables considered and the different policy res-ponses of individual regions, as indicated above. Moreover, these models fail to assess the impact of regional policies on national objectives (cell C), a severe lim-itation for regional policies meant to assist, for example, a large underdeveloped region.

Models built according to the 'bottom-up' principle seem more appropriate, be-cause for such models the national variables are correctly computed as the aggre-gates of the respective regional variables, for instance with respect to employ-ment, consumption, exports, etc. The tight interdependence assumed in multi-re-gional, bottom-up models between the regional and the national economy, permits to estimate the effects which a country's interregional structure may have on the transmission mechanism of national policies (cell a). Moreover, they clearly make the evaluation possible of the feedback from regional effects to the national level (cell C).

However, econometric models, even if they are integrated with input-output tables, are severely constrained by their macro-economic characteristics. While perhaps useful for the evaluation of short-term effects of such traditional macro-economic policies as monetary, fiscal and exchange-rate policies, they seem inad-equate for the evaluation of long-term effects, and do not allow for the details required to assess the impact of such national structural policies as are considered in this volume.

Therefore, to identify the relations among regional and national policies, the structure of the sub-systems in the national economy to which structural policies address themselves needs to be analysed more thoroughly. Only thus can the con-nection between the objectives and instruments of such policies and the economic development of the regions be established.

In view of the many problems involved, to devise a research method accounting for all complexities in the system seems an impossible task. Some simplification is unavoidable.

First, we shall leave aside any relations among the subjects of the various chap-ters of this book (between agricultural and monetary policy, for instance).

Second, we shall leave out of account the feedback from regional to national and Community levels. The analyses of the following chapters of the book will

concentrate on the unilateral effect exerted on regions by non-regional policy instruments. This effect may give rise to actions of regional policy.

1.5.3. The weight of EC policies

In the past, national states have increasingly intervened in economic life, as is evident from the rising number of civil servants dealing with policy, the extending
volume of legislation and regulations, and the size of the budget devoted to certain programmes. Typically, public budgets in European countries now take up
some 40 per cent of GDP. Theoretically, the national governments have thus created a great potential of means to influence regional equilibrium through regulations and pogramme budgets. However, the effective use of that potential depends
on the efficiency of mechanisms of policy co-ordination and the effect of the political process on the desirability of the actions concerned.

EC policies are likely to affect the regions far less than national policies. For
one thing, the EC carries in general much less weight than nations, as witness the
smallness of the total Community budget (only 3 per cent of those of the national
states in Europe), and the correspondingly few civil servants and (in comparison to
nations) limited body of regulations. That does not mean, however, that EC policy
should not be an interesting subject; the absolute size of budgets in some areas
and the regulative power of the EC in others are significant enough.

Let us look a little closer at the various fields of activity. In 1985, the budget of
the EC was divided as indicated in the table hereafter. This table suggests that
the three major policies to be considered in the present book are those concerned
with agriculture, social and employment, and industry. Three other major policy
areas (with the corresponding budgetary categories) will be disregarded, however.
Outlays for regional policy itself are made expressly in specific regions and hence
are not part of the book's subject matter. Operational costs refer mainly to manpower; their regional impact obviously concerns the places where the institutions
are located. Finally, development aid is left out because the idea of tailoring aid
to developing countries to comply with regional objectives in Europe is getting
very little political support.

Table 1.4
Share (%) of policies in total EC budget (1985)

	Category	%
1.	Agriculture and fishery (EOGFA)	74
2.	Regions (ERDF)	6
3.	Social and employment (ESF)	6
4.	Industry, energy, transport, technology	3
5.	Development aid (EDF)	4
6.	Operational cost and various	7
	Total	100

Source: European Documentation.

1.6. Organisation of the book

The choice of subject areas to be treated in this book has largely been dictated by the weight specific EC policies carry in total EC activity on the one hand, and their presumed effect on regions on the other.

The first part of the book deals with the regional effects of policies concerned with the sectors of the economy. The first among them is agriculture (chapter 2), which takes up three quarters of the budget. Although the EC's budgetary outlays for the other sectors of the economy (category 4) are relatively small, we will nevertheless devote separate chapters to some sectors, namely, industry, energy, and transport. Industry (chapter 3) because the common market of manufactured goods is the core of the EC; energy (chapter 4) and transport (chapter 5) because the treaties of Rome and Paris foresaw for them separate policies more or less parallel with those for agriculture[11].

The second part of the book is concerned with policies of a more general type. Chapter 6 deals with social and employment policy, a significant item in the budget.

Moreover, two attention fields not showing up in the budget will be discussed: external trade, and macro and monetary policy. Trade is discussed because the commercial policy of the EC takes precedence over that of the member states, and trade-policy measures can make a powerful regional impact. As to macro and monetary policy: EC competences in that area are still limited, but in view of the aspiration to develop into an economic and monetary union, exploration of the possible effects of policies in that area seemed in order.

The final chapter of the book draws the principal conclusions from the separate policy chapters, and tries to distil as well some aspects common to these chapters.

1.7. Notes

1. Riccardo Cappellin has written sections 1.3 and 1.5, Willem Molle sections 1.2 and 1.4.
2. Probably, inclusion of the two Iberian countries in the calculations would not change the picture much.
3. For details of these and related indicators, see again the study of the Commission (CEC 1984a and CEC 1987).
4. We do not pretend to give a complete review of these theories. For that, readers are referred to handbooks, like Paelinck and Nijkamp (1976), Richardson (1973), or more recent ones like Aydalot (1985), which puts much weight on the modern 'endogenous' approach, or Nijkamp and Mills (eds, 1987), vol. 1, which concentrates on methods.
5. For a more extensive treatment of regional policy on the European level the reader is referred to N. Vanhove and L.H. Klaassen (1980).
6. The best known right of the Commission of the European Community (art. 93 of the Treaty) was that of prohibiting certain measures of support, regional ones among them, if these were considered incompatible with the common market.
7. See for an overview of regional aid schemes Allen (1979) and Yuill and Allen (1985).
8. See for an early survey, CEC (1979); many more have since been made (SEC 1984b).
9. Discussed already at Messina in 1956, proposed formally by the Commission in 1969.
10. See for further information on the realisation of the Fund: Talbot 1977, and for its working in the last 10 years: CEC 1985a.

11. We have grouped the fast evolving sector of telecommunications with the transport sector because both types of service use (public) infrastructure (networks), the latter to convey goods and persons, the former to convey data. There is an infrastructural aspect as well to energy (transmission systems, for example) and agriculture (land, water); it will be given due attention in the relevant chapters.

1.8. References

Albegov, M., A.E. Anderson and F.Snickars (eds.), Regional Development Modelling, Theory, Practice, North Holland, Amsterdam.

Allen, K. c.s. (1979), Regional Incentives in the European Community; a Comparative Study, EC collection studies, Regional Policy Series No.15, Brussels.

Aydalot, Ph. (1985), Economie Régionale et Urbaine, Economica, Paris.

Bailly, A.S., D. Maillat and M. Rey (1985), Tertiaire moteur et développement régionale: le cas de petites et moyennes villes, Revue d'Economie Régionale et Urbaine, no. 1.

Berg, L. van den (1986), Urban Systems in a Dynamic Society, Gower, Aldershot.

Berg, L. van den, L.S. Burns and L.H. Klaassen (eds.) (1986), Spatial Cycles, Gower, Aldershot.

Biehl, D. (1980), Determinants of Regional Disparities and the Role of Public Finance, Public Finance, no. 35.

Borts, G.H., and J.L. Stein (1984), Economic Growth in a Free Market, Columbia University Press, New York.

Camagni, R., and R. Cappellin (1981), European Regional Growth and Policy Issues for the 1980s, Built Environment, no. 3/4.

Camagni, R., and R. Cappellin (1981), Policies for Full Employment and Efficient Utilisation of Resources and New Trends in European Regional Development, Paper presented at the XXI European Congress of the RSA.

Camagni, R., and R. Cappellin (1984), Changement structurel et croissance de la production dans les régions européennes, Revue d'Economie Régionale et Urbaine, vol. 25, no. 2, pp. 177-217.

Camagni, R., L. Diappi and G. Leonardi (1986), Urban Growth and Decline in a Hierarchical System, Regional Science and Urban Economics, no. 16.

Cappellin, R. (1983a), Osservazioni sulla distribuzione inter ed intraregionale delle atticità produttive, in G. Fuà and C. Zacchia (eds.), Industrializzazione senza fratture, Il Mulino, Bologna.

Cappellin, R. (1983b), Productivity Growth and Technological Change, Giornale degli Economisti ed Annali di Economia, vol. 42.

Capellin, R. (1986a), The Development of Service Activities in the Italian Urban System, in S. Illeris (ed.), The Present and Future Role of Services in Regional Development, Commission of the European Communities, Brussels, FAST Occasional Papers, no. 74, 1986.

CEC (1961), Document de la Conférence sur les économies régionales, vol. II, Brussels.

CEC (1964), Reports by groups of experts on Regional Policy in the European Economic Community, Brussels.

CEC (1969), A Regional Policy for the Community, Brussels.

CEC (1971), Regional Development in the Community: Analytical Survey, Brussels.

CEC (1973), Report on the Regional Problems in the Enlarged Community (Thomson Report), Com.73/550, Brussels.

CEC (1977), Regional Policy of the Community, Supplement 2 to the Bulletin of the European Communities, Brussels.

CEC (1979), The Regional Development Programmes", Brussels, Regional Policy Series, nr. 17.

CEC (1981), The Regions of Europe; first periodic report, Brussels.

CEC (1984a), The Regions of Europe; second periodic report on the situation and socio-economic evolution of the regions of the Community, Brussels.

CEC (1984b), Les programmes de développement régional de la deuxième génération pour la période 1981-1985), Collection Documents, Brussels.

CEC (1985a), The European Community and its Regions, 10 Years of Community Regional Policy and of the ERDF, European Documentation, Luxemburg.

CEC (1985b), Main Texts Governing the Regional Policy of the European Communities, Collection Documents, Brussels.

CEC (1987), Regional Disparities and the Tasks of Regional Policy in the Enlarged Community (third periodic report), Brussels.

Ciciotti, E. (1984), L'ipotesi dell'incubatrice rivisitata: il caso dell'area metropolitana milanese, Rivista Internazionale di Scienze Sociali, no. 2-3.

Ciciotti, E., and R.W. Wettmann (1981), The Mobilisation of Indigenous Potential, Commission of the European Communities, Brussels, Internal Documentation on Regional Policy in the Community, no. 10.

Clausse, G., J. Girard et J.M. Rion (1986), Evolution des disparités régionales dans la Communauté, 1970-1982, Analyse statistique et comparative, EIB paper, September, pp. 17-35.

Courbis, R. (1981), Integrated Multiregional Modelling in Western Europe from one Country's Regional Models to a Multicountry, Multiregional Model for Western Europe, IIASA, Laxenburg.

Crum, R.E., and G. Gudgin (1977), Non Production Activities in U.K. Manufacturing Industry, Commission of the EEC, Brussels, Collection Studies, Regional Policy Series, 3.

Daniels, P.W. and B.P. Holly (1983), Office Location in Transition: Observation on Research in Britain and North America, Environment and Planning, no. 15.

Ewers, H., and R. Wettmann (1980), Innovation Oriented Regional Policy, Regional Studies, no. 14.

Fielding, A.J. (1982), Counterurbanisation in Europe, Pergamon Press, London, Progress in Planning.

Fua', G., and C. Zacchia (eds.) (1983), Industrializzazione senza fratture, Il Mulino, Bologna.

Garofoli, G. (1983), Industrializzazione diffusa in Lombardia, Franco Angeli - I.Re.R., Milan.

Giersch, H. (1949), Economic Union between Nations and the Location of Industries, Review of Economic Studies, vol. 17, pp. 87-97.

Goddard, J.B. (1975), Office Location in Urban and Regional Development, Oxford University Press, Oxford.

Gudgin, G. (1978), Industrial Location Process and Regional Employment Growth, Saxon House, Farnborough.

Hall, P., and D. Hay (1980), Growth Centers in the European Urban System, Heinemann, London.

Hamilton, F.E.I. (ed.) (1978), Contemporary Industrialisation, Longman, London.

Hansen,N.M. (1967), Development Pole Theory in a Regional Context, Kyklos, vol. 20.

Haselen, H. van, and W. Molle (1980), Regional Disparities and Assisted Areas in a European Community of Twelve, NEI/FEER 1980/22; also in Revista de Estudios Regionales no. 6, pp. 153-198.

Henry, P., Study of the Regional Impact of the Common Agricultural Policy, Luxemburg, 1981.

Hirschmann, A.O. (1958), The Strategy of Economic Development, Yale University Press, New Haven.

Holland, S, (1976), Capital versus Regions, McMillan, London.

Issaev, B., P. Nijkamp, P. Rietveld and F. Snickers (eds) (1982), Practice and Prospect of Multiregional Economic Modelling, North Holland, Amsterdam.

Kaldor, N. (1980), The Case for Regional Policies, Scottish Journal of Political Economy, no. 17.

Klaassen, L.H., W.T. Molle and J. Paelinck (eds.) (181), Dynamics of Urban Change, Gower, Aldershot.

Klaassen, L.H., and W. Molle (eds) (1982), Industrial Mobility and Migration in the European Community, Gower, Aldershot.

Klaassen, L.H., and P. Drewe, (1973), Migration Policy in Europe, Saxon House, Farnborough.

Lebon, A., and G. Falchi (1980), New Developments in Intra European Migration since 1974, International Migration Review, vol. 14, pp. 539-573.

Leone, R., and R. Struyck (1976), The Incubator Hypothesis: Evidence from five Smsa's, Urban Studies, no. 13.

Maillat, D. (ed.) (1982), Technology: a Key Factor for Regional Development, Saint-Saphorin.

Malecki, E.J. (1983), Technology and Reginal Development, International Regional Science Review. vol. 8.

Molle, W., with B. van Holst and H. Smit (1980), Regional Disparity and Economic Development in the EC, Saxon House, Aldershot.

Molle, W. (1983), Technological Change and Regional Development in Europe, Papers and Proceedings of the Regional Science Association, vol. 52.

Molle, W. (1986), Regional Impact of Welfare State Policies in the European Community, in J.H.P. Paelinck (ed.), Human Behaviour in Geographical Space, Gower Press, Aldershot, pp. 77-91.

Myrdall, G. (1957), Economic Theory and Underdeveloped Regions, Duckworth, London.

Nijkamp, P. (1986) (ed.), Technological Change, Employment and Spatial Dynamics, Springer Verlag, Berlin.

Nijkamp, P., and E.S. Mills (eds) (1987), Handbook of Regional and Urban Economics, North Holland, Amsterdam.

North, D. (1953), Location Theory and Regional Economic Development, Journal of Political Economy, June.

Noyelle, T., and T.M. Stanback (1984), The Economic Transformation of American Cities, Rowman & Allaheld, Totowa.

Paelinck, J. (1965), La théorie du développement régional polarisé, Cahiers de l'ISEA, no. 159, L. 15.

Paelinck, J.H.P., and P. Nijkamp (1975), Operational Theory and Method in Regional Economics, Saxon House, Farnborough.

Pedersen, P.O. (1970), Innovation Diffusion within and between National Urban Systems, Geographical Analysis no. 2.

Perroux, F. (1955), Note sur la notion de pôle de croissance, Economie Appliquée, no. 7.

Pollard, S. (1981), Peaceful Conquest, Oxford University Press, Oxford.

Pred, A. (1977), City Systems in Advanced Economies, Hutchinson, London.

Richardson, H.W. (1973), Regional Growth Theory, McMillan, London.

Richardson, H.W. (1978), Regional and Urban Economics, Penguin Books, Harmondsworth.

Salt, J. (1976), International Labour Migration, the Geographical Pattern of Demand, in J. Salt and H. Clout (eds), Migration in Postwar Europe: Geographical Essays, Oxford University Press, Oxford.

Siebert, H. (1969), Regional Economic Growth: Theory and Policy, International Textbook Company, Scranton.

Stohr, W.B., and Todtling (1978), Spatial Equity - Some Antitheses to Current Regional Development Doctrine, Papers and Proceedings of the Regional Science Association, vol. 38.

Talbot, R.B. (1977), The CEC's Regional Fund 1977: Progress in Planning, vol. 8, part 3, pp. 183-281.

Thompson, W.I. (1968), Internal and External Factors in the Development of Urban Economies, in H.S. Perloff and L.Wingo (eds.), Issues in Urban Economics, John Hopkins University Press, Baltimore.

Thwaites, A.T. (1982), Some Evidence of Regional Variations in the Introduction and Diffusion of Industrial Products and Processes within British Manufacturing Industry, Regional Studies, vol. 16.

Vanhove, N., Klaassen, L.H. (1980), Regional Policy, a European Approach, Gower, Farnbourough.

Vernon, R. (1966), International Investment and International Trade in the Product Cycle, Quarterly Journal of Economics, no. 80.

Williamson, J. (1976), The Implication of European Monetary Integration for the Peripheral Areas, in Vaizey, J. (ed.), Economic Sovereignty and Regional Policy, Gill and Macmillan, Dublin.

Yuill, D., and K. Allen (eds) (1985), European Regional Incentives, CSPP, University of Glasgow.

2 Agriculture

D. STRIJKER and J. DE VEER

2.1. Introduction

In this chapter we analyse the relation between the Common Agricultural Policy (CAP) of the EC and regional development. Agricultural policy, a concern of the EC right from its foundation in 1958, has come to be among the most elaborate policy areas, taking up three quarters of the EC budget.

The discussion will be structured as follows. The first section briefly describes the agricultural sector of the EC in relation to other sectors and to agriculture outside the EC. The subsequent sections analyse the causes of divergent regional development, among which, besides differences in spatial and natural conditions, the structural development process makes much impact. After that, a section is devoted to the effect of EC agricultural policies on regional differences. The chapter will conclude with some remarks on possible future development and some conclusions.

2.2. Description of the sector and the policy

2.2.1 Agriculture as part of the economy

Formerly the mainstay of the economy, agriculture now generates less than 4 per cent of gross national product[1]. Nevertheless, it tends to get more attention than is warranted by its share in total value added, for several reasons.

First, agriculture is still the main source of income and employment in some regions. In Greece and in the southern regions of Italy, the agricultural sector produces between one sixth and one quarter of the regional product, and accounts for about one third of employment. Even in the highly industrialised countries in the North West of Europe, agriculture is relatively important in rural regions. In the Dutch province of Friesland, agriculture contributes 9 per cent of the regional product, and about 13 per cent of total employment[2].

Second, agriculture generates income and employment in an indirect way. Approximately one half of Europe's food-processing industry depends on agriculture, the remainder mostly on imports (cocoa processing, for instance)[3]. Moreover, to many industries the agricultural sector provides a market for their products (fertilisers, machinery, etc.). Such indirect effects bring the total contribution of agriculture and related industries together to an estimated 6 per cent of GDP.

Third, agriculture is the greatest user of open space. More than 60 per cent of the EC's total acreage is given over to agriculture, and changes in the state of agriculture therefore make a great impact on the landscape and natural environment in rural areas.

Fourth, agriculture produces goods for basic needs, with supply and demand elasticities such that small changes in production and consumption bring about great changes in prices and income. So, a minor change in the level of production or delivery counts for much in terms of consumers' welfare.

Last, agricultural products and food are important factors in international trade (about 12 per cent of intra-EC and 9 per cent of extra-EC trade). France and The Netherlands range immediately after the USA as the world's second- and third-largest exporters of agricultural produce. The EC's greatest agricultural importers are West-Germany and the United Kingdom. Imports from third countries consist partly of raw materials for fodder (imports for the agricultural sector) and partly of raw materials for the food-processing industry.

For the EC as a whole the share of agriculture in value added appears to be lower than its share in employment, a reflection of the somewhat backward agricultural practice in some parts of the EC, marked by a low income level or even subsistence production, a surplus of labour and outdated techniques. In some regions agricultural practice has hardly changed for decades[4]. However, in extensive parts of the EC agriculture has expanded as rapidly as the rest of the economy. In the countries in the North West of the EC, labour productivity increased even faster in agriculture than in industry between 1950 and 1980 (Van der Meer, 1983). Agriculture in these parts is of the modern, intensive kind, with intermediate consumption representing more than one half of final production (and still relatively increasing)[5] and a high amount of capital being invested per worker (in the years 1979-1983 amounting, for full-time farmers, to an average 25,000 ECU in the EC; in the UK and the Netherlands the investment was about 100,000 ECU per farm[6].

Productivity in agriculture has risen considerably in the last few decades. The EC averaged 4.7 per cent per annum in the period between 1973 and 1983. EC countries vary much as to the development of agricultural labour productivity. In the period 1973-1983 (three-year averages) the annual growth of gross value added per worker was, for instance, 3.4 per cent in Greece, 3.9 per cent in France, 5.3 per cent in the United Kingdom and 5.8 per cent in the Netherlands.

The basic organisational unit of EC agriculture is the family farm. In nearly all countries the percentage of family workers, including the holder, is above 90, the United Kingdom being the only exception (63 per cent in 1977). In all countries, except Belgium, the operator owns more than half the total cultivated area. That has important implications for the farmers' response to market forces and for the pressure on policy makers. The normal economic reaction to a strong increase in labour productivity and a stagnating demand for output is to reduce the input of labour. On family farms, however, the family income may be reduced unless alternative employment opportunities are available. In a situation of uneven distribution of land and capital, this will result in strong pressure on farmers' incomes, which in turn may be a reason for compensatory price-policy measures.

2.2.2. Short description of the CAP

The treaty to found the EC (the Treaty of Rome) lays down that the EC was to pursue a common agricultural policy. Article 39 of the Treaty already gives the principal objectives of such a policy, namely:
- to increase agricultural productivity by promoting technical progress;
- thus to ensure a fair standard of living for the agricultural community;
- to stabilise markets;
- to ensure the availability of supplies;
- to ensure that supplies reach the consumer at reasonable prices.

Apart from the aims, the Treaty also indicated as basic elements for a CAP:
- a common market organisation;
- a common price policy;
- the creation of a Common Fund.

On that basis, the EC has progressively developed the CAP on the following principles:
- unity of markets: agricultural products may flow freely from one country to another; the product markets must therefore be organised similarly in all member countries;
- preference for EC producers: protection from third- country producers up to a certain point;
- financial solidarity: the cost of the various measures will be borne by all members and paid from the Agricultural Fund, fed by the budget.

In practice, two types of policy have been developed: a market/price policy, paid for by the Guarantee Section of the European Agricultural Guidance and Guarantee Fund, and a structural policy intended to improve the production structure of European agriculture, paid for by the fund's Guidance Section.

The price policy has traditionally been the most commented and costliest part of the CAP. Its practical issue is the management of the markets, by a system of border levies, export subsidies, and intervention at guaranteed prices. In the last 20 years, production has increased considerably, leading to a corresponding decline of imports, and a growing need to dispose of surplus produce on world markets, where the prices are generally lower.

The structural policy, intended to help accomplish structural adjustments in EC agriculture, is less far advanced. It covers some recurrent EC interventions with member states. The EC helps farmers with a variety of instruments to modernise their production, and grants subsidies to activities concerned with the marketing of agricultural produce (slaughter houses, etc.) and with infrastructure.

The regional objectives of the CAP are not very clear. Article 39 (2) of the Rome Treaty mentions only in passing that in the implementation of the Common Agricultural Policies the regional variation of farming structures and natural conditions should be taken into due account.

At the Conference of Stresa, which prepared the EEC treaty, the link between regional policy and the CAP had been more explicitly mentioned (Meester, 1980, pp. 44-64). Even clearer were the Proposals of the Commission of 1960, which stated that the structural policy should be geared to both the reduction of production surpluses and the increase of productivity in backward regions, in order to achieve a more equitable regional income distribution. The proposals also stated that the role of the EC in that respect would be modest. Apart from some lip service, until recently the regional dimension of the CAP was not given much attention.

2.2.3. EC agriculture in the world

Common Agricultural Policy (CAP) has greatly influenced the size and structure of European agriculture. High guaranteed prices have not only made the EC more and more self-sufficient in agricultural products, but even made it a net exporter of quite a number of products. Between 1973 and 1982 the net self-sufficiency of EC 9 for all agricultural products together, increased from 83 to 95 per cent (Thiede, 1984).

Increasing self-sufficiency and a rising export surplus, if based on competitive strength, are not to be considered negative. The condition is not fulfilled for most agricultural products, however. Domestic prices are kept well above world-market level, and exports are achieved by considerable subsidies. As long as the surplus was small and the EC had only a minor share in total world exports, no serious problems ensued. When, however, the share of exports in total sales rose - first of all for dairy products - and the EC became a major supplier (Meester and Oskam, 1984), the situation changed: the flood of EC exports began to influence significantly the prices on the world market. The revenues from export fell rapidly as supplies increased, and increasing quantities together with higher unit subsidies caused the budgetary costs of surplus disposal to soar.

So, the rapid growth of production made serious inroads into the EC budget, of which agriculture takes up three quarters. From 1973 to 1984 the budget increased from 3,800 to 20,100 million ECU, an increase of more than 400 per cent. In 1985, budget expenditures amounted to about 13 per cent of the value of agricultural production. Total government expenditure for agriculture is even higher, for national governments also spend large sums on agriculture. Clearly, such a growth rate was not acceptable for a declining sector, especially not in times of budgetary deficits and moves were made to reconsider the CAP and its effectiveness. In the next sections of this chapter we will deal with the regional effects of the CAP and the possible consequences of changes in that policy.

2.3. Regional differences in input and output

2.3.2 General

Until recently, the regional distribution of European agricultural capacity and production was badly known for lack of basic information. To remedy that situation, EC institutions initiated some research projects in the 1970s (Jacobs and De Boer, 1979; CEC, 1981; Rainelli and Bonnieux, 1978; Van Hecke, 1983). Partly as a result of these projects, more regional data on agriculture have become available; they are now published in the Yearbooks of Regional Statistics (for instance Eurostat, 1984). For a short description we will use the publication by Van Hecke, who classified the 102 EC regions by their dominant subsector. Map 2.1 gives an idea of the typology thus achieved.

Arable farming scores highest in the north-western regions of France, the central regions of Germany, the north-eastern regions of Italy, and some Dutch, Belgian and Danish regions. Very low scores are recorded in Ireland, Wales, Scotland and large arts of France (the south). Horticulture is heavily concentrated in contiguous regions of Belgium and The Netherlands and in some mediterranean regions, and somewhat around large cities (Paris, London, Hamburg, Rome, etc.). Perennial cultures score high in most regions of Italy and mediterranean France and the famous wine regions of France and Germany.

Herbivores, especially dairy cattle, are concentrated in The Netherlands and Belgium and to a lesser extent in the northern and southern regions of Germany. Finally, intensive animal husbandry is concentrated in the northern regions of Belgium, the southern regions of The Netherlands, and the north-western regions of

Germany. This sector has also some importance in central Germany, Bretagne and the Po area.

2.3.2. Input differences

That the input structure of agriculture varies among regions of the EC is common knowledge, but relevant quantitative information is scarce. One important production factor that is well documented, is labour. The data show large differences among regions of the contribution of agriculture to total employment: in the United Kingdom and the industrialised regions of West Germany it is under three per cent, while in the southern part of the EC percentages between 25 and 30 are not unusual (Abruzzi-Molise, Puglia, and others).

The input of land is another well documented variable. From the statistics, the regional variation of area per worker follows largely the same pattern as that of the labour supply. The RICAP-study (CEC,1981) found that the area per worker is eight times higher in British regions than in the south of Italy. Not only the area per worker, but also the quality of the land and the workers (education) is known to vary. The connection between the quality and the yield of the land appears to be a loose one (Jacobs and Strijker, 1981, pp.77-83). That is hardly surprising, because land use, man/land ratio and yields are affected as well by the quality of infrastructure, the climate, the nearness of non-agricultural resources or large consumption centres.

As to the other inputs in agricultural production: on a national scale, intermediate consumption varies from less than 40 per cent of total production value in Greece and Italy, to about 65 per cent in Denmark and West Germany. Depreciation, a practical yardstick of the use of capital goods, ranges from less than 70 ECU/ha in Ireland to more than 500 ECU/ha in the Netherlands (Commission of the European Communities, 1985).

2.3.3. Differences in the productivity of land

Jacobs and Strijker (1981) have published a rather detailed analysis of varying yields of many crops among the regions of Europe. The data on which it is based are not more recent than 1973, but as a major finding was the stability of the regional differentials in crop yields, we think the results of the study still useful.

In most of the 341 regions of the EC 9, the annual average growth rate of physical yields of the main crops did not deviate much from the EC average. For most crops, the highest growth rates, on or even above the general EC level, were recorded in the French regions. The central and southern parts of Italy were the only regions lagging behind; already among the lowest yielders of the EC in 1950, they were put back even more by their relatively low growth rate. Interregional differences in yield, especially between the northern and southern parts of the EC, remain large. In the early years of the EC, the 20 per cent of regions with the highest wheat yields were all situated north of Paris, while the 25 per cent of regions with the lowest wheat yields were all situated south of that city. The same clear geographical separation line between high- and low-yielding regions holds for barley and potatoes. The gaps between the lowest and highest yields have not significantly changed since 1960, although some areas have much improved their position.

27

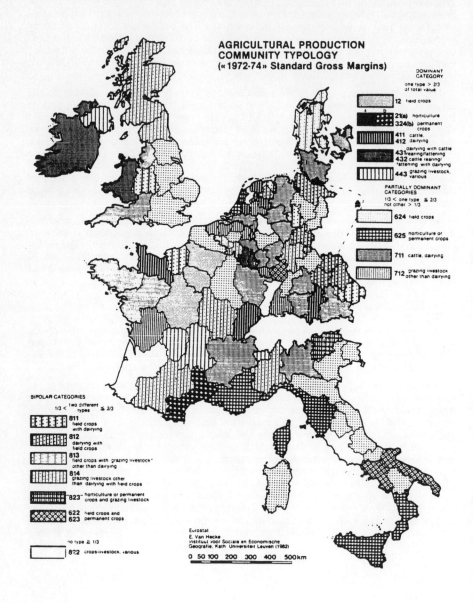

AGRICULTURAL PRODUCTION COMMUNITY TYPOLOGY
(«1972-74» Standard Gross Margins)

DOMINANT CATEGORY
one type > 2/3 of total value

12	field crops
21(a)	horticulture
324(b)	permanent crops
411	cattle,
412	dairying
431	dairying with cattle rearing/fattening
432	cattle rearing/fattening with dairying
443	grazing livestock, various

PARTIALLY DOMINANT CATEGORIES
1/3 < one type ≤ 2/3
not other > 1/3

624	field crops
625	horticulture or permanent crops
711	cattle, dairying
712	grazing livestock other than dairying

BIPOLAR CATEGORIES
1/3 < two different types ≤ 2/3

811	field crops with dairying
812	dairying with field crops
813	field crops with grazing livestock other than dairying
814	grazing livestock other than dairying with field crops
823	horticulture or permanent crops and grazing livestock
622 / 623	field crops and permanent crops

no type ≥ 1/3

822	crops-livestock, various

Eurostat
E. Van Hecke
Instituut voor Sociale en Economische
Geografie, Kath. Universiteit Leuven (1982)

0 50 100 200 300 400 500km

Figure 2.1

28

Among member states, for most crops, the country with the highest yield scores twice as high as that with the lowest yield. In 1982, the average wheat yield was 3010 kg in Greece and 7380 in The Netherlands; for barley the yields were 2740 kg in Greece, 3010 kg in Italy, and 5690 kg in Belgium. In 1981-82, one ha of sugar beets yielded an average 4800 kg in Ireland and 8330 kg in France. In 1983, the average milk production per cow varied from 3470 kg in Italy to 5280 kg in the Netherlands.

The regional differences are even more pronounced. In 1979, the average wheat yield in the isle of Crete was about 1300 kg; at the other end of the scale, the south-western provinces of The Netherlands yielded an average 6400 kg. Potato yields range from under 10 ton/ha in the Italian regions of Molise, Basilicata and Umbria, to more than 40 tons/ha in some Dutch regions.

2.3.4. Regional concentration of production

Regional production depends on the area used for various crops and the yields per ha. Following Meester (1980) we can calculate the regional concentration of agricultural production by ordering the production of all regions by increasing yields. The graphical reproduction is a concentration curve (Lorentz curve) of the type often used to present (changes in) income distribution (see also CEC, 1981). We have calculated such a curve for wheat from the data gathered by Jacobs and De Boer (1979) for the EC 9 and for the years 1951 and 1972 (Fig. 2.2).

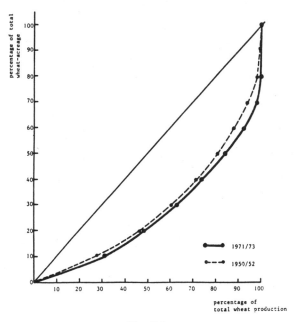

Fig. 2.2
Cumulative distribution of Production,
EC 9, 341 regions, wheat, 1950/52 and 1971/73

From this figure, in both years half the production of the six EC member countries appears to be concentrated on less than a quarter of the EC area. A comparison of the two curves shows that regional concentration has somewhat increased between

29

1951 and 1972: in 1951, 27.5 per cent of wheat production was concentrated in the first decile; in 1972 the percentage is 31.8. At the other end of the curve, 2.6 per cent of total wheat production was generated in the lowest two deciles, against about 0.3 per cent in 1972. There is evidence that the tendency has continued into recent years. The cumulative distribution of wheat production in the years 1963 and 1977 on the basis of a regional divison of the EC 6 into 42 parts also indicates a progressive concentration of production (Meester, 1980). However, this development does not extend to all other crops. Meester's figures show a comparable development for potatoes and milk, but not for barley, rye and sugar beets. Intensive livestock production also shows increasing regional concentration.

The pattern found for the EC 6 is also valid for the EC 9, as is shown by an analysis based on the division of the EC 9 into 38 regions and on developments between 1958 and 1980-81 (Meester and Strijker, 1985).

Regional concentration of production is not the same as regional specialisation, a fact to be kept in mind. The high-yielding regions in the northern part of the EC, especially in France and The Netherlands, have relatively large shares in the EC production of many agricultural products. Evidently, while production is more or less concentrated in those regions, they are not at all specialised in any product. That belies the wide-spread belief that a common market would favour regional specialisation and thus help to alleviate regional problems in the EC.

2.3.5. Income differences

The differences in input/output ratios and in concentration of production among the regions of the EC bear heavily on regional incomes. The regional differences in agricultural income are analysed in detail in the RICAP study (Regional Impact of Common Agricultural Policy; CEC, 1981). In that study, Gross Value Added (GVA) per working-year unit, as a measure of income, is divided into two components: one for intensity (GVA/ha), and one for structure (ha/unit of labour). Figures are calculated for the regions of the EC 9 and for two benchmark years. Figure 2.3 gives the picture for the year 1976-1977.

Let us first consider the results of the breakdown into two components. In the first few years of the Common Market (1968/69), regional differences in GVA/ha varied from 1 for the Irish to 6 for the Dutch regions; agricultural income per working-year unit varied from 1 for the southern part of Italy to 6 for the vicinity of Paris or regions in the north of Germany. In the period 1968/69 - 1976/77, average GVA in the EC per working-year unit, in real terms, increased at the rate of 5.5 per cent per annum. One fourth of the increase could be attributed to intensification (GVA/ha), and three quarters to structural change (ha/worker). The differences among member countries were great, annual growth of GVA varying from 1.9 per cent per working-year unit in Denmark to 6.7 per cent in Ireland. The composition of growth also varied considerably. In Belgium, France, Luxemburg and Denmark, the growth of GVA per worker is connected mainly with the agricultural area available to each worker. In Germany, Italy and Ireland growth can be attributed for two thirds to an increase in the area per worker and for one third to an increase in real production per ha. In the United Kingdom and especially in The Netherlands, income growth mostly springs from intensification (growth of production/ha).

A second analysis in the RICAP study compares regional GVA per agricultural worker in the periods 1968-69 and 1976-77. Four types of development can be distinguished:
(1) income per worker above the EC average and increasing (The Netherlands, northern parts of Belgium and Germany, Scottish Lowlands, north-eastern regions of France);

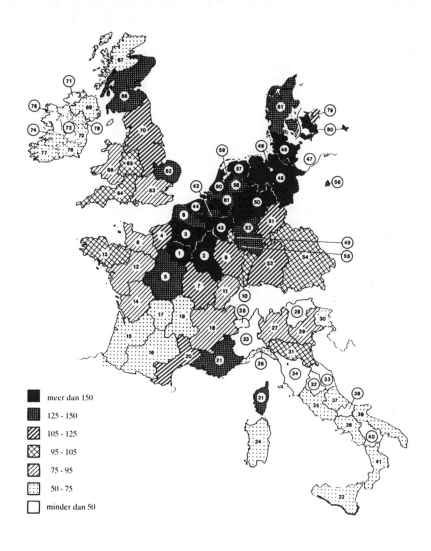

meer dan 150

125 - 150

105 - 125

95 - 105

75 - 95

50 - 75

minder dan 50

Figure 2.3
Gross value added per man year, 1976/77, EC 9 = 100

31

(2) income per worker above the EC average but declining (north-western and southern regions of France, Denmark, north-eastern part of Italy, Ireland);
(3) income per worker below the EC average but increasing (south-western regions of the UK, western regions of France, north-western and southern regions of Italy);
(4) income per worker below the EC average and declining (central and southern regions of France, north-western and southern regions of Italy).

Corresponding figures can be calculated for most regions for the year 1980. The results of the analysis for 1977-1980 differ quite a bit from those for the previous period; this time the four groups are composed as follows:
(1) most French regions, the United Kingdom;
(2) Belgium, The Netherlands, the northern part of Germany, Denmark, the north-western regions of France;
(3) Ireland, the south-western part of France, most Italian regions;
(4) the southern regions of Germany, Sicily, Campania.

The conclusion is that between 1968-69 and 1976-77, the regional concentration of agricultural income tended to increase, but that the tendency was reversed afterwards: after 1976-77, the regional differences in GVA per worker had diminished. The Lorentz curve (RICAP study, p. 154) for 1980 appears to remain inside the curves for 1968-69 and 1976-77. In particular Ireland and most Italian regions, starting from very low levels, had come closer to the EC average (from 20 to 30 per cent below the EC average in 1980). The relative position of the central part of the EC (north-west France, Belgium, The Netherlands, Denmark, Germany) had deteriorated, but managed to keep income per agricultural worker at between 30 and 100 per cent above the EC average, with the sole exception of central and southern Germany. The Federal Republic as a whole was still on the EC average in 1980, but the south had already dropped far below.

The method used has an important drawback: it only gives information about the income per agricultural worker as far as generated in agriculture, while we know for certain that on many German farms, for instance, much of the family income is earned by work of the owner or the members of his family outside his farm. We have no way of knowing whether, and how much, the non-farm income of farms in regions with low GVA growth per worker has increased.

2.4. Causes of divergent regional development

2.4.1. Structural adjustments

At the early stages of modern economic development, agricultural productivity was raised mainly by intensified land use and rising crop yields. In those days, the ensuing greater agricultural production was still compensated by the growth of consumption (both the population and per capita consumption increased), particularly of livestock products, vegetables and fruit. Higher productivity due to new land-saving and crop-boosting technology did not yet entail the need to reduce the agricultural labour force. At the next stage, labour-saving technologies were introduced under conditions of a slackening demand for agricultural produce and a limited area of agricultural land, creating employment problems on the farms and in the entire sector (Maris and De Veer, 1973).

To adjust the scale of operations to the efficient use of modern farm equipment and modern farm systems without enlarging the farms themselves, farms were specialised and diversified, farm implements used co-operatively and contractors employed. Still, in many rural areas most farms became too small to provide employment and income for the farmer and his family. In a slow and gradual process the number of farm workers was reduced by laying off first the hired workers and next the dependent family workers. Finally, the number of farms had to be reduced as well; that was accomplished mainly by the retirement of older farmers without successors, and far less by farmers changing to other occupations.

The reduction process had advanced to different stages in the various regions; at present it is seriously hampered by the shortage of alternative employment opportunities.

In the more prosperous, economically more developed regions, with favourable alternative employment opportunities, the process started earlier and progressed more rapidly than in the poorer, economically less developed regions in southern Europe, Ireland, and some isolated mountainous and hilly rural regions elsewhere, mostly also agriculturally the less endowed areas.

The type of adjustment varied. In some regions, particularly in central and southern Germany, the problem was partly solved by switching to part-time farming. The switch was favoured by industrial decentralisation providing employment opportunities at commuter distance. In the peripheral, isolated and less industrialised regions, that solution was not feasible; the majority of farm workers and young people without prospects in farming were forced to migrate to industrial centres. In many of these regions a cumulative process of underdevelopment was thus set going, with the concomitant phenomena of a declining and ageing regional population, poor employment and investment opportunities, and deteriorating physical and social infrastructures.

The relative importance of agriculture as a source of employment and income was declining in all regions. Even in the most rural areas, most workers are no longer employed on farms. Most arable land and agricultural production is in the hand of a minority of large farmers; typically, between 70 and 80 per cent of the total farm output is produced by the 20 to 30 per cent large farms[7]. Particularly in the more developed regions, these farms are large enough for efficient modern farming and full employ of the family labour force. Most of the smaller holdings on the contrary have poor prospects; most are exploited by senior farmers without successors, or as part-time and hobby farms.

In Western Europe, the transition to modern farming tends to be more hampered by historical obstacles than in the farming regions of North America and Australia, which developed later. For centuries, agrarian structures and the division of rural areas has been tuned to self-sufficiency at the maximum density of population under the prevailing ecological and technical conditions (Slicher van Bath, 1962). Self-sufficiency of farms and farmer's families and of local markets has brought about diversity in land use and farm production. The settlement patterns, parcelling and use of land, farming and socio-cultural structures, and road system remained geared to that situation until after the Second World War. Therefore, the structural adjustment that the CAP was to bring about concerned not only the number of farms and farm workers but mostly also the lay-out of rural areas, the use of arable land, and regional physical infrastructures. The comprehensive rural reconstruction and land-consolidation programmes that were required, would upset the social life of the population, affect the historically developed landscapes as well as the, partly man-made, diversity of natural vegetation and wildlife, and in general conflict with the desire to preserve the European heritage.

2.4.2. Spatial and physical conditions

Transportation costs, though losing weight with technological advance in storage, conservation, processing and transport, still largely determine the location of agriculture and food industries. Especially the production of livestock is still strongly resource-based, as processed livestock products are mostly cheaper to convey over land than the fodder needed to produce them. For that reason, herbi-vores, like cattle and sheep, are almost invariably kept on the same farms which produce grass and fodder. But even intensive livestock industries, such as pig, poultry and veal production, based on the use of more easily storable and convey-able feedstuffs, locate preferably where in particular feed cereals are available from local production or overseas imports. As Western Europe, and in particular the European Community, produces more feed cereals and becomes less dependent on imported fodder, coastal regions will lose their comparative advantages - near-ness to ports of entry and consumption centres - for pig and poultry production in favour of more centrally situated regions with cereal surpluses.

So long as animal husbandry needs to locate where fodder is available, there is little sense in encouraging its expansion as a basis for regional agricultural devel-opment in remote and isolated regions with small potential for feed production. With the present food-consumption pattern in high-income countries, about 70 per cent of the capacity for vegetable production, that is, arable land, is used for the production of fodder for livestock. Evidently, the impact on the entire spatial dis-tribution of agricultural production is great.

For vegetable production, natural conditions still dominate the input-output ra-tio and, therefore, determine the location of crops and indirectly of livestock pro-duction. As distances and transportation costs become less important, regional specialisation may be based increasingly on comparative advantages springing from the variation in natural conditions. The tendency towards more uniform and less nationally and regionally differentiated food habits will reinforce that trend.

That holds in particular for climatic conditions, which are hard to change. The expansion of the mediterranean production of fruits, vegetables, wine, and decor-ative plants in response to a strong increase of demand in other EC countries is a striking example. Of course, the support and protection provided by the Common Agricultural Policy has helped to keep this expansion within the Community. Still, the total area of land involved in the production of fruits, vegetables, wine and decorative plants is relatively small, even in the mediterranean regions. Most ar-able land yields crops either for human or for mainly land-based livestock con-sumption.

Natural conditions, such as the quality of the soil and the availability of water, are more susceptible to human intervention than climate. Deficiencies can increa-singly be overcome by modern yield boosters, adapted farming systems and cultiv-ation practices, and the development of suitable crop varieties. Soil and water conditions are moreover to an increasing extent man-made. With modern technol-ogy, land can be levelled, soils ameliorated and water-management systems con-structed or reconstructed.

2.4.3. Economies of scale and linkages

At first glance, economies of scale seem hardly relevant to agricultural produc-tion. Even modern farms in Western Europe are still relatively small, with a labour force of one or two permanent workers (Bergmann, 1975). To make efficient use of modern farm outfit, out of reach to individual farms, farm implements are used co-operatively, contractors employed and services provided by downstream or up-stream industries. The same principle of external organisation is applied to such supporting activities as research and development, marketing, accounting, and all manner of expert advice that cannot be performed efficiently on the scale of in-dividual farms.

Modern farming is indeed embedded in a complex of geographically and organ-isationally interrelated industries, which provide farm inputs and process and mar-ket farm produce, including servicing firms and government-controlled research institutes, veterinary and quality-control services, etc.

The farmers and the industries and private services with which they are linked by commercial and contractual bonds, form together with the governmental supporting services so-called agro-industrial complexes. Thus, interregional competition has to a great extent become a competition between agro-industrial complexes.

The scale requirement of some components of these complexes may affect regional competitiveness if regional supply is too small for a sufficient scale of operation. On the other hand, the geographical concentration of agro-industries may imply that farm inputs and outputs have to be transported over longer distances. The concentration should allow industrial processing on such a scale, that the scale economies are greater than the increases in internal transportation costs. If the complex is too small for the components of agro-industrial complexes to function efficiently and for efficient interindustrial linkages to be established and infrastructures to be provided, the handicaps may be hard to overcome, especially in regions mainly oriented to agriculture. Seasonal unterutilisation of processing, marketing and transport capacities can be another serious disadvantage. Diversification of the regional supply of fruit and vegetables is particularly important for the full utilisation of the capacity in dependent industries and the efficient functioning of marketing organisations.

There are also dynamic aspects to economies of scale as a locational factor. Those who have introduced modern systems of production, processing and marketing at an early stage have a lead on competitors entering the market at a later stage, because for further development they can draw on experience and on an institutional framework of input supply, processing marketing services and last not least research, professional education and extension services. That the fast diffusion of new knowledge and experience in highly specialised areas is important as well, is the conclusion from a comparative analysis of greenhouse and hothouse cultures in various regions of The Netherlands (Verhaegh, 1975).

Linkages, and static and dynamic economies of scale, reinforce the tendency to divergent agricultural developments. As large-scale industrial processing and marketing grow in importance, and science-based and computer-aided farming systems are more and more accepted, modern agriculture, like modern manufacturing, will increasingly profit from the advanced research and education, the specialised servicing industries, and the leisure-time amenities that are scarce and difficult to establish in remote and isolated areas.

2.5. Effects of the CAP

2.5.1. Effects of the price policy

The Community's systems for the protection and support of agricultural production vary among products. For the main products of temperate zones, such as cereals, sugarbeets, dairy produce and beef, together covering more than 90 per cent of total agricultural land, certain guaranteed prices are set which combine external protection with the possibility of intervention on the domestic market. The systems have allowed production to expand far beyond the limitations of the domestic EC market and have resulted in the production of large surpluses, which have to be disposed of on the world market at prices generally far below the domestic level. Practically the same unlimited price guarantee prevails for a range of other crops for which the Community still has a considerable import surplus and supports the producers with deficiency payments. Thus, producers' prices for all the products involved are politically determined, the only link with the market situation being the urge to keep budgetary expenditures within bounds. With respect to that kind of agricultural enterprise, the special feature of interregional competition within the Community is that the expansion of regional production in one region neither lowers the prices nor confronts other regions with a shrinking market outlet.

For other agricultural sectors, such as pig and poultry production, horticulture, and some arable crops (potatoes, onions), the prices depend mainly on domestic supply and demand. Common-Market regulations, if they exist, hardly if at all intervene in the internal market, while external protection is on the whole much less prohibitive than with the former categories. As a result, interregional competition operates under the condition of limited commercial demand. Now what are the regional impacts of these regulations ?

The heavy price support given to a limited number of agricultural products indirectly aids other, non-supported products as well; therefore, to assign the financial CAP-support to individual products is difficult. One might argue that the regional benefits of price support are distributed according to the regional shares of a particular product in total EC-production, or, more crudely, according to regional gross production per worker[8] or per unit of agricultural land. The calculations will, of course, have different results according to the method chosen; in the latter case, regions with a high production per unit of labour or per unit of land (the western provinces of The Netherlands, the northern regions of Belgium, the northern regions of France, the areas around Paris and Copenhagen) will appear to be the beneficiaries of the price policy.

The RICAP study assumes that the more a region produces of a certain product with high price support, the more it benefits from the price policy. To assess the impacts, a so-called "nominal protection index" was calculated for each region in the following way. First the differences between internal EC-prices and world-market prices were calculated for all agricultural products; next, the weighted average difference between intra-EC and world-market prices was determined on the basis of the regional product mix. The regional price differences can then be related to the difference between weighted intra-EC price and the world-market prices, which in 1976/77 was 80 per cent. By that calculation, regions more or less specialised in the production of milk or sugar (approximately the north-east part of the EC) would be the beneficiaries of the price support, while regions specialising in fruits and vegetables (the southern regions of France and Italy) for example, would fall far below the EC-average. A serious drawback of this calculation is that the difference between the intra-EC and the world-market price depends in part on the level of world-market prices, which in turn are not for all products independent from the EC's market and price policies. The actual world-market price for dairy products is far below the one that would prevail if there were no EC policy. Should that be taken into account, than not only the regions specialising in dairy produce but also those specialising in cereal production would gain significantly from the EC price support.

The same study also suggests a more synthetic way to assess the regional gains from price support. A compound index is built up from the price difference between the EC and the world market, the qualitative effectiveness of internal price support, and the qualitative effectiveness of protection against imports from third countries, and computed for each region. The results are slightly different from those of the previous index, because not only the average price but also price variation is taken into account. With this index, regions that produce cereals and olive oil come up as the main winners, while regions specialising in fruits, vegetables and meat are hardly affected by the market and price policies of the EC.

Evidently, the results of the RICAP calculations depend very much on what is assumed or how the calculations are actually made. That is even more true if the influence of the CAP on regional agricultural development is analysed. The RICAP-study also tries to assess those consequences. For that purpose, the indices of regional price support mentioned before are confronted with the regional growth rates of agricultural production per unit of agricultural land (1968/69 - 1976/77). No significant correlation has been found. Quite a few regions combined a high level of price support with a low growth rate (regions in the vicinity of Paris, French mountain areas, some German and Italian regions). Other regions, on the other hand, combine a low level of price support with a high growth rate of production (regions specialising in the production of vegetables, flowers, quality wines, etc.). The RICAP-study points out that most of the growth of regional agricultural production can be explained by that of milk production, which, obviously, is largely due to the relatively high prices for dairy products. The low level of support to certain mediterranean products is taken to explain in part the relative stagnation of production in some mediterranean regions.

2.5.2. Structural policy[9]

The market and price policy is only one of the two pillars on which the common agricultural policy rests. The EC has also developed a structural policy which aims at raising productivity at backward farms and in backward regions. As early as 1960 Commission submitted proposals for structural policy emphasising the role of the individual member states and stressing the idea that structural backwardness of agriculture could only be overcome if other sectors in the region were growing. The proposed Community activities were confined to financial support to national projects. Several years went by before new proposals in the field of structural policy were submitted. The Mansholt-proposals, inspired by a concern for the continuing growth of production and the unsatisfactory development of agricultural income, aimed at larger and more economic farms and a considerable outflow of agricultural workers into non-agricultural jobs. The effects of the Mansholt-proposals were limited. Only in 1972 were some decisions made which introduced a restricted structural policy, with emphasis on the modernisation of viable farms and the closing of farms without prospects of development. A few years later (1975) financial support to agriculture in less favoured areas was decided on (Directive 72/268/EC on mountain and hill farming in certain less favoured areas). In that same year the Council decided to establish the European Fund for Regional Development. Though designed to develop backward regions in a general economic sense, the fund also increased the chance of an effective agricultural structural policy.

Production surpluses continued to grow, and made changes inevitable. Proposals to modify the CAP were launched, one element being the attempt to achieve a market equilibrium by setting lower prices, another the use of structural policy to bring about the modernisation of farms to diminish income discrepancies. Because modernisation by itself probably would not be enough to attain a reasonable income, the possibility of direct income support was stressed.

Until recently, the pursuit of positive regional redistribution by measures of structural policy was hampered by two facts. First, most programmes were not geared specifically to problem areas, but operated in all parts of the EC; besides, they were not very specific. That applies in particular to the projects initiated by individual member states and partly financed by "Brussels", but neither did EC-measures in the proper sense always give priority to agriculture in problem areas. From calculations, in the first five years in which Directive 72/159/EC "on the modernisation of farms" was in force, by far most farms with a certified Development Plan were situated outside the less favoured areas. In normal areas 1.7 per cent of farms had a Development Plan, in the less favoured areas 0.6 per cent.

Improvement of physical conditions and adaptation of agricultural technology tend to require heavy public investments in land-consolidation schemes, rural reconstruction programmes, irrigation and drainage systems, and in agricultural research, farm development, and support services. Such public investments tend to be biased towards the economically more developed and agriculturally more advanced regions. Public funds for investments in agricultural infrastructure and in research and development (see Evenson and Kisler, 1975) are generally more abundant in economically developed countries and regions. They are often granted to quiet farmers who complain about increasing income disparities due to rapid economic development and rising incomes in other sectors of the national or regional economy.

The accumulation of capital within agriculture, still the most important source of finance in farming, also tends to be higher in the agriculturally better endowed areas. As a result, the agriculturally more favoured and advanced regions tend to offer the best prospects for profiting rapidly and in full from improvements in physical conditions, infrastructure, and new technology, and therefore, for effective and profitable public investment (de Veer, 1983).

Of course, serious natural handicaps such as an extremely adverse climate and a highly accidented landscape, are difficult to compensate for.

As structural policies within the European Community are still mainly pursued and financed by national and regional authorities, they show a tendency to reinforce existing regional differences. Until recently, most activities in the area of structural policy had a micro character. In principle, the object of structural policy was to improve the production potential of a group of backward farms to give them better income prospects. But because the demand for agricultural products stagnated, additional production brings down average prices, thus worsening the income prospects of all other farms. Thus, the gap between comparable income and actual income at the tail end of agricultural income distribution is not closed. The only probable result is that one group of farms replaces another, and in most cases not even that happens. Now that second shortcoming of structural policy deserves to be watched closely if structural policy is to be used for raising overall agricultural income. Indeed, without specific additional measures, structural policy can even aggravate the economic problems of agriculture.

From 1975 onwards, when the regulations for agriculture in the less favoured areas were issued, structural policy has become more and more specifically regional. That 1975 directive, which covered one fourth of EC agricultural area, 15 per cent of the farms and 12 per cent of production, for the first time recognised the specific regional handicaps for farming. Until then, of the dichotomy of sectoral structural policy and regional structural policy, the former had been more emphasised. With the 1975 rules, packages were introduced for specific problem areas (irrigation in Southern Italy, reconstruction of vineyards in mediterranean France, hydraulic works in Hérault, infrastructural works and improvement of processing and marketing conditions in the Mezzogiorno, draining projects in Western Ireland, and so forth). In 1981, three integrated projects were decided on (for Lozère, the Western Isles of Scotland, and the less favoured areas of Belgium), for which the efforts of three Community funds (Agriculture, Social, Regional) were co-ordinated. Recently the same line of conduct showed in the proposals for large-scale reconstruction works in the mediterranean area, inspired by the entry of Spain and Portugal into the EC.

2.5.3. Monetary compensatory amounts (MCA)

A specific feature of the common agricultural policy with considerable effect on regional competition within the European Community, is the system of monetary compensatory amounts (MCA). We will not go into the details of the system here, but content ourselves with a few remarks. The EC sets guaranteed prices in ECU (formerly "units of account"). The obvious effect has been that the price in national currency which farmers received depended on the exchange rate to the ECU.

38

Devaluation of a currency meant higher, revaluation lower national prices to far-mers. Governments of devaluating and revaluating countries alike were opposed to those effects, the former because they tended to push up inflation, the latter because they went against the interest of the farmers. In 1969, the EC estab-lished the system of monetary compensatory amounts, meant to correct the ex-change rate for recent adjustments (introducing the so-called "green rates"). In practice the national prices are maintained by a system of border taxes and sub-sidies. In revaluating countries, price drops are prevented by subsidies on exports and levies on imports, while in devaluating countries exports are taxed and im-ports subsidised.

The system was intended to be temporary but has persisted in practice. Once established, MCA were slow to be reduced, while exchange-rate adjustments led to new compensations. Thus, the ultimate effect has been the continuous protec-tion of agricultural production - especially cereals, sugar and livestock products - in strong-currency countries such as the Federal Republic of Germany and The Netherlands, and continuous discrimination against the corresponding agricultural sectors in weak-currency countries such as France and Italy (Ritson and Tanger-mann, 1979, de Veer, 1983). As the division between countries with strong and weak currencies largely coincides with that between rich and poor countries, the MCA have clearly favoured affluent regions and set back already poor producers.

The system of MCA has offset most of the negative effects that the existence of such strong exporting sectors as capital goods in Germany and natural gas in The Netherlands would have had on the competitiveness of agriculture in these countries. The system offsets to a great extent the impact of strong non-agricultural export sectors, such as the capital-goods sector in West Germany and natural gas in The Netherlands, on the terms of trade for agriculture. Likewise it curbed the growth of agricultural production in weak-currency countries.

2.5.4. Financial efforts

The importance of measures with regional components can be summed up in terms of money. Three financial flows can be distinguished:
(1) support directly connected with the CAP:
   - outlays of the Guarantee section of EAGGF for measures of price policy;
   - outlays of the Guidance section of EAGGF for measures of structural agricultural policy;
(2) regional EC programmes;
(3) national measures.

The outlays for the price policy are substantial: in 1984 more than 18,000 mil-lion ECU were paid by the guarantee section, which is more than 200 ECU for one ha of agricultural land. This sum was geographically very unevenly spread, how-ever; the average support per unit of agricultural land can be estimated at only 100 ECU in poor regions like Sicily and Calabria in Italy, against more than 350 ECU in, among others, The Netherlands.

EC structural policy is less detrimental to poor regions; in 1982 the amounts paid under that budget line were calculated at 8 ECU per inhabitant in the poor regions of the Italian Mezzogiorno, against an EC average of 2.5.

More important than these agricultural structural supports are the joint efforts by other EC funds for regional development (EFRD, European Social Fund, ECS, special subsidies). According to the budget, in 1984 a total of 3,700 million ECU was spent on agricultural and non-agricultural structural measures (14 Ecu per in-habitant, 13.5 per cent of total EC outlays). Quite a lot of support was given to the less developed areas, for instance 55 ECU per inhabitant to the Mezzogiorno and 12 ECU in the Mediterranean part of France.

National efforts for regional purposes differ very much in budgetary recording, and the impact of measures taken by national governments to stimulate agricultural activities defies quantification. That is the more regrettable as crude estimates suggest that this type of regional support is the most important, in financial terms. Seebohm (1981, p. 126) has calculated that between 1974 and 1976 total national support to the agricultural sector in the EC 9 amounted to about twice the total EC budget for agriculture[10]. Most national efforts are structural in nature; as our study is concerned first and foremost with the regional aspects of EC agricultural policy, we will not elaborate them here.

2.6. Future developments

The relatively high price level of agricultural products has much stimulated the development of the European agricultural sector. Obviously, most of the recent intensification of EC agriculture is due to the relatively high and guaranteed prices. The ensuing sharp increase in the production of most products combined with a stagnant demand created a rapidly widening discrepancy between demand and supply. Until recent years, the surplus production could be sold on the internal market, replacing imports, but the internal market is getting saturated. Export refunds are expensive and create untenable international trade relations. Indeed, the prospects for further growth are poor.

Increasing surpluses with the concomitant rise of budgetary expenditures and risks of retaliatory international trade intervention will force the European Community and national governments to accept lower prices. The national governments or the Community will probably start making direct payments to farmers to compensate them for loss of income. Hence the stimulating effect of the price policy on production and employment in the whole range of European regions will be undone.

Large parts of the EC are still far behind in agricultural yield and income. To develop them economically, their agricultural production would have to be expanded, but without competitive outlets for the additional production such a development is difficult to envisage, and conflicting interests of EC regions are likely. Probably, the solution lies somewhere between the two extreme regional distributions of agriculture sketched below:

(a) Concentration of EC agriculture in the core regions of the EC (between Copenhagen and Paris, Hannover and London, perhaps including the Po valley). Such concentration would be limited only by the costs of agricultural congestion. The regions in the periphery of the EC would have room only for slow development of agricultural and related non-agricultural activities.

(b) Balanced development of EC agriculture, presupposing an effective system to curb the intensity of agricultural production in the central parts of the EC and leaving some scope for its more remote areas.

Which of the two scenarios is the more likely ?

On the assumption of decreasing prices, greater mobility of resources, in particular labour and capital, may reduce agricultural production in the more developed economies. On the other hand, greater productivity, efficient processing, marketing and servicing infrastructures and flexible farming systems in developed regions may work the other way. Our personal feeling is that the scales will tip towards widening regional differences in agricultural development and a reinforced tendency to concentration in certain regions of the European Community. Furthermore, if plans for agricultural development of backward regions are observed merely to add to production and depress prices, the odds are that political support to them will be diminished (Weinschenk, 1984).

40

The alternative scenario was based on a policy of direct supply control (such as system of "super-levies" on the milk production). Any system setting delivery quota for individual farms or regional dairy industries tends to preserve the existing regional distribution and to impede further regional specialisation and concentration of production. However, by deliberatly reallocating the quotas, such systems could also be used to change regional distribution and create room for expansion in the hitherto less developed areas with potential locational advantages. The enlargement of the milk-delivery quota for Irish dairy farmers may be considered such an endeavour to enhance the opportunity of exploiting potential comparative advantages and supporting development in a sector that is of great importance to total employment and income in certain regions.

Vested national and regional interests, however, are sure to oppose strongly to such direct intervention to change the regional distribution of production and achieve a more balanced regional economic development. Strong pressure may be expected to make the quotas transferable not only among farms but also across regional and national borders. Transferable quotas would offset the negative impact of frozen production structures, but presumably also favour further concentration of production in the regions best endowed for agricultural production and boasting the most efficient agro-industrial and marketing structures.

There is, however, a factor which may counterbalance the tendency to concentration, namely, the care for the environment. Indeed, modern agricultural development not only damages historically developed rural landscapes and the diversity of natural vegetation and wildlife, but also raises other environmental problems. The increased use of chemicals in combination with the specialised cropping plans of modern arable farming, threatens to pollute the soil and the surface waters, with unacceptable ecological consequences. High livestock densities, in particular the concentration of pig and poultry production on the basis of imported feedstuffs in the north-western coastal regions, produce far too much manure. If more manure is spread on agricultural land than is needed to feed the plants, then the soil, the surface waters, groundwater reservoirs and the air are polluted to an unacceptable degree, and costly measures are required to cart the surplus manure to other regions or destruction works (Wijnands and Luesink, 1985). The advantages of specialisation and concentration in such areas are increasingly wiped out by the rise of environmental costs.

Agricultural production and industry in regions with high population densities and a strong concentration of industrial activity, are apt to face increasing environmental costs for two reasons: because they add to the pollution from other sources, and because the standards of emission control in such areas are raised. Thus, their locational advantages for modern agro-industrial development are reduced. Therefore, to redirect agricultural policy to a more even regional distribution of agricultural production might be beneficial to the protection of rural scenery, the national environment, and a more balanced regional development (Weinschenk and Kemper, 1982; Van der Weijden et al., 1984). The restrictive measures which such a policy would imply, would face strong opposition from the national and regional agro-industrial interests in the economically and agriculturally more developed and advanced countries and regions.

Finally, an alternative policy option that may lead to a better regional equilibrium, is to control not production, but a production factor, in this case agricultural land. Since governmental action to create room for further agricultural development in backward areas will be strongly opposed by regions enjoying competitive advantages, a recently suggested alternative for the Common Agricultural Policy is the active withdrawal of agricultural land from production. Such a policy might possibly be designed such as to affect all parts of the EC in a more or less balanced way. It may open some perspective to the development of agriculture in backward areas. On the other hand, the negative economic effects of the with-

41

drawal of agricultural land in backward areas might be enormous while achieve only a marginal effect on EC production.

2.7. Concluding remarks

On the whole, the Common Market has created better opportunities for regional specialisation. On the other hand, the Common agricultural market and price policies have not contributed to a more even distribution of agricultural production across the Community, nor reduced existing divergences in regional agricultural development. For the products of the main temperate zone, which are subject to a strict system of market regulation, regional competition was mitigated by the unlimited market outlet provided by the Common Agricultural Policy. National and regional policies favouring physical and social infrastructures, farm development, research and extension, have much effect on such land-based products, and tend to reinforce the position of agriculture in the more advanced and developed regions, in particular in economically developed and prosperous countries. The Common Agricultural Policy has done little to counter that tendency. The funds available for supporting agricultural development in the agriculturally less advanced and economically less developed regions of the Community were small in proportion to the outlays made by national and regional governments. The central question for the future is whether the tendency to concentrate production in a limited part of the EC will be maintained. To the more peripheral regions of the EC, the diminishing market prospects for most agricultural products spell a scanty chance of growth and development. A policy of deconcentration implying the limitation of agricultural production in the central regions will find little favour among farmers and agricultural decision makers there. Yet, "agricultural congestion" (manure, landscape) makes such limitation of production, or at any rate of its growth, desirable. Some deconcentration will be an absolute necessity if prospects are to be kept open to peripheral areas. Whether there will be enough political support to such a redirection of agricultural policy, is questionable, however.

2.8. Notes

1. Unless stated otherwise, the figures in this chapter are from: Commission of the European Communities, The Agricultural Situation in the Community, 1983 and 1984, reports 1984 and 1985.
2. Calculated from: Eurostat, 1984, table III.2, and LEI, 1984, table 31A.
3. Commission of the European Communities, The Agricultural Situation in the Community, 1982 Report, 1983, pp. 27-40.
4. In these regions other sectors are often also stagnating or declining; see, e.g., de Veer, 1981, or Strijker, 1982.
5. Calculated from Eurostat, Economic Accounts agriculture, forestry, 1978-1983, Luxemburg, 1985.
6. Vide 5. Investments are supposed to be depreciated in 10 years.
7. This situation is typical of agriculture in highly industrialised countries. See for the USA: Penn, 1981, and Brewster et al., 1983.
8. At least if the costs of production per unit are assumed constant. In the situation of increasing unit costs, a decreasing unit price leads to a less than proportional decrease of income.
9. Largely based on Meester, 1980, pp. 49-64.
10. The same figure has been used in the detailed study of national structural policy in the EC (Balz, Meimberg and Schöpe, 1981, part 1, p. 14).

2.9. References

Balz, M., R. Meimberg and M. Schöpe (1981), Die Agrarstrukturpolitik in den Ländern der Europäischen Gemeinschaft, IFO-Studien 21/1-3, München.

Bergmann, D. (1975), Background Thoughts and Elements for a Discussion on Agricultural Structures in Europe 1980-1990, European Review of Agricultural Economics, 2 (4), pp. 459-480.

Brewster, D.E., et al. (1983), Farms in Transition, Iowa State University Press, Ames.

CEC (1981), Regional Impact of the Common Agricultural Policy, Commission of the European Communities, Regional Policy Series 21, Brussels/Luxemburg.

CEC (1986), The Agricultural Situation in the Community 1985, Commission of the European Communities, Brussels/Luxemburg.

Eurostat (1984), Yearbook of Regional Statistics 1984, Luxemburg.

Evenson, R.E., and Y. Kislev (1975), Agricultural Research and Productivity, Yale University Press, New Haven/London.

Hecke, E. van (1983), Regionale struktuur van de landbouwproduktie in de Europese Gemeenschap, Commissie van de Europese Gemeenschappen, Brussel.

Jacobs, H., and T. de Boer (1979), Guide to the Agricultural Data Collected for the Regions of the Countries of the EC, 1950-1973, Institute for Economic Research, Groningen.

Jacobs, H., and D. Strijker (1981), Yields of Agriculture in the EC-regions 1950-1973, Institute for Economic Research, Groningen.

LEI (1984), Landbouwcijfers 1984, LEI, The Hague.

Maris, A., and J. de Veer (1973), Dutch Agriculture in the Period 1950-1970 and a Look Ahead, European Review of Agricultural Economics, 1 (1), pp. 63-78.

Meer, C.L.J. van der (1983), Growth and Equity - Experience in Developed Countries with a Market System, in A. Maunder and K. Ohkawa (eds.), Growth and Equity in Agricultural Development, Gower, Aldershot.

Meester, G. (1980), Doeleinden, instrumenten en effecten van het landbouwbeleid in de E.G., LEI, publikatie 1.15, The Hague.

Meester, G., and A. Oskam, (1984), Analysis of World Demand for Dairy Products from the European Community, in K.J. Thomsom and R.M. Warren, Price and Market Policies in European Agriculture, University, Newcastle upon Tyne.

Meester, G., and D. Strijker (1985), Het Europese landbouwbeleid voorbij de scheidslijn van zelfvoorziening, WRR-voorstudies en Achtergronden V46, Staatsuitgeverij, The Hague.

Penn, J.B. (1981), Economic Development in U.S. Agriculture, in D.G. Johnson (ed.), Food and Agricultural Policy in the 1980s, American Enterprise Institute for Public Policy Research, Washington and London.

Rainelli, P., and F. Bonnieux (1978), Situation et évolution agricoles de la Communauté, Informations sur l'agriculture nos. 52, 53, 54, Brussels/Luxemburg.

Ritson, C., and S. Tangermann (1979), The Economics and Politics of Monetary Compensatory Amounts, European Review of Agricultural Economics 6 (2), pp. 119-164.

Seebohm, G. (1981), Nationalstaatliche Landwirtschaftsförderung und Europäische Agrarpolitik, Agrarwirtschaft, Sonderheft 89, Hannover.

Slicher van Bath, B.H. (1963), The Agricultural History of Western Europe (500-1800), E. Arnold, London.

Strijker, D. (1982), Regional Disparities in Agriculture, Institute for Economic Research, Groningen.

Thiede, G. (1984), 10 Jahre Versorgungsberechnung für die E.G., Agrarwirtschaft, 33 (15), pp. 136-142.

Veer, J. de (1981), Theory, Analysis and Methodology, European Review of Agricultural Economics, 8 (2/3), pp. 409-424.

Veer, J. de (1983), Gli effetti nazionale dei cambiamenti nella PAC, Città & Regioni, no. 1, February, pp. 134-149.

Verhaegh, A.P. (1975), De positie van de bedrijven met glastuinbouw buiten de grote centra, LEI, publikatie 4.67, The Hague.

Weinschenck, G. (1984), Neue Wege in der Einkommenspolitik - Notwendigkeiten und Realisierungschancen, Schriftenreihe der Gewisola, Band 21, Münster-Hiltrup, pp. 795-815.

Weinschenck, G., and J. Kemper (1981), Agricultural Policies and their Impact in Western Europe. European Review of Agricultural Economics, 8 (2/3). pp. 251-281.

Weyden, W.J. van der, H. van der Wal, H.J. de Graaf et al. (1984), Bouwstenen voor een geïntegreerde landbouw, WRR-Voorstudies en Achtergronden V44, Staatsuitgeverij, The Hague.

Wijnands, J.H.M., and H.H. Luesink (1985), Transport en verwerking van mestover-schotten in Nederland, LEI, publikatie 3.130, The Hague.

3   Industry and Services

W. MOLLE

3.1. Introduction

The present chapter aims to review methods to establish the impact of measures of industrial policy taken by the EC. To that end various elements will be analysed.

First we will briefly discuss the industrial policy of the EC. Sectorally, the term "industrial' is to be understood in a fairly specific sense, to the exclusion of 'agriculture, forestry, fisheries' and the 'building', 'energy' and 'transport' sectors. Industrial policy, however, is understood in a fairly broad sense, that is, to include large parts of technology and innovation policies, but exclusive of competition policy. This chapter is concerned, then, with structural policies for most of the manufacturing and service branches.

Next we will briefly indicate some theories about how industrial growth leads to regional development, theories that should govern the empirical study of the regional impact of industrial change. Special attention will be given to technology and innovation aspects.

Studies made to assess the impact of changes in specific industries and actions of regional policy undertaken to compensate for any negative effects in specific regions will be analysed next. The generalisation of such studies to more or even all sectors gives a more complete picture of the effects of total industrial change on all European regions; the fourth section of the chapter will discuss some approaches in that direction.

All such approaches presuppose fairly simple direct relations between sectors and regions. In a more sophisticated approach, interindustrial and interregional effects are accounted for as well, as has been done in the FLEUR model, briefly discussed in the fifth section of this chapter.

Some conclusions will show that to tackle the problem in hand satisfactorily, there is still ample scope for improvement of methods and concepts.

3.2. A sketch of EC industrial development and policy

3.2.1. Introduction

From very scanty beginnings, the EC has gradually developed an industrial policy of its own. This policy has up till now been mostly confined to a small number of declining sectors; only recently have growth sectors been given some attention. The EC uses a panoply of instruments to implement its industrial policy. After a review of the main instruments, we will picture the differential growth of the various branches of the economy.

3.2.2. Legal basis of political structure

The measures of industrial policy which the EC has issued in the last few decades have different legal bases, which explains the variety in outlook and instruments for different sectors.

The Treaty of Paris, which created the European Coal and Steel Community (1952), gives very detailed rules for a steel policy. It empowers the Commission (formerly the High Authority) to regulate markets (by production quotas, minimum prices, import controls, etc) under certain conditions. Moreover it enjoins upon the Commission to carry out a policy of structural improvement, in particular by giving investment aids but also by controlling investment to prevent overcapacity.

The Treaty of Rome, which created the European Economic Community (1958), is not very explicit on industrial policy. The philosophy of this Treaty was that a sound competition policy should be sufficient to regulate market forces, without the need for governments to regulate prices, quantities etc. Competition was also supposed to stimulate continuous modernisation. However, when after some time it became apparent that in many cases competition alone was not sufficient to bring about the structural changes of European industry needed to ensure continuous growth, the modalities of a positive industrial policy for the EC began to be considered (see e.g. Toulemon et Flory 1974).

The main arguments for such a policy on the EC level are:
1. the competitiveness of European industry on international markets would improve;
2. a larger financial resource base would be created, enabling European industry to undertake projects of which the risks are unacceptable to individual countries;
3. scale economies would ensue from co-operative European efforts (to that effect the Commission might even have to relax its views of competition);
4. technological innovation would be stimulated so as to develop new products and European technical standards (mostly new branches);
5. the balanced restructuring of the older sectors is inadequate if done for each country separately; a European framework is often needed.

As far as institutional aspects are concerned, the industrial policy in the narrow sense of the word is largely hammered out by DGIII, Industry and Internal Market, while important parts of innovation policy are designed by the Directorate General XII, Research and Technology.

3.2.3. Differences among sectors

After a period of trial and error, the role of the EC in the improvement of industrial structures is now fairly generally accepted. Indeed, the industrial policy of the EC has focused on declining branches of activity, and has only recently got involved in the more modern branches. While in the 1970s much attention was

46

given to the restructuring of the older sectors like textiles, shipbuilding and steel, to help them cope with the effects of the depression, recently new sectors (information, communication, etc) have been stimulated in their attempts to build up a strong competitive position, for instance by the Esprit programme (European Strategic Programme of Information Technology, CEC 1984a). Although some important modern service sectors are in the same basket with manufacturing sectors because some services and products are closely allied, most of EC policy appears to be concerned with manufacturing.

Indeed, the service sector has been less in the limelight, for several reasons. For one thing, the EC considers many services, which tend to follow the population, to be a national rather than an EC concern (sector 6 Commerce, part of sector 8, Business Services, and the public and non-market services of sector 9). Banking and insurance (most of sector 8), being closely related to monetary policy, are often dealt with in that framework. Transport (sector 7), for which the Treaty of Rome gave a set of special rules, will on that account be treated in a special context.

Surveying all sectors we find that a well-defined EC policy for services is lacking. Some more attention for the service sector may be expected in future, however, in particular for those services that are internationally tradable; indeed the EC is now discussing, internally as well as with other contracting parties in GATT, the possible further liberalisation of the service trade.

3.2.4. Instruments

Like national states, the European Community can use instruments to carry out a positive industrial policy for the structural improvement of European industry (CEC 1982, see also OECD 1980; Rothwell and Zegveld 1981, Pelkmans 1984 for a comprehensive description of policies with respect to EC industrial development, and Jacquemin 1984 for a discussion of various elements of European industrial policy).

Because a large European market makes it possible to profit from economies of scale and keep the lead in the technological race, the EC is concerned first of all with removing all obstacles to a homogeneous internal market. Next, it aims at creating a favourable environment for industrial restructuring, with stable exchange rates, macro-economic growth, etc. The hard core of its industrial policy consists in using the following instruments:
-   economic and technical information: spreading existing information to relevant partners, aid to the creation of data banks and the execution of prospective studies;
-   financial measures: provision of grants and loans to industrial development; so far, this has been done on a modest scale on the EC level;
-   public procurement contracts: the EC regulations ensure equal access of all producers to these contracts;
-   external relations: protecting the EC market by trade agreements from being flooded by imports;
-   research and development: co-ordination of national programmes on the EC level, joint EC programmes, and dissemination of their results.

3.2.5. Industrial development pattern

The development of the various branches of industry in the EC depends on many factors, such as consumer preferences, technology change, final demand, international competitiveness, natural-resource potential, and human capital. Industrial policy influences these determinants to some extent, and through them the levels of production, productivity, and employment by branch. Most often employment is the principal indicator selected, for obvious political reasons.

Table 1 gives an idea of the differences in long-term growth of employment among branches and sectors. The figures for 1950-1980 show clearly a gradual decline of employment in manufacturing and a consistent growth of the services. As to the individual branches, we observe how employment decline first seized on textiles, next spread to all other manufacturing branches except chemicals. Finally, chemicals fell a victim to decline as well (see for some causes Molle and Wever 1984, and for a more comprehensive description of the developments in several branches of industry De Jong 1981). The service branches, on the contrary, continued to grow, often at high rates, all through the period 1950-1980. The figures for 1980/1990, speculative as they are, mostly indicate a further decline of the manufacturing sectors and growth of the service sectors; this implies that employment-wise Europe has clearly entered the "de-industrialisation stage" (see, for example, Jacquemin 1979). Output-wise, the situation is different; from data supplied by Freeman et al. 1982, the following three stages can be identified for the EC of Nine:

- from 1950 to 1966 both industrial output and employment expanded fairly steadily;
- from 1967 to 1973 output continued to grow rapidly while employment stagnated;
- since 1973 output has continued to grow, if more slowly, while employment has declined substantially.

Freeman and his colleagues contend that the change in the relation is due to the rationalisation investments consistent with the standardisation phase of the long cycle, and the increasing availability and exploitation of scale economies. The development has been accelerated by the European integration process (see, for example, Pelkmans 1984, and Jacquemin and De Jong 1977). We will come back to these points in section 3.3.

The "autonomous and "policy-induced" components of the changes in individual sectors as presented in table 1 are seldom separated; even less common are attempts to assess how much the development of employment in specific sectors varies with the intensity with which a certain instrument is applied.

3.2.7. Conclusion

EC industrial policy, which is complementary to the member states' own industrial policies, aims at an efficient restructuring of the older and a balanced development of new sectors to strengthen the position of EC industry on both the home and export markets.

3.3. Some theory; industrial and regional development

3.3.1. Introduction

The previous section described the patterns of long-term industrial decline and service growth in the EC. These phenomena are causing structural adaptation problems to many regions in the European Community, mostly manifest in bad labour-market conditions. Evidently, one needs to understand the phenomena before setting out to study their impact.

The previous section also touched upon the industrial policy of the European Community. New patterns of industrial specialisation and growth springing from technological development are highly relevant to that policy. Technological change, and more particularly automation and robotisation, have a negative effect

Table 3.1. Average yearly employment growth (%) by branch and sector
(1950-1980), EC10

Code	Sector	1950/60	1960/70	1970/80	1980/90
31	Food	0.8	0.0	-0.8	-0.9
32	Textiles, clothing	-0.8	-1.8	-3.4	-3.0
33	Wood	0.1	-0.3	-1.2	-1.3
34	Paper, printing	2.9	1.1	-0.8	-1.1
35	Chemicals	3.4	1.8	0.1	-0.5
36	Non-metal minerals	2.2	0.2	-1.7	-1.1
37	Metal industries	3.6	1.1	-0.8	-0.8
38	Transport equipment	2.6	1.8	-0.7	-1.0
39	Other manufacturing	2.8	1.7	0.1	-0.2
61/62	Trade	2.5	0.7	-0.1	0.1
63	Hotels	0.5	1.1	0.6	0.5
71	Transport	0.7	-0.2	0.1	0.0
72	Communication	1.8	1.8	1.4	0.6
81/82	Finance and insurance	3.8	3.6	2.5	2.1
83	Business services	4.7	4.6	3.0	2.3
84	Personal services	3.4	0.6	2.3	1.1
91	Public administration	1.4	2.9	2.7	1.4
92	Education	4.1	4.3	3.2	1.5
93	Medical	2,7	3,8	3,3	1,8
94	Social services	0.2	3.5	2.5	1.4
95	Leisure and culture	2.2	1.3	2.3	1.0
1	Agriculture	-2.9	-4.9	-2.2	-1.9
2	Mining	-1.3	-5.8	-2.7	-2.3
3	Manufacturing	1.8	0.5	-1.1	-1.1
4	Public utilities	1.2	1.0	-0.6	-0.1
5	Construction	2.9	1.2	-1.3	-0.1
6	Trade	2.1	0.8	0.1	0.2
7	Transport	1.0	0.3	0.4	0.2
8	Business services	4.0	3.1	2.6	1.9
9	Community services	2.3	3.4	2.9	1.5
T	Total	0.9	0.3	0.1	0.1

Source: NEI, FLEUR study.

on employment in existing industries; on the other hand they stimulate the development of new industries, thus creating new employment. The ideal industrial
strategy should enhance employment and productivity simultaneously, but that
ideal is generally understood to be extremely difficult to achieve; many would also
argue that in the present situation any improvement depends on the degree to
which the production process can be renovated by mastering new technologies.
Before entering the debate, let us consider some details of a few relevant theoretical aspects.

3.3.2. Technology and innovation

Technology is not a static quantity, it changes constantly.

Following Schumpeter, we distinguish three stages in the process of technological change:

1.   invention: a new idea takes shape;
2.   innovation: the idea materialises in a product, and a production process;
3.   development: the product is improved and adapted to market needs.

The first two stages cover 'Research', the third 'Development'. Inventions may be the result of systematic basic research (in universities and government institutes, or in the laboratories of industries), but may also be accidental. To carry through innovations is mostly the task of individual firms, as is, evidently, development. We will use the term 'innovation' as encompassing the stages 2 and 3: Innovation and Development.

The countries of the EC vary considerably in the amounts they spend on R&D, and there are also wide differences in that respect between EC countries, the US, and Japan (see, for instance, OECD 1980). Empirical studies have shown that industrial research-and-development is a very important source of technical change and hence a determinant of growth. The low growth figures of Italy and Spain may indeed be due to their low level of R&D expenditure (Cuadrado c.s. 1982). However, economic growth also depends on the capacity to transform the results of R&D efforts into marketable products. Mediterranean countries seem to do better; many of them follow a strategy of early adoption or imitation, focusing on the Development rather than the Research side. Some of their regions create substantial GDP growth without much R&D. The opposite may also occur; indeed, high expenditure on R&D that is not followed by successful marketing will not create much GDP. There are indications that the low growth record of the United Kingdom is partly due to failure to master that part of the game (Broadbent and Meegan 1982).

3.3.3. Technology and sectoral growth

All through history, technological progress has time and again changed the entire organisation of economic life. Gradually the dynamics of the process has become known; the fragments of knowledge gained have found general expression in the theory of the life cycle (Kondratieff 1926, Kuznetz 1930, Tarde 1962, Utterback and Abernathy 1974). This theory distinguishes four stages in the life of a product, namely, introduction, growth, maturity, and stagnation, marked by different needs for research and development (R&D), market strategy, etc. (Freeman et al. 1982, De Jong 1981). Because important innovations that spark off new product cycles tend to come in clusters, the theory develops into a macro-growth theory, explaining significant ups and downs of the economy (long cycles) by the superposition of life cycles. An essential step is the translation of product cycles, via groups of related products, into sector life cycles (see, e.g., Van Duyn 1982). This translation is easiest for sectors producing homogeneous products or dominated by one type of product. Examples of sectors dominated by a few well defined products are automobiles and shoes. Textiles are an example of a sector that reached the end of its cycle some time ago; automobiles appear to be well into the later stages, and so are many chemicals. By contrast, the information sector is still at the early stage of the cycle. The degree to which a nation can gain a competitive edge in modern sectors still at the beginning of their life cycles, largely determines its future growth chances. Along these lines attempts have been made in a number of studies to single out the principal factors behind the differential national patterns of sectoral growth (for instance, CEC 1979).

3.3.4. Regional growth patterns and technological change

The locational advantages and disadvantages of a region determine, together with the requirements of investors, the location of economic activity, and hence its regional distribution. Investors' requirements change as time passes and technology develops. The spatial counterpart of the life-cycle theory (Thomas 1975) states that at each stage of a product's life cycle a certain type of region is best suited for the location of production facilities. This theory is generally associated with the "filtering-down theory" (Vernon 1971, Wells 1972). The various stages are characterised as follows:

1. At the growth stage, process and product innovations are frequent and therefore the needs for information and communication great. Neither the products nor the production processes are standardised; therefore production will take place in the innovating country or region. Note that innovations are introduced in the country that is technologically most advanced and offers the largest initial market. Part of the production will be exported to countries with an equal or slightly lower level of technological development.
2. At the maturity stage the new product becomes more and more standardised and product innovation gives way to process innovation. The need for information and communication with the market decreases. The high production costs in the technologically more advanced countries will lead entrepreneurs to try and increase labour productivity by rationalisation and by transferring production to countries with lower cost levels.
3. At the stagnation stage, finally, production is standardised so far that production ceases in the initially innovating country and is transferred to low-cost, often low-wage countries.

The above analysis, originally intended for consumption goods and international trade, can also be applied to investment goods and interregional trade. Klaassen and Molle (1983), for instance, have shown how general is in the EC the trend of manufacturing industries to emigrate from central areas to more peripheral ones. Differences in location factors (like innovativeness and labour costs) can indeed be as powerful among regions as among nations, and may lead to similar spatial behaviour.

Thus, well developed (and often highly urbanised) regions, are found among the inventors or early adopters, frequently followed by regions in the next layer of the urban hierarchy, while peripheral agricultural and backward areas tend to bring up the rear.

3.3.5. Space and the selection environment

The filtering-down theory is evidently highly schematic; some authors have questioned its relevance in general and the realism of the related hierarchical diffusion model in particular (see, for example, Ewers and Wettman, 1980). Alternative efforts such as the industry-specific diffusion model or the firm-specific diffusion model, are not satisfactory either. A new way to generalise the notions is to use the concept of regional selection environment, with its various facilitators and constraints.

The definition of selection environment refers mostly not to a region or a community but to the progress of a specific technological trajectory (Nelson and Winter, 1977). The type of environment is usually characterised in terms of management science, systems analysis, or decision theory rather than in terms of geographical factors. In our view (Boeckhout and Molle 1982, Molle 1983a) the selection environment has a spatial aspect as well. Our extended concept of selection environment can be defined, then, as the set of facilitators and constraints with respect to a particular technological trajectory, including the attitudes of local decision makers with respect to innovative efforts.

Many innovations are, in principle, generally available "at a price". However, geographical barriers and local constraints tend to make their adoption and hence their diffusion across space uneven.

Spatial differences in rates of innovation may also spring from differences in creativeness among regions. Innovations may indeed be introduced because the situation in specific regions is felt to be so bad or to have deteriorated so much that only a specific technological breakthrough can reverse the decline. When in the middle of the eighteenth century the exhaustion of the wood resources used for making charcoal brought about an energy crisis, the rise of coal mining brought new life to European steelmaking.

The success of such locally initiated innovation processes and of the adoption of innovations developed elsewhere depends on the innovative capacity and stimulus on the one hand and on the, mostly restraining, elements of the selection environment on the other. Together they determine what one might call the innovative potential of a region.

3.3.6. Accessibility and receptivity

A region is developed by the activities of actors located there (Maillat, 1982, Malecki 1981; Thomas, 1981). Their attitude and behaviour together with the production (selection) environment in which they operate, determine the growth prospects. Traditionally the selection environment has been described in terms of location theory only, specifying the advantages and disadvantages to new investors. That view is too restricted, however: the earlier stages in the development process, invention and innovation, need to be included as well. Such an extension of traditional theory, to achieve its full meaning should be complemented with the concepts of accessibility and receptivity (Mignolet, 1983).

Access to ideas, innovations, etc., is the first. Whether an individual entrepreneur can gain access to an innovative idea and materialise it into an investment in a certain region, depends on many innovation facilitators and constraints in his selection environment, for instance telecommunication infrastructure, mechanisms of technology transfer, etc. A region with access to a new product at the early stage of its invention, innovation and development, will mostly be in a good starting position to attract investments within its borders; the final effectuation evidently depends also on the region's access to sources of finance.

Actors may have (physical) access to innovative ideas but not be receptive to them. That may be a matter of attitude or of skill. To both problems, education programmes are the answer.

Even if entrepreneurs have good access and are highly receptive to new ideas, other actors (for example trade unions, farmer organisations, local pressure groups) may be overtly hostile to them. Such attitudes and pressures can be seen as important elements of the regional selection environment.

3.3.7. Conclusions

Traditionally, the theory of regional development has allotted limited weight to technological change. Recently that situation has changed, for two reasons: (1) the increased attention for innovation as a source of enhanced macro-economic growth, and (2) the conviction that regions will no longer be able to draw on spill-over effects, but have to engender indigenous growth. That is possible if a region can mobilise its potential by developing an adapted production technology, each region identifying its potential on the one hand and on the other the major

facilitators and constraints that characterise its productive structure and selection environment, including such objective factors as access to information and
more subjective ones like receptivity to change.

3.4. Regional impact of industrial change; sectoral analysis

3.4.1. Introduction

Industrial change has a direct influence on regional economic development. Many
factors contribute to industrial change, for instance consumer tastes, technology,
and industrial policy. To separate the effect of industrial policy from those of all
other factors is very difficult, and so is, consequently, the analysis of the regional
impact of industrial policy per se, as this would assume a quantitative distinction,
on the European level, between the 'autonomous' and the industrial-policy effects
of employment change by branch. Because in practice such a distinction is not
feasible, so far all regional assessments have considered the whole decline of employment in industrial sectors, irrespective of its origin.

The problems confronting both the researcher and the policy maker differ according to the stage in the life cycle which the industry to be analysed has
reached. Running through the cycle backwards, we will briefly review the situation for declining and growth sectors.

Next to studies concentrating on one sector of industrial activity, more general
studies are needed. Many instruments of industrial policy are indeed generic
rather than industry-specific. Stimulation of new technology is generic, for instance: new production methods may enhance productivity in many sectors and regions; new products may lead to completely new sectors. To assess the impact of
such instruments, the analysis of just one sector of the economy is not enough. For
that reason we will review some studies that cope with several sectors at once.

3.4.2. All sectors: a view of the past

The regional patterns of declining manufacturing industry and growing service
sectors have been studied for the EC by several authors. We will briefly discuss
the results of three investigations.

The first, by Molle c.s. (1980), concerns the period 1950-1970 for the EC of
Nine. The analysis shows that the disparities in the distribution of manufacturing
and service employment among the regions decreased by half in the two decades
of study, owing to the generally low or even negative employment growth of certain sectors in regions where they were heavily represented, and their fast growth
in those regions where they were underrepresented. The index figures of Table 3.2
show that the general tendency prevailed in both manufacturing and services in all
regions and periods. The employment trends in manufacturing can be explained in
part by the decentralisation of manufacturing industries (Klaassen and Molle
1983); the trends in service sectors are caused in part by the flourishing of welfare
services, and for the remaining part by the fact that decentralising manufacturing
industries and non-market services as well as income transfers tend to enlarge the
market for market services (see Molle 1986).

A second study considers branches and regions in more detail, concentrating on
the developments in the 1970s (Eversley et al. 1984). The authors found that the
large conurbations of Europe's heartland are the areas most heavily struck by industrial decline. Moreover, other conurbations and their surrounding regions all
over Europe economically dependent on declining industries, suffered great employment losses (iron and steel, textiles, shipbuilding). With very few exceptions,
the growth of employment in manufacturing is confined to the less industrialised

Table 3.2. Annual (%) growth of employment (EC9) in manufacturing (I), services (S) and total (E), by period (1950-1960-1970) and category of region (shares of I and S in E in percentages)

	Region	1950-1960			1960-1970		
		I,S	E	index	I,S	E	index[a]
I/E	over 50	1.1	1.1	100	-0.3	0.1	96
	40-49	2.1	1.5	106	0.5	0.5	100
	30-39	2.5	0.9	116	1.6	0.4	112
	under 29	2.0	-0.8	125	1.7	-0.4	123
S/E	over 45	1.8	1.1	103	1.7	0.7	109
	35-44	1.5	0.5	110	1.6	0.1	116
	25-34	2.9	1.2	118	2.3	0.3	122
	under 24	2.3	-0.1	127	2.8	-1.6	155

Source: Molle c.s. 1980.
a) Index calculated as 10 years' growth index of I or S divided by ten years' growth index of E.

parts of Europe, the trends there being mostly a continuation and acceleration of those of the 1950s and 1960s.

A third study, by Camagni and Cappellin (1984), is quite different from the two previous ones. The authors' objective is to reveal, by analysing regional data on employment (E) and production (P) by branch, the different strategies of industrial change which EC regions followed in the 1970s. From the position of each region with respect to the average growth of E, P and P/E in the EC, they group regions according to seven types of strategy, each strategy (reconversion, conservation, closures etc.) reflecting the regions' capacity for seizing the advantages of new industrial growth. The authors show that this capacity is related to the regions' socio-economic characteristics (or, in terms of shift/share analysis, the differential effect) rather than to their initial industrial structure (structural effect). This casts serious doubts on the validity of any analysis of the impact of industrial change based solely on an industry's present location patterns and macro growth.

3.4.3. Declining sectors: past and present

To evaluate the extent to which problem regions are the result of the structural decline in manufacturing employment (and production), seems important from the point of view of regional policy.

In a typical impact analysis, the size, structure and employment of certain pre-determined declining industrial sectors in the various regions of the EC are assessed and problem regions identified; the second periodic report (CEC 1984b) shows the outcomes of such analyses of the shipbuilding, textile, and steel branches.

The attention given to declining sectors is no surprise; indeed, one of the chief missions of EC regional policy (CEC 1984b) is the reconversion of declining industrial regions.

The analysis is mostly followed by some action of regional policy: investment in new sectors is stimulated with a view to supporting the industrial reconversion of backward regions. Industrial policy is involved only insofar as the measures of regional policy are to some extent differentiated (for instance in the rate of closing down steel plants). Regional policy has the primacy over industrial policy mainly because in the realm of industrial development, unlike in that of agriculture, there is nothing to compare with the powerful financial resources of the European Fund for Regional Development (EFRD).

Regional policy actions take the form of a so-called 'Specific Community action for regional development'; three action programmes with respect to steel, ship-building and textiles were recently agreed upon by the Council (Official Journal 31-1-'84 art. 27; Regulations art. 216/84 and 219/84). In principle, these programmes apply only to selected areas satisfying, with respect to the declining sector (DS), the following specific criteria:
1. minimum number of jobs in DS;
2. high dependency of regional economy on employment in the DS;
3. considerable loss of employment in DS in past years;
4. significant worsening of regional employment problems if jobs in DS would be cut back further;
and two general criteria:
5. eligible for national regional aid;
6. having regional problems above the EC average (measured by GDP and unemployment).

The regions thus designated are often fairly small (labour-market areas). The aid given by the EFRD is designed to remove obstacles to the development of new economic activities in the regions concerned. The specific programmes give much attention to SME: small and medium-sized enterprise. A whole panoply of instruments is used, aid being given to governments (e.g. infrastructure) as well as companies (e.g. for consulting services).

So far, analyses have been made, and regional-policy actions undertaken on behalf of regions suffering from declining sectors. But what about regions specialising in stagnating industrial sectors that may well become the <u>future problem sectors</u> ? While the present location of stagnating industries is known, the spatial differentation of their decline is difficult to foresee at this stage[1], so one cannot select regions by criterion 3, nor assess the problems by criterion 4. That may be why regional policy so far has not been very specific about stagnating sectors. Presumably, the method described above will be applied as soon as the sectors concerned pass from stagnation to decline.

3.4.4. Growth sectors; evaluating future trends

For some industrial and service sectors, growth rates of value added and employment far above the average are generally expected. Such sectors are often called 'growth sectors'.

In the past, most models have been built for manufacturing growth sectors. An example of a model for services is Cappellin 1986, which has been made operational for Italy only. Empirical models of growth-sector location are few and far between, and non-existent on the EC level.

To assess the regional impact of growth-sector developments, an entirely different approach is needed, prospective rather than empirical. For one thing the future growth of employment in the industry as a whole should be appreciated. For another the likely future location dynamics of the firms in the branch concerned needs to be evaluated. Finally the impact of the changes on different types of regions has to be assessed. In all three stages much is uncertain[2].

One such study of a modern sector is the one made of new information technology (NIT) (CURDS 1984), an industry actively promoted by the EC in the framework of its industrial policy. The first part of the study is an empirical analysis of the industry's present location patterns. The next part is of the prospective type; it deals in a qualitative way with the future spatial dynamics of NIT firms, taking account of future developments of such factors as product and production technology, labour needs, etc. The study shows that the less favoured regions of the European Community risk missing out on the benefits of NIT while suffering direct and indirect losses. To create a strong NIT sector in Europe is an imperative object of industrial policy, but the available social and regional policy instruments fail to compensate the least favoured regions for the losses. So, the study suggests adding a specific NIT component to regional policy.

3.4.5. All sectors: prospective analyses

Several attempts at a more general view of future development have recently been made, of which we have selected Molle c.s. 1982 and Bartels c.s. 1983, as relevant to the impact of industrial policy. We will briefly analyse the approaches followed in each of these studies and indicate the results.

In the PRESTO study (Boeckhout and Molle 1982, Molle c.s. 1982, Molle 1983a) an attempt has been made at evaluating the impact of different technological developments on regional employment in Europe. This attempt is based largely on the analysis of theoretical factors such as innovation and regional development, presented in section 3.3. First, from the leading technologies, micro-electronics and the information complex were selected and their future employment effects on different sectors estimated. Next, the locational impact of their future use was studied. Some in-depth studies of a more empirical nature were carried out of these and other sectors with respect to industrial restructuring regions (UK) and agricultural/peripheral regions (Mezzogiorno, Andalucia). An attempt was then made to generalise the empirical and prospective components to the future development of all sectors and regions in the EC. The general conclusion was that stimulating micro-electronics would probably lead to considerable employment losses in all types of regions, losses which in some regions, mostly the high-amenity areas in the vicinity of central regions, may be compensated by gains in the information and communication sectors. Suggestions were made to improve the potential of regions for indigenous growth by enhancing their accessibility and receptivity to change, in particular industrial innovation. Apart from technology, affecting regional development through industrial change, the study underlined the importance of numerous other factors, such as industrial organisation, social structures, and labour attitudes.

The study by Bartels c.s. (1983) of the prospects for the regional development of the tertiary sector initially follows the same approach as PRESTO. After an analysis of the employment change in five service branches (together covering the whole service sector) between 1974 and 1981 in three types of regions (central, peripheral and intermediate), the authors identify and quantify the effects of a number of technological and social changes on the future level of employment by service branch in each type of region. The authors conclude that while there is a considerable potential for job creation in the service sectors, there are indications that such a positive overall development may be accompanied by increasing regional disparities, the less favoured regions losing ground to the more developed ones.

3.4.6. Technology and innovation; a crucial factor

In recent years the body of literature on the regional aspects of technology change had grown steadily. In many research papers, attention has been given to the location of hi-tech industries, the different birth and death rates of firms in various regions, the regional distribution of R&D (both public and private), the possibility of improving the transfer of knowledge, the use of robots (for instance Camagni and Cappellin 1984; Camagni, Capellin and Garofoli 1984; Molle 1985; the 1986 conference of the French Regional Science Association). These analyses have confirmed that a good research and technology infrastructure is in general a prerequisite for industrial restructuring. They have moreover given a wealth of detail concerning specific aspects, suggesting a need for a regional innovation policy. To bring together the elements available in the EC countries and arrange them such as to provide clues for a regional dimension to EC R&D policy, the Commission recently started the co-operative STRIDE study - Stimulation of Research and Technology Development in Regions), covering all member states. Possibly, the study may produce an outline programme for action by the Regional Development Fund for the creation of innovation centres, transfer points, research institutes, etc.

3.4.7. Conclusions

European regional policy aims at compensating certain regions for the losses they suffer from the restructuring of declining industrial sectors. Declining sectors being a well known problem case, the policy action to be taken for reconversion regions is well defined and specific. The same cannot be said of the other sectors.

Prospective and empirical elements are to varying degrees used in approaches which try to generalise sectoral development; such studies tend to be more qualitative than quantitative. They all assume one-way relations between an industry and a (set of) regions.

3.5. Regional impact of industrial change; using the FLEUR model to cope with interregional and intersectoral effects

3.5.1. Introduction

All the studies discussed so far have attempted to assess the impact of industrial change on regions by specifying and quantifying a fairly direct relationship between one sector and the regions in which it is located; for a more complete picture, some of them generalised the approach by adding up the results for several sectors and/or several regions. However, that approach hardly does justice to the real world, in which sectors of industry influence one another and developments are propagated from one region to another through interregional linkages. To take such interregional and intersectoral relations into account requires a more sophisticated approach. The FLEUR model (Factors of Location in Europe), developed to analyse the influence of a number of factors of location on the regional distribution of sectoral growth in the European Community, satisfies the requirements. Up till now the model has not actually been used to assess the impact of industrial policy or more generally of industrial employment changes in Europe[3]; let us see how far its basic characteristics would fit the purpose.

3.5.2. The explanatory model

The basic idea underlying the FLEUR model is that the total production and employment growth of a branch on the European level is determined by variables associated with the long-term cycle. So, total employment in the EC as a whole is an exogenous variable.

The next idea is that the location (that is, the national and regional distribution) of the activity in question changes under the influence of different sets of factors, among which the factors enumerated in section 3.3 take pride of place.

Many considerations have guided the construction of the theoretical FLEUR model, too many to be discussed here; for an in-depth discussion, see, for instance, Molle 1983b; Ancot and Paelinck 1983. The basic features of the model can be outlined as follows. The FLEUR model explains the changes, in the course of a certain period, of the share each region of the EC had in the total European employment of a sector of economic activity. The model consists of a set of identical equations, one for each sector of activity. For some sectors we do not use the model, but introduce the changes in regional employment exogenously. An equation summing the results of the sectoral equations to find total employment (share) by region in the last year of a period completes the model.

The development of a typical sectoral equation of the FLEUR model is too involved to be reproduced here. Again, the reader is referred to the studies mentioned earlier. Suffice it to say that practical problems and theoretical considerations have led us to choose particular specifications for each variable and that estimation problems have induced us to transform the theoretical model into an estimable model, specified as follows:

$$_i\text{CESR}_r^t = a._i\,\text{INSTR}_r^{t-1} +$$

$$b_1._i N_i\,\text{LIOMT}_r^{t-1} + {}_i\text{LIOMT}_r^t 0 +$$

$$b_2._i N_i\,\text{IOMT}_r^{t-1} + {}_i\text{IOMT}_r^t 0 +$$

$$c_1._i N_i\,\text{LISMT}_r^{t-1} + {}_i\text{LISMT}_r^t 0 +$$

$$c_2._i N_i\,\text{ISMT}_r^{t-1} + {}_i\text{ISMT}_r^t 0 +$$

$$d.\text{NCL}_r^{t-1} + \text{CL}_r^t 0 +$$

$$e.\text{NAL}_r^{t-1} + \text{AL}_r^t 0 +$$

$$f.\text{NURB}_r^{t-1} + \text{URB}_r^t 0 +$$

$$g.\text{RPS}_r^{t/(t-1)} +$$

$$h.\text{CD}_r^{t/(t-1)} + \tag{3.1}$$

$$\varepsilon$$

where:
i = sector, t = year, and r = region;
a, b, c, d, e, f, g, and h = coefficients;
1 and 2: denote, respectively, the coefficient for the linear and log terms of the interregional variables;
CESR = corrected employment by sector and region;
INSTR = instrumental variable (proxy for CESR at t-1);
IOMT and LIOMT = interregional output-market tension;

ISMT and LISMT = interregional input-supply market tension;
CL = cost of labour;
AL = availability of labour;
URB = urbanisation;
RPS = regional policy;
CD = country dummy.

3.5.3. How does the FLEUR model work ?

Some explanation of the working of the FLEUR model is in order (for details the reader is referred to Molle 1983b).
The FLEUR study distinguishes 53 standard sectors of activity (i).

The model is based on decennial reference years (t): data are available for 1950, 1960 and 1970; 1980 data are being prepared. The explanatory model describes changes in 76 standard regions (r) of the EC of Nine. The essential indicator of growth in the model is employment (E); policy makers tend to focus their attention on it, and the data situation is better than for other indicators.

The dependent variable of the model (CESR) is the change in employment in a sector i in region r between two points in time t (for instancer, 1950/1960 or 1960/1970), defined as shares in the EC total).

The model accounts first for the influence of national sectoral employment change on regional developments, an element that is indispensable because the model is intended to deal in the same way with all regions of the European Community, to whatever member country they belong (that is to say, it does not consist of a national layer with a set of regional sub-models). The differential effect of the sectoral development of employment in the member countries of the EC on regional employment is accounted for in the model by correcting the regional shares at the end and beginning of each period for the national situation. The corrected share of a region in sectoral employment at the end of a period is now explained by that same region's share at the beginning of the period (t-1) plus a number of characteristics of that region. Further transformation proved necessary as estimations progressed. First it proved practical to have only the employment situation at the end of the period as dependent variable, putting the corresponding situation at the beginning of the period as first independent variable. Next it proved necessary to replace this first independent variable (lagged employment by sector, accounting for the endogenous dynamics of the system) with an instrumental variable to avoid estimation difficulties.

A set of location factors were introduced as explanatory variables, The list of explanatory variables has been drawn up from an analysis of the factors showing up in empirical studies of location decision. After a careful examination of the available data needed to quantify these variables, the following independent variables were included to account for the regional dynamics of sectoral employment change: (1) output markets (OM), (2) input-supply markets (SM), (3) transport (T), (4) labour costs (CL), (5) labour availability (AL), (6) urbanisation (URB), and (7) regional policy (RPS). The model makes a distinction between variables with only a regional effect, and variables exerting also an interregional influence. We will give a brief comment on both.

CL, AL, URB and RPS are all considered regional variables, that is, variables exerting an influence in their own region only. The effect of these regional variables can be explained by the example of the regional differences in labour availability: the idea is that the more labour is available in a region during a period of analysis, the higher will be (ceteris paribus) the region's share in sectoral employment.

IOMT and ISMT are _interregional_ variables; they have influence in other regions as well, beyond a certain point decreasing as the distance (T) becomes longer.

The interregional effects are somewhat more complicated. Take output markets as an example; in the FLEUR model, a region's share in sectoral employment will be higher as the market outlets in the regions are larger, and also, as access from the own region to markets in other regions is easier. So, when accessibility improves, for instance because of improved transport infrastructure (e.g., a new motorway replacing a former small road, permitting higher average speed) or when the markets in neighbouring regions grow (for instance because sectors have developed there which use the products of the sector in question as inputs), the market potential of the region under study will increase and the region's share in the total European employment of the sector under study is expected to grow also.

One more feature of the model should be recalled, namely, that it is _intersectoral_, a feature that is contained in the two market variables (OM and SM). Take, for example, the machine-tool industry, needing steel products for its production process; the location of machine-tool production in a particular region increases that region's market potential for the steel industry, so one may expect its share in employment in the steel industry to grow. On the other hand the presence of this machine-tool factory may be important to sectors requiring machine tools, so the increase in the input-market potential indicates the region's heightened attractiveness to such activities as the construction of non-electric machinery, and the region's share in the employment in such sectors may be expected to grow as well.

The country dummy added to the model takes care of imperfections in the data and for national factors not further explicited; this variable's only purpose is to achieve correct estimations of the various parameters.

Theoretically, we should have liked to make a distinction between the initial effect, being the influence of the situation with respect to certain variables at the beginning of a period, and the final effect, being the effect of the same explanatory variables at the end of the period; however, as this did not probe possible in practice, we had to take the two together, which implies that we can compute only the average 'period' effect.

The model uses the input- and output-market tension variables twice, once in a logarithmic version (for example, LIOMT), and again in a linear version (for example, IOMT). In that way, from the composite estimated coefficients b_1, b_2 and c_1, c_2, can be derived the original coefficients of the model, consisting of the distance friction) (of interregional effects), the propensity parameter (q) and the adaptation parameter (a). From the coefficients d through h, together with a, the original propensity coefficient and the adaptation parameter a are derived.

3.5.4. Estimation results

The FLEUR model has been estimated for 41 selected sectors, the twelve others being precluded for various reasons; the final results are given in Molle (1983b).

For each sector a separate equation was estimated on the basis of two cross-section analyses, one for the period 1950-1960, the other for the period 1960-1970. The period 1970-1980 will be added as soon as the dataset for 1980 is completed. For each sector three types of coefficients were calculated from the original estimated parameters, namely, a distance-friction coefficient (for the interregional variables OM and SM), propensity coefficients for all variables, and an adaptation coefficient applicable to the whole sector.

The adaptation parameter indicates the speed at which a sector adapts to new conditions (represented by the independent variables). The adaptation parameter lies between 0 and 1, 1 denoting a complete adaptation during the 10-year period, 0 no reaction to locational factors at all. The propensity parameters give an indication of the degree to which the sector is responsive to a specific locational factor, and are sector- and variable-specific. Finally, the distance-friction coefficients denote the rate at which interregional influences diminish with increased distance; one distance friction coefficient is computed for the supply variable, and another for the demand variable (see for details Molle 1983b).

Without describing the results in detail, we want to emphasise that for all sectors the degree of explanation was high, most parameters agreeing in sign and size to theoretical expectations. It means that we have been able to make operational a tool with which to explain the regional effects of past industrial change.

A few exercises have also been made with a FLEUR projection model (1990-2000) (Paelinck 1983, Ancot, Molle and Paelinck 1984), including policy simulations to optimise future regional trends of industrial change.

3.5.5. Conclusions

The FLEUR model regionalises primarily the European and national developments of a given industrial sector; because demand and supply market variables change under the influence of change in other sectors and regions, the model accounts also for intersectoral and interregional effects of industrial change. Its aptitude for policy-impact analysis has been demonstrated but needs to be further explored.

3.6. Final remarks

The objective of the present study was to give some insight into the methods that have been used to assess the impact of industrial policy measures on regional equilibrium in Europe.

A first conclusion from the review of the relevant literature is that up till now all studies have considered only the total impact of industrial change, not splitting it into policy-induced and other industrial change. In recent times the attention has been diverted from aid to investment to other forms of aid, for instance, aid to R&D or innovation, aid to professional and entrepreneurial training facilities, etc. Many of these types of assistance are geared to small and medium-size industries. However, on the European level the idea must still be translated into policy (the STRIDE-programme is now being elaborated). So long as we do not know basically how to split up the effects, it is hardly surprising that the further specification of, for instance, the influence of specific measures of industrial policy (such as subsidies to R&D, or demand stabilisation through government procurement) on regional equilibrium, is still in an embryonic stage too.

A second conclusion is that the methods used to assess the impact vary considerably. They combine varying proportions of empirical and prospective elements; most of them depend heavily on a combination of qualitative arguments and the simple treatment of statistical data (CEC 1984b, CURDS 1984, Molle c.s. 1982, Bartels c.s. 1983). The few more formalised approaches (Carnagni-Cappellin 1984, Molle 1983b) have up till now proved valuable only for analysing the past; how far they are useful for projecting the regional impact of industrial change for the future still wants proving.

A final conclusion is that industrial change is only one of the factors influencing regional equilibrium. Several studies (Camagni-Cappellin 1984, but also Van Haselen c.s. 1983, Van Haselen and Molle 1984) have shown that other factors, notably manpower and demography, make an important impact as well.

3.7. Notes

1. A few studies have been made, however, a notable one being EIU 1983.
2. Some insight into future problems of growth sectors could be gained from the analysis of their locational dynamics in the past, but only if the same kind of industry is involved.
3. For a first step in that direction, see Ancot and Paelinck (1983), and Ancot, Molle and Paelinck (1984).

3.8. References

Ancot, J.-P., and J.H.P. Paelinck (1983), The Spatial Econometrics of the European Fleur Model, in D. Griffith and A.Lea (eds.), Evaluating Geographical Structures, Mart. Nijhoff Publishers, The Hague, pp. 229-246.

Ancot, J.-P., W. Molle and J.H.P. Paelinck (1984), Modelling the European Regional System: some experiences with the FLEUR model, in A.R. Kuklinsky and J. Lambooy (eds.), Societies, Boundaries, Regions, UNRISD Series, Geneva.

Bartels, C.P.A., D. Boomstra and B. Vlessert (1983), Prospects for the Regional Development of the Tertiary Sector, study carried for the EC Commission, Oudemolen (mimeo).

Boeckhout, I.J., and W.T.M. Molle (1982), Technological Change,Location Patterns and Regional Development, PRESTO-project, FAST Occasional Papers no. 16, EC-DG XII, Brussels.

Broadbent, A., and Meegan, R. (1982), New Technology in Older Industrialised Regions, PRESTO-project, FAST Occasional Papers no. 57, EC-DG XII, Brussels.

Camagni, R., et R. Cappellin (1984), Changement structurel et croissance de la production dans les régions européennes, Revue d'Economie Régionale et Urbaine, vol. 25, no. 2, pp. 177-217.

Camagni, R., Cappellin, R., and Sarofoli, G. (1984), Cambiamento technologico e diffuzione territoriale, Franco Angeli, Milano.

Cappellin, R. (1986), The Development of Service Activities in the Italian Urban System, in Illeris (ed.), Present and Future Role of Services in Regional Development, FAST occasional paper no. 74, CEC,Brussels.

CEC (1979), The evolution of the sectoral structures of the European economies since the oil crisis 1973-1978, Special number of European Economy, Brussels.

CEC (1982), The European Community's Industrial Strategy, manuscript by P. Maillet, European Documentation 5, Luxemburg, 66 pages.

CEC (1984a), Draft Council Decision adopting the 1984 work programm for the European Strategic Programme for Research and Development in Information Technologies (ESPRIT), Official Journal of the EC, E47, vol. 27. pp 1-67.

CEC (1984b), The regions of Europe, Second Periodic Report, COM (84) 40 final 2, Brussels.

Cuadrado, J.L, Arioles, J., and Granados, V. (1982), Andalucia, a case study in technological development and regional growth, PRESTO-project, FAST Occasional Papers nr. 30, EC-DG XII, Brussels.

CURDS (1984), The effects of new information technology on the less favoured regions of the Community, Newcastle upon Tyne.

Duyn, J.J. van (1982), The Long Wave in Economic Life, Allen and Unwin, London.

EIU (Economic Intelligence Unit) (1983), Impact régional de la politique communautaire dans le secteur de l'automobile, vol. 2, Régions, Internal EC report, Brussels.

Eversley, J.F., Gillespie, A.E., and O'Neil, A. (1984), Régional Disparities in Industrial Decline, paper for the RSA Conference, Milan.

Ewers, H.J., and Wettmann, R.W. (1980), Innovation Oriented Regional Policy, Regional Studies, vol. 14, pp.161-180.

Freeman, C., Clark, J., and Soete, L. (1982), Unemployment and Technical Innovation; a study of Long Waves and Economic Development, Frances Pinter, London.

Haselen, H. van, c.s. (1983), Analysis and Projection of Regional Labour Market Balances in Europe (LABEUR), Internal Documentation on Regional Policy in the Community, no. 14. Brussels.

Haselen, H. van, et W. Molle (1984), Analyse et projection des marchés du travail en Europe: le modèle LABEUR, in Ph. Aydalot (ed.), Crise et Espace, Economica, Paris, pp. 322-348.

Jacquemin, A., and De Jong, H. (1977), European Industrial Organisation, Mac-Millan, London.

Jacquemin, A. (1979), Le phénomène de désindustrialisation et la Communauté Européenne, Revue Economique, VI, pp.985-999.

Jacquemin, A. (ed.) (1984), European Industry; Public Policy and Corporate strategy, Clarendon Press, Oxford, 377 pages.

Jong, H.W. de (1982), Dynamische markttheorie, Stenfert Kroese, Leiden.

Jong, H.W. de (ed.) (1981), The Structure of European Industry, Nijhoff Publishers, The Hague.

Klaassen, L.H., and Molle, W.T.M. (eds.) (1983), Industrial Mobility and Migration in the European Community, Gower Press, Aldershot, 1983.

Kondratieff, N.L. (1926), Die langen Wellen der Konjunktur, Archif für Sozialwissenschaft und Sozialpolitik, pp. 573-609.

Kuznetz, S. (1930), Secular Movements in Production and Prices, Houghton Mifflin.

Maillat, D. (ed.) (1982), Technology a Key Factor in Regional Development, Georgi, Saint Saphorin.

Malecki, E.J. (1981), Public and Private Sector Interrelationships, Technological Change and Regional Development, Papers of the Regional Science Association, vol. 47, pp. 121-137.

Mignolet, M. (1983), Les processus de diffusion des innovations dans l'espace et le redéploiement économique régional, Ph.D., Namur (roneotyped).

Molle c.s., W.T.M. (1980), Regional Disparity and Economic Development in the European Community, Gower Press, Farnborough.

Molle, W.T.M., c.s. (1982), Prospects of Regional Employment and Scanning of Technological Options, PRESTO-project, Synthesis, FAST Occasional Papers, no. 31, EC-DG XII, Brussels

Molle, W.T.M. (1983a), Technological Change and Regional Development in Europe, Papers of the RSA, 22nd European Congress, pp. 23-48.

Molle, W.T.M. (1983b), Industrial Location and Regional Development in the European Community, Gower Press, Aldershot.

Molle, W.T.M., and Wever, E. (1984), Oil Refineries and Petrochemical Industries in Western Europe, Gower Press, Aldershot.

Molle, W.T.M. (ed.) (1985), Innovatie en regio, Staatsuitgeverij, The Hague.

Molle, W.T.M. (1986), The Regional Impact of Welfare State Policies in the European Community, in J.H.P. Paelinck (ed.), Human Behaviour in Geographical Space, essays in honour of L. Klaassen, Gower Press, Aldershot, pp.77-91.

Nelson, R.R., and Winter, S.G. (1977), In Search of a Useful Theory of Innovation, in K.A. Stroetmann (ed.), Innovation, Economic Change and Technology Policies, Birkhäuser Verlag, Basel.

OECD (1980), Technical Change and Economic Policy, Paris.

Paelinck, J.H.P. (1983), Investment and the Development of Backward Regions, in A. Heertje (ed.), Investing in Europe's Future, Blackwell, Oxford.

Pelkmans, J. (1984), Market Integration in the EC, Studies in industrial organisation, Vol. 5, Nijhoff Publishers, The Hague.

Rothwell, R., and W. Zegveld, (1981), Industrial Innovation and Public policy: preparing for the 1980's and 1990's, F. Pinter, London, 251 pages.

Tarde, G. (1962) La psychologie économique (translation of E.C. Parsons, The Law of Imitations), reprint.

Thomas, M.D. (1975), Growth Pole Theory, Technological Change and Regional Economic Growth, Papers of the Regional Science Association, vol. 34, pp. 3-27.

Thomas, M.D. (1981), Growth and Change in Innovation Manufacturing Industries and Firms' Process and Product Innovation, IIASA Collaboration Paper, Vienna.

Toulemon, R., et J. Flory (1974), Une politique industrielle pour l'Europe, PUF, Paris, 272 pages.

Utterback, J.M., and Abernathy, W.J. (1974), A Test of a Conceptual Model Linking States in Firms' Process and Product Innovation, Working Paper HBS, 74-34 Harvard Business School, Cambridge (Mass.).

Vernon, R. (1974), International Investment and International Trade in the Product Cycle, Quarterly Journal of Economics, pp. 190-207.

Wells, L.T. (ed.) (1972), The Product Life Cycle and International Trade, Division of Research, Harvard Business School, Boston.

4 Energy

B. BOURGEOIS

4.1. Introduction

Energy policy covers a wide and complex area; it concerns, on the one hand, the exploration and production of primary sources of energy (coal, oil, gas, etc.), the transformation of these primary sources into energy products (oil products in refineries, electricity in power plants), and their distribution to the consumers. On the other hand it deals also with energy consumption policy. It influences price formation and the quantities produced and delivered in each sub-sector of the energy economy, co-ordinates activity in these sub-sectors, regulates the quality of the products and the emission of pollutants.

To define and implement such a variety of policies naturally involves many actors. In the energy sector, at least as far as supply is concerned, the Member State generally takes precedence over the region and the Community. While the objectives of the Member States in our period of study have been to some extent the same, the priorities given to realisation have been different. To keep in line with the presentation of other sectors in this study, we shall first describe the main themes of the Community's energy policy during the past decade and its intervention in that regard in the regons. Next, we shall raise some theoretical and methodological points of the political interface between energy and region.

The body of this chapter we shall devote to the analysis of the regional imbalances of energy supply in the European Community, focusing on the vulnerability of regions to changes in the dominant type of energy. That leads us, finally, to a critical study of the orientation of EC energy policy, and to suggestions for future action.

4.2. Community energy policy

4.2.1. Introduction

The term "Community energy policy" is of recent date. In the review "Energy and Europe", the Commission refers to the year 1967, when the executive institutions of the three Communities merged, as that of the "first Community energy action".

The notion of "Community energy policy" was first diffused publicly in 1980, when the Community committed itself to energy objectives to be realised by 1990. The proposal was approved, and given a minimum of political support, by the Member States, and concerned all the main problems of energy policy. We will review these objectives as they are contained in the Community's strategies, as well as the methods that have been used to realise them.

4.2.2. Objectives

The existence of a Community energy policy appears clearly from the approval of quantitative and/or qualitative "Community energy objectives" set by the Council of Ministers for a certain time horizon. On June 1980, the Council set five sectoral objectives to be reached by 1990, three quantitative and two qualitative ones. Of the quantitative objectives, one concerned primary energy demand ("to reduce the gross primary energy consumption/GNP elasticity to 0.7"), and two related to energy supplies, more in particular the dependence on oil ("to reduce the share of oil in gross primary energy consumption to less than 40 per cent), and electricity production ("to meet 70-75 per cent of primary energy requirements for electricity production using solid fuels and nuclear energy"). The two qualitative objectives relate to the setting of energy prices and the increase of the share of alternative and renewable energies.

The Community's quantified objectives were based on projections made for the individual Member States and received their approval, unofficially at any rate. No such objectives have been set for the Member States individually; therefore, the degree to which the policy objectives have been achieved in the various countries is difficult to assess. We do know, however, that some Member States have achieved better results than others. The disparities are largely due to national differences of:

1. the availability of national fossil energy resources;
2. the ability to modify the national energy system through appropriate investments;
3. the relative priority of energy policy objectives among the overall policy objectives.

In 1985, the Commission submitted to the Council "new Community energy objectives" for the year 1995. These objectives were based on an analysis of the past results of each Member State's energy policy, and the projection of energy supply and demand to the years 1995 and 2000 (specified in "Energie 2000").

Some progress had meanwhile been made. In particular the fact had been recognised that energy policy together with other Community policies interacts with the definition of horizontal objectives of a qualitative nature. That is why objectives have now been proposed for such various matters as foreign policy, the integration of the energy market in the Community, guaranteed supplies, energy pricing, environmental impacts, technological development and regional development. The Community aims specifically at "reinforcing the Community's energy policy by appropriate measures in the less favoured regions". Obviously, then, the Commission has become aware that efforts to attain the Community energy objectives in regions that are underdeveloped or experience severe industrial decline encounter specific difficulties, and that the situation calls for appropriate responses, in particular that of "encouraging energy developments which will have considerable local impact" in the former, and "developing new activities" in the latter type of region.

In the following section we will set out the arguments by which the GD XVI (Regional Policy) justifies both orientations.

More consideration is now also given to the uncertainty besetting the forecasts and projections which serve as the basis for quantified sectoral objectives. This uncertainty is largely due to the fluctuations of oil prices and economic growth in each Member State.

Six sectoral objectives have been set for 1995, namely:

- to reduce the intensity of final energy by at least one quarter (final-energy-demand/GNP ratio);
- to reduce the dependency of total primary energy consumption on oil to one third of the oil imported (48 per cent in 1983);
- to maintain and, if, possible increase the relative share of solid fuels whilst continuing to restructure the Community's coal industry;
- to maintain and, if possible, increase the relative share of natural gas (18 per cent in 1983);
- to restrict the share of hydrocarbons in total fuel for electricity production to a maximum of 10 per cent (22 per cent in 1983);
- to increase the contribution of nuclear energy to electricity production to 40 per cent;
- to triple the share of new and renewable energies.

4.2.3. The means

To realise its energy objectives, the Community relies, apart from ad hoc regulations and treaties, mainly on technological energy programmes and on structural financial funds to support investments in energy.

The Community's technical programmes fall apart into those to support research and those devoted to development, a distinction sometimes hard to keep up.

One objective of the first Community Research and Development Programme (1984-1987) is "to improve the management of energy resources and reduce energy intensity". Apparently, at the beginning of 1985 most of the one milliard ECU of the Community's financial resources were already committed to nuclear objectives and 300 million ECU to non-nuclear objectives (renewable energies, the rational use of energy). Probably the results obtained with non-nuclear energy will make more impact on the economy and the energy supply in the Community's peripheral regions than those for nuclear energies; the very high energy power levels generated even with minimum economic size makes nuclear energy unsuitable for the thinly populated peripheral regions.

The programmes most oriented to development are the "demonstration programmes". At a recent meeting (on November 11, 1985), the Energy Council decided in principle to set aside some 500 million ECU for the period 1986-1989 in favour of energy savings, alternative kinds of energy, coal gasification and liquefaction, and support to the technological development of hydrocarbons. A 1984 report highlights the positive aspects of the Community's practical programme undertaken between 1978 and 1984, and shows that their success reflects the increasing number and progressive diffusion of demonstration projects. Once more, the spatial/regional dimension should be considered in the distribution of innovations.

Structural financial tools - whether loans or subsidies - have done much to support investments in energy. Loans have been granted by EIB, NCI, ECSC and EURATOM, while ERDF Special UK-Deutschland measures and interest rebates account for most of the subsidies. In 1983 - apparently a record year for this type of financing, cumulative Community aid (loans and subsidies) represented 7.9 per cent of the energy sector's gross investment.

Table 4.1
Subsidies and loans provided by various Community financial sources
for energy investments between 1975 and 1983

SUBSIDIES			LOANS		
Instru-ment	Total	of which energy	Instru-ment	Total	of which energy
	in m ECU	m ECU %		m ECU	m ECU %
ERDF	9 407	1 328 (14)	EIB	20 446	8 008 (39)
EAGGF	4 727	34 (1)	NCI	3 017	808 (27)
ECSC	903	24 (3)	ECSC	7 495	2 303 (31)
Social Fund	7 963	0	Euratom	367	367 (100)
EMS[a]	1 017	0			
Special	4 915	1 188 (24)			
TOTAL	28 932	2 574 (9)		31 325	11 486 (37)

Source: DG XVI.
a) Intrest rate subsidies

Three comments can be made on the allocation of these loans and subsidies.

The Commission is aware of the fact that, for the most part, subsidies help "finance national rather than Community energy programmes". If, in spite of the difficulties involved (for instance the existence of "multi-regional programmes"), the loans and subsidies are distributed among the regions where the investments are made, the per capita subsidies on energy investments are found to have been higher as the regions rank higher on the priority list for Community regional policy; the only exception is the United Kingdom, because of so-called "additional measures" in the period 1981-1983.

On the other hand, from the same per capita ratios, loans appear to depend largely on the ability of Member States to present large-scale projects (gas pipelines, nuclear-power stations, district heating networks), which obviously favours countries which are already reasonably developed; here the exception is Ireland.

An intra-sectoral analysis of the allocation of funds shows that in the period 1973-1984 4 per cent of the subsidies and 5 per cent of the loans were invested in the rational use of energy and local energy (new types of energy, and lignite and peat). The so-called 'dense energies' - electricity production, transportation and distribution - accounted for about 65 per cent).

4.2.4. Community action to solve problems of energy policy in the regions

Proceedings involving energy mostly evolve between the Community and the national governments, but the Commission tries to establish relations with regional governments as well. Such relations always require the consent of the governments of the Member States concerned, and are sometimes regarded by them as infringements of national sovereignty.

Regional energy policies are not in general far developed, so there is no point in comparing them here. Table 4.2 just highlights some noticeable differences between Member States with a decentralised, federal structure, and those where the State has much and local actors have very little say in the matter of energy (see Lucas and Papaconstantinou (1985)

Table 4.2
Support given by local actors and territorial
communities to the energy-supply sector

Significant	Poor	Practically none
West Germany	Netherlands	United Kingdom
Denmark	Belgium	Ireland
	Italy	Greece
	France	

The contrasts shown in the table refer mostly to the supply of energy; the role played by local actors with respect to energy demand, consumption and/or substitution is mostly more important, even in countries with poor or virtually absent support to energy supply.

Apart from the loans and subsidies represented in Table 4.1, two other types of Community Aid to energy have been given to regions.

(i) Investment support has been granted by the European Regional Development Fund (DGXVI) to develop renewable kinds of energy and energy savings in the Mezzogiorno region and in the Greek islands, and for the extenson of the gas pipeline network in Ireland; the amounts involved were in the order of 5, 20 and 32 million ECU, respectively. The execution of the Mezzogiorno project encountered some difficulties, but it is early days to pass judgment on the overall effects.

As a counterpart to this more or less defensive action ("to compensate the negative effects of other Community policies"), those responsible for the Community's Regional Policy have proposed a "Community Programme concerning the development of certain underprivileged regions within the Community by developing potential endogenous energy" (CCE)[1]; the reasons and methods of that new type of Community aid will be set forth in the third section of this chapter.

(ii) Financial aid for regional and local energy studies has been granted by the Commission since 1982. At the suggestion of the GDXVII, twenty-odd local and regional energy studies have been supported, out of the one hundred which were to be launched (Community budget of approximately 3.44 million ECU; see Table 4.3 hereafter). Some important themes of these studies are: the establishment of local or regional energy balance sheets, an analysis of the determinants of energy demand and of energy-demand forecasting, the use of local/regional energy sources and the rational use of energy; some studies plead evaluation of the impacts which energy investment programmes make on the local economy.

The wide variation in situations, problems and methods make the results of these studies very difficult to compare. However, in their variety, the studies highlight what is at stake in actions involving energy demand and local energy supplies coupled with those of the large national networks, a point that is useful when investments programmes are developed.

Table 4.3
Energy and local analyses financed by the EC

Project name		Location Area 1000 km2	Inhab. Mio.	Type	Project Content	Aims	Dura-tation/ months	Project Situ-ation	Work needed H/M a)	Principal	Represen-tative	EC subsidies in 1000 ECU
Aquitaine	F	41.3	2.6	R	E	IED	36	i.D.	100	EC-region	Aquitainergie	320
Berlin	D	0.5	1.9	S	E	IE	24	i.D.	80	EC-Land	InnoTec	341 (1)
Brussels	B	0.2	1.0	S	E	IE	18	i.F.	36	EC-region	Region	60 (1)
Bornholm	DK	0.1	0.05	R	E(N&E)	IED	10	i.D.	20	EC-region	Region	67
Flanders	B	13.5	5.6	RS	E	IE	18	i.D.	110	Region-EC	SESO, M&R	157
Ireland	IRL	70.3	3.4	R	E	IE	24	g		EC-State	State	150 (1)
Cyclades	GR	2.6	0.1	R	E(N&E)	IE	24	i.D.	144	EC-region-State	State,region, Cons.	231 (1)
Lombardia	I	23.9	8.9	RS	E	IE	24	I.D.	70	EC-region	Univ. bodies	160 (1)
Lozère	F	1.0	0.4	R	E	I	36	I.D.	80	State-EC	NCRS	66
Luxemburg	L	2.6	0.4	RS	E	IE	24	g	50	EC-State	IWS Consult	100 (1)
North Brabant	NL	5.1	3.2	S	W/K	IE	24	i.D.	50	EC-State	TNO	100
North Frisia	D	2.0	0.2	R	E	IE	24	i.D.	50	EC-State-Land	Var.private companies	150
NE England	GB	7.3	6.5	RS	E	IE	24	g	50	EC-Ind.-region	March-Cons.	150 (1)
High Palatine	D	0.7	1.0	R	N&E	IED	16	a	50	EC-region	Z.V.Oberpfalz	267
Provence-Alpes-Côte d'Azur	F	31.4	3.9	RS	E	IED	36	i.D.	100	EC-region-state	ARENE	188
Apulia	I	19.3	3.9	R	E	IED	36	i.D.	50	EC-region	CSCE-Bari	167 (1)
Saar	D	2.6	1.1	RS	W	IED	36	a	150	State-EC-region	Z.V.S. Fern-wärme	260
Storstrom	DK	0.2	0.3	R	E	IED	10	i.D.	20	EC-region	Cowi-Cons.	61
Wallonia	B	16.8	3.2	R	E	IE	36	i.D.	120	EC-State-region	I.W.Namur	287
Westland	NL	1.3	0.1	R	E	IED	16	i.D.	50	EC-State	NEOM	160
TOTAL		250	50									3,440
Methodical EC-studies, comparative analyses		1,658	271		Evaluation Various,current/complete					EC	Various institutions and consultants	
Portugal		92	9.9	RS	E(N&E)	36				EC-State	ERA/PE	100 (1)

(1) Financing still incomplete.
(a) Estimates (including conversion of part-time to full-time collaboration; excluding auxiliary and clerical staff).

Legend
Type: R = region
            S = town (or built-up industrial area)
            RS = highly urbanised region
Content: E = energy market as a whole
            W = heat market (low temperature)
            N&E = new and renewable energies (including rational use of energy)
Aims: I = improved information basis, particularly with regard to demand
            E = development of decision bases
            D = elaboration of feability plans
Position: i.D. = in progress
            g = projected
            a = completed
Source: Von Scholz.

4.2.5. Some intermediate conclusions

From the above rapid examination of the objectives and resources of the Community's energy policy in the period 1973-1985, some progress apears to have been made towards an energy strategy, or policy, of the Community. This progress has been hampered:

-   by the differences among Member States in situation and energy priorities. Some Member States are highly dependent on oil imports; others have succeeded in reducing their dependence. Member States also have different fossil fuel resources;
-   by the reluctance of some Member States to delegate part of their sovereignty to the Community, an attitude not peculiar to the energy sector alone. Because of it, the very notion of a Community energy policy is still very fragile.

Recently, the Community has included energy considerations in its actions of regional policy. Such actions are undertaken either to support economic development in the less favoured regions, or to help adjust potential energy supply to energy requirements. In the near future, they may coincide with elements of the VALOREM programme briefly described in the introductory section. The integration of the two may be the key to success for Community actions in the region-energy interface.

4.3. Energy policy and regional policy: theory and methodology

4.3.1. Theoretical aproaches

In the course of the last decade, many theoretical works have been published on the relation between the energy system and the spatial economy. Four orientations may be quoted:

1. Some studies treat energy as a production factor, to be replaced or complemented by other production factors: capital, labour, and, should the need arise, other raw materials. The long- and short-term development, in connection with price elasticities, are examined. Several American authors have walked this theoretical path, among others:
    -   Lakshmanan (1984) et al., who, with the help of the Allen econometric estimation of substitution elasticities, show regional variations in the complementarity between energy and two forms of capital, for a given sector;
    -   Garofalo and Malhotra (1984), who estimate input demand and substitution elasticities (energy, capital, labour) for 9 regions through two periods (1963-1966 and 1974-1977).
2. Some other studies analyse the local and regional impacts of large-scale energy projects, often evaluating the environmental impacts as well (Lakshmanan and Johansson, 1985; Guesnier, 1983; Kneese et al., 1981).
3. There are studies which discuss the interaction between energy supply and demand on the one hand, and on the other either the spatial distribution of activities (demonstrated by Nijkamp 1983, by an analysis of the systems), or evolutions in the urban sector (Lundqvist, 1983; Downs and Bradbury, 1984).
4. Finally, some studies aim at detecting and possibly measuring interregional income flows between energy importing and energy exporting regions (Miernyk, 1976, 1977; Manuel, 1982, 1985).

A synthesis of the territorial impact of changes in the conditions of energy supply - which to the best of our knowledge, no author has yet attempted - might be made along the following lines.

1. Arrange regional inequalities, first within the framework of the national economy, then within the international framework, which is known increasingly to affect economic flows.
2. Integrate the various types of impacts, both direct (on energy-intensive sectors; increased household energy bills) and indirect (macro-economic impacts on the regional level).
3. To measure their relative importance on the regional level, dissociate the impact of energy changes from those caused by the economic crisis (downward tendency in the growth of external activity, increased pressure from competitors ...).
4. Outline these numerous and complex interactions within a temporal framework for a period of at least five to ten years.

Perhaps this programme is a little too ambitious in comparison with existing models and in view of difficult manipulation and validation presented by the existing models.

With France as an example, a system of two linked models comes to mind.

1. Integrate models, giving an account of the interaction between energy and national economic growth. An example is the Mini-DMS Energy model (Brillet et al., 1985), a long-term dynamic model of Keynesian approach; it shows, on the macro-economic level, three production sectors (Sector 1: Industrial equipment; Sector 2: Protected sector: Agriculture, Tertiary and Public-works industries; Sector 3: Energy), and five institutional sectors (1: companies; 2: households; 3: administration; 4: financial institutions; 5: foreign). Past econometric links are estimated (a) between the macro-economic bloc and the energy sector; for example: influence of the level of activity in the production sectors and their investments on intermediate energy consumption; (b) between the energy bloc and the macro-economic bloc; for example: influence of the price of energy products on prices in general, and on household consumption and foreign trade.
2. National integrate regional models, of which the REGINA model (Courbis 1979) is an example; it is based on the hypothesis of jointly established national and regional accounts. However, the demands on data and consistency are so high that to use such a model to study energy impact is not realistic. In that respect, Aydalot (1985) wonders whether the abandoning of the REGINA model is not "symptomatic of a certain disenchantment with large-scale models" and whether researchers will perhaps be forced to restrict the scope of their theoretical question, particularly as regards regional economies, for which it is much more difficult to obtain information and statistics than for national economies.

Leaving aside the idea of integrate models, we will now concentrate on some selected topics. Those listed at the beginning of this section do not seem equally relevant to the question this book is addressing, while some really important ones are not on that list. We have therefore selected a new range of topics for further discussion, focusing on the role of the energy price in the reduction of regional disparities, the regional impact of energy investments, and the regional distribution of innovation in energy production.

4.3.2. The price of energy as instrument to reduce regional inequalities

There is an enormous difference in the cost of energy supply and distribution between areas that are difficult to get to (mountainous land, and certain island

areas), and those that are easily accessible (industrial or port areas), between urban and rural zones, and between industrial and agricultural zones.
The differences in the unit cost of energy supply can be largely explained from two factors:

1. the density and volume of energy consumption;
2. the sensitivity of energy infrastructures (production, transport, distribution) to economies of scale.

To optimise the allocation of resources, setting prices in correspondence with the costs is sound economics. We know, however, that a system which strictly links prices to supply costs is not practicable: in some peripheral areas prices would rise to prohibitive levels to domestic consumers with a lower-than-average income, and to companies handicapped by other high costs.

During the 1960s, some of those responsible for regional policy, following growth-pole theory, defended the idea of a completely different tarification. They argued that the history of industrial development in industrialised countries or regions had demonstrated the "driving force" of certain basic sectors, usually the energy-intensive ones. So, to attract these sectors to the peripheral regions, one only had to offer them "favourable" energy prices, that is, lower than the national average. The following sequence was assumed:

1. the newly settled industries can make the very capital-intensive energy infrastructure profitable; cheap energy can then be offered to other industrial or domestic consumers;
2. the products and by-products of the basic industries can be transformed by downstream industries which will spring up close to the basic industrial complexes.

Other factors cast doubts on the effectiveness of the process, however. For one thing, energy-intensive industries may be highly sensitive to the price of energy, but that factor is only one of many to be considered when choosing a site for a particular industry; in under-industrialised regions and countries, for instance, the additional investment costs may run to 50 or even 100 per cent of capital expenditure; to compensate for the investment-cost differentials, the energy-price differential must be even greater. Nor is there a mechanism to ensure the liaison between the establishment of intermediate industries and the development of downstream ones; the model assuming industrialisation by upstream capital-intensive industries functions only if numerous other conditions are met. Whether that type of industry will be the "driving force" of the 1980s and 1990s, remains doubtful. Furthermore, such "artificial" lowering of prices causes increasing economic distortions in a market where energy prices are high. Finally, since the middle of the 1970s, intermediate industries have been moving to oil-exporting countries (see Molle and Wever, 1984); therefore, price-lowering tactics cannot be seriously considered in the countries they have left.

A less voluntarist orientation, with the same intention of reducing regional inequalities, consists in establishing systems of total or partial tariff equalisation within a particular Member State, either between rich, industrialised regions and peripheral, rural ones, or between urban and rural areas. To assess the reality of that proposal, the evaluation would be required of all advantages and disadvantages of equalising regional energy prices, such as:

- the political and economic cost of the institutional system required to equalise areas with a deficit and those with a surplus: either a (public) company will be given a monopoly for the whole territory, or the deficit areas receive specific subsidies, which must be revised every year;

73

- the twofold perverse effects of a system of price equalisation: if the consumption of energy increases with the drop in price, the deficits to be compensated will steadily increase, or the low price of a particular form of energy may prevent its rational use and the economic development of local competitive resources.

4.3.3. The regional effects of various forms of investment in energy

During the 1950s and 1960s, the energy strategy was mostly to optimise investments in energy supply, particularly from imported primary sources of energy. The changes that have come about since 1973, especially with regard to the leading oil price, have shown the economic importance of investments in energy saving, energy substitution and renewable and/or local energy supplies, the choice from these three being free to some extent. Meanwhile, policy priorities have also evolved; slow economic growth and the shift of leading sectors has forced the less favoured regions to rely no longer on growth "imported" from developed regions (Klaassen and Molle, 1985), but to look for indigenous growth potential. Indeed, "the stimulation of the endogenous potential of regional development" more and more "becomes the heart of the regional development problem" (Giolitti, 1984). The question is, which type of energy investment is the best to mobilise the potential of the less favoured regions.

Investments in energy, like any other, have regional socio-economic effects, which depend on (1) the ability of the region to realise and exploit the new energy unit; (2) the reduction of the energy bill, and (3) the spatial distribution of energy products. Investment in "local" energy and the rational use of energy stimulate the endogenous development potential in two ways. For one thing, local energy is, by definition, exploited locally. For another, local participation in the construction and exploitation of these investments is mostly higher than in large-scale energy networks. Still, investment in the more traditional, large-scale units in peripheral regions gives energy advantages, too, and often stimulate a significant local contribution. On the other hand, all too often a large part of the output is re-exported to the more central, industrialised regions, so that the permanent local economic impact of such large sites is often lower than that of rational use of energy and local energy investments.

4.3.4. How energy innovations are distributed

The regional distribution of innovations in energy systems is the concern not only of large energy companies but also of local and regional actors, both public and private. Indeed, to find ways to save energy and develop local sources and to choose the most up-to-date techniques to exploit them, requires a minimum of economic and technical understanding of these techniques. In the first section we have seen that the Community recognises their importance and in its programme favours practical demonstrations. However, regions differ in their ability to take advantage of new technology. That in certain Member States, France and Italy for instance, the most industrialised and developed regions took the initiative in that respect, is not just chance: the scientific and technical infrastructures, technical expertise, hi-tech industries are found more easily in industrialised than in rural or peripheral regions. Obviously, a proper understanding is required of the mechanics and factors that slow down the diffusion of energy innovations and those that may mobilise the energy potential in the less favoured regions. Those responsible for the Community's regional policy, realising this, have launched "software measures" for the express purpose of making the less favoured regions more capable to evaluate, and decide on, new investments from within.

4.4. Regional disparities and energy imbalance in the European Community be-tween 1973 and 1985

4.4.1. Introduction

The European Commission has carried out or financed several studies to evaluate the regional impact of the Community's energy policy; these studies have tried to "diagnose" the regional repercussions of the energy crisis, and to propose measures to correct the negative effects of the evolution of the energy sector or its sub-sectors in distressed Community regions. In this section we will analyse the stud-ies, and give our personal interpretation.

Between 1982 and 1984, at the request of DGXVI several experts[2] carried out a study of "the regional impact of the energy crisis". In the next sub-sections we will present the diagnosis that is the main result of this study, and supplementary results obtained by work carried out in 1984-1985. In the last sub-section will be presented the measures the Commission has decided on to lead the developments of the energy sector in problem regions in the right direction.

Changes in the energy sector can be evaluated by looking either at energy pri-ces or at energy investments.

For the period 1970-1980, the study has found contradictory evidence on the relation, on the Community level, between energy prices, by type of energy by type of energy and by type of consumer, and socio-ecnomic indicators in the re-gions of level 2. While on the one hand regional comparisons on the Community level have shown that energy prices in ecu per Gigajoule are ofthen higher in the most developed - urban, central - regions than in the peripheral ones, on the other hand, in Member States where no national policy of energy-price equalisation "er-ases" regional differences in the cost of supply to the consumer, high energy pri-ces (compared to the national average) tend to prevail in poor regions, and low energy prices in rich ones. The paradox can be explained mainly by (1) exchange rates, and (2) the fact that in the early 1980s, the governments of Italy and Greece pursued a policy of artificial low prices, to the detriment of the financial viability of energy firms.

The isolated regional influence of the price of each type of energy leads to par-adoxical conclusions on the level of the Community's regional policy. Considera-tion of the supply structures and the investments modifying them, may - with cer-tain reservations - generate more workable results. The reservations refer in par-ticular to the fact that there are hardly any statistical data concerning regional energy supplies and investments, so that a "detour" through the Member States is necessary to reach any conclusions on the regional level; fortunately, there are significant exceptions with respect to certain island areas and certain energy sub-sectors.

4.4.2. A picture of the national investment structures

In the course of the last 15 years, many national energy systems had become ob-solete. Considerable efforts have been made to adapt them; given the extreme capital-intensiveness of the sector, these have led to an increase in the relative share of energy investments in the Gross Fixed Capital Formation (GFCF) of Member States. Logically, the high level of investment gave rise to a very high investment rate (GFCF of the energy sector divided by its gross value added): it varies by year and by country between 30 and 60 per cent.

Notwithstanding the lack of statistics for some member states, the table clearly shows:

Table 4.4
Gross fixed capital formation of the energy sector,
by Member State

	Belgium	Denmark	Germany	Greece	France	Ireland	Italy	Luxem-burg	Nether-lands	United Kingdom	EUR10
1974											
GFCG p.c, in ECU	1031	1269	2223	391	1934	462	579	1397	955	604	840
% of energy bearers	6.3	3.6	7.6	-	5.8	5.3	7.4	4.1	8.4	10	7.3
GFCF fuel and power products, ECU p.c.	65	46	85	-	60	24	43	57	80	60	61
1980											
GFCF, ECU p.c.	1822	1753	2175	723	1923	1148	999	2393	1813	1235	1580
% of energy bearers	6	5.2	6.1	-	9.3	7.1	8.6	2.8	6.8	13.5	8.6
GFCF fuel and power products, ECU p.c.	109	91	133	-	179	82	86	67	123	167	136

Source: EUROSTAT, Review 1974-1983.

- the relative importance of the effects in terms of energy supply: 6 to 8 per cent in 1980;
- the increase in average investment within the Community from 7.3 to 8.6 per cent in the period 1974-1980;
- the specific, high rates for the United Kingdom (investments in North-Sea oil) and France (investments in nuclear power stations), and of low rates for Luxemburg.

With the exception of these three countries, the differences in energy investment are mainly explained by differences in per capita GFCF, which itself depends on the national GNP-levels.

But we have to consider the structure as well as the level of investments. Unfortunately, statistical information on investments in energy sub-sectors and in efforts to save or substitute energy are even more difficult to establish than those on total investment. The Commission's departments (GDXVII) have only given estimates of the composition of energy investments on the Community level in 1980, and those with reservations. According to these estimates, out of a total of 50,000 million ECU of energy GFCF, 80 per cent were allocated to the supply of energy (50 per cent to electricity and nuclear energy, 10 per cent to solid fuels, and 20 per cent to hydrocarbons); 20 per cent were allocated to the rational use of energy (15 per cent to energy saving and 5 per cent to alternative energies).

We cannot quantify our earlier statement that energy investments differ as to their socio-economic impact on the regional level, by an exhaustive survey of such impacts, on account of the lack of information about different energy investments and the low relative share - (on average 2 to 3 per cent) - of value added , investments and employment in the energy sector. Indirect and intra-sectorial approaches can be used to advantage, however. We know, for example, that specific national energy policies have led to the concentration of energy investments in one or two sectors and thus to preferential regional impacts. Let us look at some examples.

- In France, investments in the production and distribution of electricity represent just under 70 per cent of total (supply-side) investments in the energy sector in the period 1975-1981 (Source: Eurostat, Annual Investments Fixed Assets 1975-1981). Approximately 60 per cent of this amount is taken up by the cost of nuclear power stations, brought on line between 1973 and 1982.

However, the construction of these power stations had local and regional impacts on the areas where they were built, and also on the industries of capital goods based in certain regions.

Two regions (Rhône Alpes and Centre) have received 49.2 per cent of the 57.643 MWe either in operation or due to go on line between now and 1989, eight other regions sharing the remainder. The same two regions have benefited from 56,250 of the 102,850 manyears of local manpower (direct, indirect, or induced employment), who helped to construct these plants.

A study prepared by the Ministry for Industry shows that 28 per cent of the total cost of a power station came from the Burgundy region, 23 per cent from the Paris Region, 14 per cent from the North, 11 per cent from Lorraine, and 9 per cent from Rhône Alpes. The unequal regional distribution of such an investment programme is thus easily measured, although its overall effect goes beyond the aspects mentioned.

- In the United Kingdom, investments in oil and natural gas represent 52.4 per cent of total investments in the energy sector in the period 1975-1981. These investments in off-shore exploration and production had multiple economic effects, but have benefited only certain regions, such as Scotland, and certain urban areas, such as Aberdeen.
- In Ireland, the sales of peat extracted by the Bord Na Mona rose very substantially between 1979 and 1984. Most of the production and the labour involved - around 7,000 jobs in total - are based in the Midlands and County Kildare.
- In Greece, lignite seems to be one of the most important national energy sources (recoverable reserves are in the order of 700 million tons of oil equivalent (toe). The national electricity company, the PPC, is also responsible for exploiting the mines producing the lignite for its thermal power stations. Having already spent large sums of money on the extraction, the PPC intends to allocate another 1,100 million ECU) to it in the period 1985-1990. Most lignite mines currently in operation, as well as the thermal power stations close by, are centred in the central and western regions of Macedonia, providing these regions with a surplus of permanent economic activity. That makes it possible to detect and evaluate the regional impacts of sectoral energy investments, at least if they have a certain minimum size and last for a certain time.

These examples show that in the period 1973-1983, member states could develop energy investments corresponding to the priorities of their own energy policy, based on the presence or absence of fossil energy sources. However, we must prevent that we cannot see the wood for the trees. In other words, looking at the investments, we must not forget the structures of energy supply. Two more analyses are called for. The next subsection will show how vulnerable the structure is on the national level, and - with the help of a case study - on peripheral islands. Although nearly all member states increased the portion of GFCF to the energy sector during the period 1974-1980, we know that the energy situation is far from homogeneous within the Community. Are perhaps some areas (member states or regions) structurally more vulnerable than others because they are more dependent on oil ? In the next sub-section, we will examine how vulnerable certain regions are to a decline in a particular branch of energy.

The general poor share which employment in the energy sector has in total employment has already been mentioned; however, in some regions is the percentage much higher, between 10 and 20 per cent. If in such regions employment in the energy sector is confined to a single branch and if that branch falls into decline for reasons specific to the energy sector, regional imbalance is likely to be the result.

4.4.3. Community areas with energy imbalances

By areas with regional imbalances we understand territories in which the energy constraints on the economic system are worse than the Community average. To identify such areas, the first step is to look at the information on energy that is comparable on the level of member states.

To evaluate the constraints we will use the indicators of supply conditions and consumption of energy that have been perfected by the Commission's services through a number of years of examining energy policies. Indicators of supply show (1) the dependence of supplies on imports, (2) their dependence on imported oil, or (3) the share of liquid or gaseous hydrocarbons in electricity production. The higher the value of these indicators, the more unfavourable will be the conditions of energy supply, the higher will be the bill for domestic and imported energy, and the greater the macro-economic constraints on national economic growth; 1983 will be used as the reference year for these indicators.

As both the European Community and the OECD have information available on Spain and Portugal, these two new member states have been included; however, their energy supply is not included in the calculation of the Community average.

- The Community average of the first indicator - dependence on imports - is 42 per cent. in decreasing order of dependence we find: 1. Luxemburg 98; 2. Portugal 88, 3. Denmark 85; 4. Italy 82; 5. Belgium 74; 6. Spain 72; 7. Greece 65; 8. Ireland 63; 9. France 62 per cent. That was the situation in 1983. The Community energy forecast for 1990 places the following countries above the average Community dependence rate of 45 per cent: Luxemburg 98, Portugal 63, Greece 59; Italy 53; Ireland 52; and Spain 50 per cent.
- By the second indicator - dependence on imported oil supplies -, the following countries are, in decreasing order, above the Community average of 32 per cent in 1983: 1. Portugal 80; 2. Italy 62; 3. Spain 62; 4. Greece 59; 5. Denmark 51; 6. Ireland 50 per cent. In 1990, the following five member states are expected to be the most dependent, compared to the same average Community dependence figure: Portugal, Greece, Italy, Ireland and Spain.
- With respect to the third indicator - the share of liquid or gaseous hydrocarbons in electricity production -, in comparison with the a Community average of 20 per cent in 1983, the following countries appear in decreasing order: 1. Ireland 73; 2. the Netherlands 65; 3. Portugal 64; 4. Italy 64; 5. Greece 28; 6. Spain 27. Probably the same countries, except Spain and Greece, will probably still above the Community average of 15 per cent in 1990.

The evolution of the indicator of energy demand is harder to interpret, as it covers very different phenomena.

It is interesting to follow the primary energy content (defined as the ratio of primary energy consumption minus bunkers divided by the GNP expressed in constant money terms at the current exchange rate) through a sufficiently long period. But the value of this ratio depends on two factors, with either cumulative or contradictory effects:

- the structure of the economy, which may be defined as the relative share of the production of energy-intensive, intermediate goods. Of course, the level of household incomes determines to a certain extent the satisfaction of energy requirements (for heating and transport);
- the technical efficiency of energy conversion, which depends on the average age, and the technology, of the equipment used.

Past observations reveal that the value of primary-energy content tends to increase noticeably during industrialisation - at rates which vary among countries with different geographies, climates and energy resources. That perfectly natural economic trend poses specific problems when energy is expensive and imported on a massive scale; the member states concerned are all the more handicapped when their energy content increases or their primary energy content decreases at a rate below the Community average. We will assume, therefore, that energy constraints are felt most in countries which in a given period reduce their energy content less rapidly than the Community average.

In the recent past - that is, in the period 1973-1982, average EC-10 energy content dropped about 19 per cent (from 833 to 673 kgoe per 1000 ECU). In comparison, there was an increase of 4 per cent in Greece, of 16 per cent in Spain and of 27 per cent in Portugal, and reductions of 13 per cent in Ireland and 15 per cent in Italy, percentages below those of the Community.

The study entitled "Energy-2000" has calculated future national and Community ratios for the period from 1983 to 2000. Compared to a Community reduction of 19 per cent (from 670 kgoe per 1000 ECU in 1983 to 540 in 2000), an increase of 6 per cent for Greece has been calculated, and decreases for Portugal (3), Spain (11), Ireland (15), and Italy (16 per cent). Although the indicators are somewhat ambiguous, the four taken together lead to one clear conclusion: Italy, Ireland and Greece are with Spain and Portugal the member states with the structurally most unfavourable energy situation in comparison with the Community average. They are the same countries which have the most underdeveloped regions. Admittedly, the overall "geographic coincidence"[3] of member states with energy imbalances and underdeveloped regions does not indicate that the underdevelopment causes the energy imbalance, nor that the energy handicaps slow down - ceteris paribus - first national and then regional growth. Indeed, these countries may attempt at least partially to compensate for their energy deficit by increasing their efforts to export manufactured products, agricultural products or services (tourist industry).

While the lack of statistics renders it impossible to construct structural energy indicators on the Community level which fit all regions, for certain island areas such data are available. For one thing they are significantly more dependent on oil than the national average, and for another, the imports and exports of goods and services can be computed more straightforwardly than in other regions. The table below gives several significant examples of that dependence on oil for the energy supply.

Table 4.5 shows that there are island areas or - in the case of Northern Ireland - quasi-islands:
-       in member states which are themselves handicapped by their energy situation - for instance, Greece;
-       in member states which, on the contrary, have a relatively favourable energy situation - for instance, the United Kingdom.

Table 4.5
Oil dependence in island areas and member states (%) (1983)

	Oil dependence for electricity production	Oil dependence for total energy supplies
1. GREECE	28	65
of which		
Aegean Isles + Krete		
+ Rhodes	90	n.a.
Cyclades	98	97
2. UNITED KINGDOM	9	-22
of which		
Northern Ireland	90	76
3. FRANCE	7	45
of which		
Corsica	65	88
Overseas territories	61	89

4.4.4. The vulnerability of regions to a downturn in a sub-sector of the energy branch

The changes in the energy sector consisted not only in higher-than-average investment levels in its sub-sectors; they were accompanied by a differentiation in the relative growth of these sub-sectors. The gas industry, the production and distribution of gas, and hydrocarbon extraction have shown higher growth rates than the sector's average. But the refining and distribution of petroleum products, and the extraction of coal have been the two sub-sectors in the Community that have been particularly hit by the downturn.

The crisis in the refining and distribution of petroleum products follows logically from the efforts of member states to decrease their oil consumption and in particular their fuel-oil consumption, because to date no economic substitute has been found for fuels. In addition, "conversion" investments had to be made to convert refineries to catalytic crackers, thermal crackers, hydrocrackers and other coking methods, while the industry was already struggling with deficits. The refining industry's use rate was reduced enormouslsy between 1973 and the beginning of the 1980s, precisely the period in which the imports of petroleum products from other countries, particularly the OPEC countries, tended to increase. The crisis in the refining industry has led, then, to the closing down of several refineries and to the modernisation and diversification of others.

The decisions to close down a refinery depends on several factors:
- the strategy of the national or international companies;
- the pressure put on the industry by member states;
- their location, particularly with respect to ports and major waterways and canals;
- the age of the plant and the presence or absence of cracking units.
In a recent report (CCE 1985c), the Commission has drawn up a table of the evolution of the Community's refining capacities through the last ten years. Between 1976 and 1985, 274 million toe of distillation capacity were totally or partially closed down. The Commission estimates that 16,000 jobs were lost through the close of 35 refineries, whose capacity was more than one million tons a year. Of

that total, 3,000 people will neither find another job nor have the right to retire. The indirect effects of these closures are in some cases even more serious. The same report states with regard to the regional impact that:

"in the case of some refineries employing large numbers of people and located in high unemployment regions, it appeared that the effects of the total loss of jobs on the local community were very severe".

That conclusion must be qualified somewhat. Although in some cases the loss of jobs has been of considerable local importance, it is less so in relation to the size of the active population. Moreover, the loss of jobs appears, with few exceptions, to be localised in the richer industrial regions, where its relative impact is less than in poorer regions. As no specific study of the subject has been carried out, we cannot go into any further detail on the regional impact of the refinery crisis.

The downturn in coal extraction in the Community is very different from that in the refining industry. The Community's energy objectives for 1990, while recommending continued efforts to rationalise the mining industry, advocated maintaining total production volume at the expense of a massive renewal of investments. Nevertheless, an analysis of the industry's performance in the four producing countries concerned (United Kingdom, West Germany, France, and Belgium) has revealed the following trends:

- a considerable increase in the exploitation deficits per ton: from 3.3 ECU/ton in 1975 to 32 ECU/ton in 1984 on the Community level. Financial help for current production increased from 742 million ECU to 5,432 million ECU in the same period;
- the loss of 112,000 jobs between 1975 and 1983, distributed as follows among the four countries concerned.
- Out of a total of 250 million tons extracted in 1981, studies made by request of the Commission have shown that
  . 50 to 60 million tons are competitive;
  . 40 million tons are totally unprofitable;
  . 150 to 150 million tons are generally unprofitable.

In total, only half this production (100 to 120 million tons) does not rely on subsidies.

Table 4.6
Employment reduction in the Community's coal industry
(1975-1983)

	1975	1983	Reduction
Western Germany	168 800	118 600	20 200
Belgium	24 500	17 100	7 400
France	68 700	42 900	25 800
United Kingdom	245 200	186 600	58 600
Community total	507 200	395 200	112 000

Source: CCE 1985a.

The table hereafter clearly shows the regions mainly affected by the decline between 1975 and 1983.

Table 4.7. Division of Community coal production [a]
by coal field and by productivity level (in 1975); unit : Mt

Coalfields with productivity below Community average			Coalfields with productivityaboveCommunity		
Coalfields	1975	1983	Coalfields	1975	1983
Aachen	6	5	Ruhr	82	71
Lower Saxony	2	2	Saar	9	11
Campina	6	6			
Southern fields	1	-			
Nord/Pas-de-Calais	8	3	Lorraine	10	11
Centre-Midi	5	3			
Scotland	10	6	Yorkshire	33	30
North	15	12	Midlands	36	34
North West	13	11	Open-air		
South Wales	9	7	exploitation	11	14
Kent	1	1			
Community total	76	56		181	171
% of Community production	29.5	24.7		70.5	75.3

a) Excluding small extraction centres.
Source: CCE 1985a.

An initial check on the 150,000 jobs potentially threatened in the Community's less productive fields (UK: Scotland, North East, West, South Wales, Kent; France: Nord Pas de Calais, Centre Midi; West Germany: Aix, Lower Saxony; Belgium: Limburg) shows that they are distributed as follows:
- 79 per cent in the regions where the variation rate of job losses in the manufacturing industries exceeded 10 per cent between 1974 and 1982;
- 21 per cent in the regions where the rate of variation of job losses is less than 10 per cent.

The reductions in oil prices,which will probably persist forecast for the next five years, will inescapably lead to increased deficits which the individual member states will not be able to cover. For this sector, the impact could in principle be assessed very precisely, both geographically and sectorally. There are sufficient indications to show that the spatial impact of this new downturn in the Community's coal industry is concentrated in approximately the same regions as the ones cited above.

To sum up: the serious regional effects of the new downturn in the coal industry, which for some time was hidden by a certain revival in the period 1975-1980, are the result of two phenomena:
1. the concentration of less productive mines in old industrial regions;

2. the fact that these same regions are hit by a severe industrial decline and have, therefore, fewer possibilities of compensation by employment in other industries.

4.4.5. The orientations of the Community's regional policy in the energy sector

The elements of the diagnosis of the regional impact on the energy sector have shown:
- that member states situated in Southern Europe, where the more underdeveloped regions are concentrated, and certain peripheral island areas are structurally more vulnerable than the Community average to disturbances in their energy supply;
- that the new regression in the Community's coal industry is mainly concentrated in the regions of Northern Europe which are already going through a severe industrial decline (United Kingdom, France, West Germany, Belgium).

In theory, those responsible for the Community's regional policy could help solve these specific regional problems either by trying to influence the definition of the objectives of the Community's energy policy before they are implemented, or by introducing specific measures to compensate for the changes in the energy sector with the greatest negative impact. In practical terms we think that there is little scope for Community regional actions of the first type, at any rate if the Community's energy policies are mainly referred to. For, although the Community's energy policy takes account of regional problems it may entail, and concentrates specific actions on the regions involved, it has but little scope to do so. For example, it is out of the question for regional policy to challenge the need for a further reduction of the Community's coal industry. The objective of regional policy is to take compensatory measures, in this case to help the regions to create new jobs in sectors of potential growth. Such measures belong to the second type of action referred to above. Moreover, while it is the Community's responsibility to redefine, for example, Community aid to the coal industry, in the end the coal-producing member states finance nearly all such aid, besides "paying" the political price of the mine closures.

Measures to remedy, in the long and in the medium term, the structurally unfavourable conditions of energy supply in the more underdeveloped regions, also belong to the second type mentioned above: they consist in efforts to increase national and Community investment in energy in the member states and regions involved.

In conclusion, the greatest merit of the first type of measure is the Community's acknowledgement that the pursuit of its energy objectives may have specific, direct or indirect, impacts on certain regions. That acknowledgement then serves to justify the allocation of additional, financial Community aid to those regions.

Compensation measures may vary widely among types of problem region, as the energy problems encountered are also very different.

In industrial regons in decline which face a massive reduction in employment from coalmine closures or from rationalisation measures, the action to be undertaken is to compensate - at least partly - the loss of employment in an energy subsector by creating new jobs in other industrial or tertiary sectors, or in other energy sub-sectors, as the case lies. This could be done by the Community's contributing to the ECSC reconversion budget, or through traditional (joint financing of industrial projects) or more specific (joint financing of programmes) EFRD actions in the regions concerned, or by giving priority to these regions in the allocation of loans by such institutions as the EIB (CCE 1985a).

In the less favoured regions the appropriate measure is rather to help the member states increase their efforts to finance additional energy investments. The question is, what type of investment ? what type of aid ? After the reform of the EFRD regulations which became legal on January 1st, 1985, funds can be allocated to the following categories:

1. studies;
2. investment projects;
3. national programmes of interest to the Community;
4. Community programmes.

Given
1. the structural nature of the difficulties encountered;
2. the link between the objectives of regional and those of the Community energy policy;
3. the Community's commitment to do something within that interface;
4. and the prospect that appropriate measures would simultaneously improve the realisation of objectives of regional policy and energy policy;
the "Community programme" as a tool must be understood in accordance with the terms of article 7 of the EFRD regulations.

Once the form of action has been established, the content of the "appropriate measures" must be defined. The orientation formally adopted by the Commission on the 20th of January 1986 is to propose to the Council a Community energy programme (see note 1) focusing on aid to energy investments that are expected to make a particularly heavy impact in the regions benefiting from the programme, that is, investments relating mostly to:
- the exploitation of the potential of alternative and renewable energies;
- the exploitation of small peat and lignite deposits;
- the exploitation of the potential of energy savings and certain oil-substituting operations in small and medium-size companies in the industrial and service sectors.

Such sectoral priorities will stimulate the development of the endogenous energy and economic potential. They complement the efforts made by the member states to improve their energy infrastructure by large investments in the networks.

The regions benefiting from this programme are those:
- eligible by the criteria of regional policy;
- located in member states "which are considerably behind (the goals of) the Community's energy policy, that is, in island territories with high energy costs depending enormously on the outside world for their energy".

Regional-policy makers have already started to evaluate and confirm the actual existence of the above-described energy potential in these regions. Particular attention is being paid to helping local and regional authorities in their investment decisions, as they do not always possess the technical and economic capabilities required to make the correct decision.

Together with the communicaton programme, this proposed Community programme ought to become one of the first two applications of the new tool of Community regional policy.

4.5. Conclusion

1. The member states in Southern Europe seem to have been more affected by the 1974 and 1979 oil crises than those in Northern Europe, because

a. they were, at the beginning of the period, far above the Community average dependent on oil;
b. the conversion to oil substitutes in the period between 1973 and 1983 was not so fast as in Northern Europe.

Because of the considerable external constraints on national economic growth, growth prospects in the regional ecnomies of the member states concerned seem to have been limited in the measure that these peripheral and rural regions were less able than others to avail themselves of opportunities to convert to new technologies.

Aware that to create or extend large-scale energy networks is of less economic interest in regions with low population and economic density than in more favoured regions, logically the Commission, within the context of a regional policy centred around the promotion of endogenous development, the Commission recently adopted an important programme to "develop endogenous energy potential" in favour of these regions. This programme emphasises investments in local energy sources (alternative and renewable energies, small peat and lignite deposits, energy savings) given their considerable local and regional impact.

2. However, the economic interest of this programme, like that of all other oil-substitute development programmes, will be reduced by the recent drop in oil prices: $ 29/barrel in November 1985 against $ 10/barrel in July 1986. That new turn-around in the energy market prompts two questions. First, whether such a drop in prices is exceptional parenthesis or long-lasting; economic factors (world oil demand, and OPEC and non-OPEC production capacities) seem to indicate that this parenthesis could last ten years or so, so long as no financial catastrophe comes along to upset the markets.

On the assumption that this time scale is approximately correct, it will noticeably modify programmes of investment in oil substitution which were viable when oil was between 20 and 30 dollars a barrel; on the other hand it offers an appreciable "lifeline" to those countries whose economies are vulnerable because of their dependence on oil.

The subject will initially be discussed by the member states and the Community, to find out whether the advantages and disadvantages of a temporary drop in oil prices will, or will not, prevail over those of a market protected by import tax. That debate brings to mind the one held during the 1960s as regards foreign competition (Japan, United States, new industrial countries), when the question was whether Community coal production should be "protected" against the "invasion" of cheap oil. However, a Community consensus in favour of an efficient and stable import-duty system may be difficult to arrive at so long as the allocation of its fruits on the macro-economic level remains uncertain.

Although hypothetically economic growth and job creation can be stimulated, to specify how to distribute them across the regions is difficult at present, as the priorities of the Community's regional policy may switch - and rightly so - either to North-European industrial regions in severe decline, or to developing regions in Southern Europe. In the short and medium term, these regions may well benefit from that lifeline, but the problems caused by their vulnerability to fluctuations in the oil market remain unchanged.

4.6. Notes

1. The proposal of the 'VALOREN programme' by the CEC (Com(85)838 fuel) has been definitively approved by the Council on the 27th of October 1986. This programme, which links regional policy to energy policy, is designed to be "strengthening the economic base in the regions concerned by improving the

conditions of local energy supply (alternative and renewable energies, namely solar and wind energy, biomass including urban waste, small-scale hydro power and geothermal energy), and the efficient use of energy (energy savings and oil substitution)". The underlying idea of this programme is to make such regions less sensitive to disturbances in the traditional energy markets, in particular oil.

2. F. Archibugi, M. di Palma, B. Bourgeois, F. Convery, Hansen, N. Merzagora, G.R. Otten, A. Silitti, M. Slesser, S. Theofanides, A. Volwahsen.

3. With the exception of Northern Italy, the Athens nomos and Dublin in the EC-10 member states.

4.7. References

Aydalot, P. (1985), Economie régionale et urbaine, Collection Economie, Economica, Paris, p. 224.

Brillet, J.L., C. d'Hose et F. Mouttet (1985), Le modèle Mini-DMS-Energie, in Energie: modélisation et économétrie, Economica, Paris, pp. 53-82.

CCE (1975), Caractéristiques de l'évolution de l'industrie charbonnière communautaire depuis 1975, Bruxelles.

CCE DG XVI (1983), Fichier interne ICEFIER (Interventions Communautaires en faveur des investissements énergétiques par région), Bruxelles.

CCE (1985a), Rapport de la Commission au comité consultatif CECA sur sa politique de reconversion, COM (85) 526 final, Bruxelles.

CCE (1985b) DG XVII, Energie en Europe, Politique énergétique et tendances dans la Communauté Européenne, no. 3, Décembre.

CCE (1985c), La situation de l'industrie du raffinage de pétrole et l'impact des importations de produits pétroliers en provenance des pays tiers, COM 85(32) Bruxelles.

CCE (1986), Proposition de règlement (CEE) du Conseil instituant un programme communautaire relatif au développement de vertaines régions défavorisées de la Communauté par la valorisation du potentiel énergétique endogène (programme VALOREN), COM (85) 838 final, 20 Janvier 1986, Bruxelles.

Courbis, R. (1979), Le modèle REGINA, modèle de développement national, régional et urbain de l'économie française, in R. Courbis ed., Modèles régionaux et modèles régionaux-nationaux, Cujas, Paris.

Downs, A., and K.L. Bradbury (1984), Energy costs, urban development, and housing, Brookings Institution, Washington DC, p. 296.

Garofalo, G.A., and D.M. Malhotra (1984), Input substitution in the manufacturing sector during the 1970s: a regional analysis, Journal of Regional Science, vol. 24, no. 1, pp. 51-61.

Giolitti, A. (1984), The Years of Community Regional Policy, An account, Milan, 28-31 August.

Guesnier, B. (1983), Les effets de choix énergétiques sur l'activité régionale de l'utilisation rationnelle de l'énergie, les énergies nouvelles et renouvelables, Revue d'économie régionale et urbaine, no. 2, pp. 193-205.

Klaassen, L.H., and W.T.M. Molle (eds) (1983), Industrial Mobility and Migration in the European Community, Gower, Aldershot.

Kneese, A.V., F.L. Brown et al.(1981), The Southwest under stress: National Resource Development Issues in a regional setting, J. Hup for Resources for the Future, Washington, p. 268.

Lakshmanan, T.R., et al. (1984), Regional dimensions of factor and fuel substitution in the U.S. manufacturing, Regional Science and Urban Economists, pp. 381-398.

Lakshmanan, T.R. and B. Johansson (1985), Large-scale energy projects: assessment of regional consequences - An international comparison of experiences with models and methods, IIASA, NH, Studies in Regional Science and Urban Economics.

Lucas, N.J.D., and D. Papaconstantinou (1985), Western European Energy Policies: a comparative study of the influence of institutional structure on technical change, Oxford University Press.

Lunqvist, L. (1983), Analysing the Impacts of Energy Factors on Urban Form. CIB. W. 72 Workshop on technological change and urban form, Waterloo, July 7-9.

Manuel, D.P. (1982), The Effects of Higher Energy Price on State Income Growth, pp. 26-37.

Manuel, D.P. (1985), Unemployment and Drilling Activity in Major Energy Producing States, The Journal of Energy and Development, vol. 10, no. 1, pp. 45-63.

Miernyk, W.H. (1977), Regional Consequences of High Energy Prices in the United States, Journal of Energy and Development, vol. 2, pp. 213-219.

Miernyk, W.H. (1977), Rising Energy Prices and Regional Economic Development, Growth and Change, vol. 8 no. 3, pp. 2-7.

Molle, W., and Wever, E. (1984), Oil Refineries and Petrochemical Industries in Western Europe, Gower, Aldershot.

Nijkamp, P. (1983), Regional Dimensions of Energy Scarcity, Environment and Planning, vol. 1, pp. 179-192.

Scholz, H.E. von (1985), Planification locale et régionale de l'énergie dans la C.E. L'action de la Commission des C.E., in Planification régionale de l'énergie dans la R.F. d'Allemagne et dans la Communauté Européenne, Séminaire Berlin, pp. 42-43.

5 Transport and Communications

B. FULLERTON and A. GILLESPIE

5.1. Introduction

5.1.1. Organisation

Traditionally, the issue of regional development has been very closely intertwined with the supply of infrastructure, particularly transport infrastructure. It is consequently of little surprise that almost three quarters of the ERDF is spent on infrastructure. For this reason alone, to study in some depth the regional effects of a policy that is mainly concerned with infrastructure seems now in order.

Transportation, traditionally preponderant in total infrastructure investment, is the subject of the first part of this chapter. Recently western society is said to have changed from an industrial society to an information society. Information is transported across (tele)communication networks. Because the future role of telecommunication will probably equal that of transportation in the past, that aspect will be discussed in the second part of the chapter. We begin with a short discussion of the problems in specifying the transport-communications/regional development into relationships, and an introduction to the societal changes entailed by the "information revolution".

5.1.2. The relation between transport and communications, and regional economic development

The crux of the argument concerning the role of transport and communications in regional economic development lies in the distinction between necessary and sufficient conditions for such development. Several studies during the last decade have sought some quantification of the undoubted relationship between investment in transport and/or communications and subsequent regional development. Funck and Blum (1986) in particular, have demonstrated the nature of the interactions between infrastructure and regional inputs. The nature of the inputs, however, varies greatly from region to region. Certainly there would appear to be strong statistical association between the provision of both transport and communication infrastructure and the level of economic development (measured in per capita income), as Biehl and his colleagues (1982) have demonstrated for the regions of Europe. The UK input to the Biehl study (see Meadows and Jackson 1984) attempted to get beyond simple association and to test for the direction of causality by the use of lagged correlation coefficients. Their analysis suggested that the provision of infrastructure services promoted regional development, rather than development leading to an increased demand for infrastructure. However, they added that "The only significant exception to this conclusion appears to be in the case of transport infrastructure, the demand for which appears to be stimulated to a significant extent by the development of a region" (Meadows and Jackson 1984, p. 279), while no consistent direction of causality could be determined with respect to the relationship between telecommunication infrastructure provision and regional development.

In policy terms, Biehl et al. (1982) are cautious about the implications of their analysis. Firstly, they point out that a successful infrastructure-led development strategy for a region is conditional on there being "at least one infrastructure category representing an actual bottleneck and hence a limiting factor to the development of the region concerned" (p. 89, emphasis added). Further, they point out the essentially double-edged impact of infrastructure provision, particularly for transport and communication improvements. It follows that providing such infrastructure as an instrument to policy is, on its own, unlikely to be beneficial and may even be harmful to the region concerned. Infrastructure provision needs to be part of a more comprehensively framed development strategy.

A region developing from an export-based economy towards a more diversified industrial structure will become increasingly dependent on the conditions of interregional transport, but the dependence may or may not require new infrastructural investment. Studies of the effects of motorways built in the last decade suggest that their effects on regional development have been variable. Schulz-Trieglaff (CEMT 1984) quotes a series of studies along motorway corridors in West Germany carried out in the early 1970s which suggested a rate of new job creation of only 300 per 50 km of motorway over a timespan of eight years. Bonnafous et al. (CEMT 1975) quote research from Lyon suggesting that the effect of a section of the Autoroute du Sud in the lower Rhone valley was to encourage development among the former trunk roads in its vicinity which were now more available for local traffic. The motorway had contributed to the public image of the region but its direct stimulus and its effects on employment were difficult to discern. Earlier studies, reported in CEMT 1975, showed, for instance, that attempts by the Netherlands government to steer development out of Randstad Holland to the north east of the Netherlands through heavy infrastructural investment in that direction failed to prevent industrial movement to the south east of the country. A number of seaport and airport investments in northern Portugal suffered a similar lack of success. The main effects of the Autostrada del Sole has been to encourage additional migration from the Mezzogiorno to more developed areas of Italy. The motorways had little effect on the behaviour of small and medium sized firms: it appears that the large firms and state enterprises which established themselves in the South were more attracted by state subventions than by improved land-transport links. It became clear that large firms had not, on the whole, become growth poles attracting smaller companies and, despite the presence of the motorway, there had not been a balanced industrial development in the Mezzogiorno. The provision of improved transport services to a region may lead to increased demand for the goods and services of that region if neighbouring regions are growing. In these circumstances transport services encourage what Kraft et al. (1971) called a "spillover" or "growth fall-out" effect from the more developed to the less developed region.

Further, the terms of economic integration are usually dictated by core-region interests and enterprise and may not operate to the benefit of firms in peripheral regions. The opening up of export opportunities for a peripheral region is also likely to expose that region to imports from other regions. If the peripheral economy is initially weak, improvements in communications and transport may serve to expose those weaknesses to outside competition. The inherently unequal nature of interregional relationships within market economies must be constantly borne in mind.

Among measures to encourage regional development, it can be argued that the relative importance of communication and transport provision is becoming less important through time. The real costs of overcoming the friction of distance have already been reduced through technological and organisational changes within the transport and communication industries. Outside the few manufacturing industries with a final product including a low value/weight ratio, transport costs now constitute only a small proportion of firms' operating costs. A recent study (Pieda 1984) of the degree to which firms in Scotland were disadvantaged by higher transport costs arising from their peripherality, for example, was able to detect only a minuscule effect, with total transport costs averaging only 4 per cent of firm turnover.

Successive rounds of investment in transport and communication infrastructure will reduce the added impact of each extra investment, as Aberle (1979) and Kraft et al. (1971) point out. Few, if any, EC regions have such a deficient transport system that major regional resources are lying untapped. The older industrial regions, such as Wallonia and central Scotland, are well provided with transport infrastructure and services to other regions. This circumstance leads Bonnafous (1979), among others, to argue that the role of transport is now marginal to regional development.

5.1.3. Communications and new forms of spatial economic organisation

There can be little doubt that the relative ease and cheapness of freight transport in the second half of the twentieth century has played a crucial enabling role in the development of new forms of spatial industrial organisation. By the early 1970s, the European network of motorways and the lorries it carried permitted (but did not enforce) a dispersal of production away from traditional industrial centres. The conjunction of new transport and communication opportunities with an increase in industrial concentration and the development of large multi-site corporations, resulted in the functional division of labour becoming associated with new and complex forms of spatial divisions of labour (Massey 1984). Different parts of the research, production and marketing processes could be optimally located and scale advantages exploited without impairing the ability of corporations to co-ordinate and manage the geographically separate components of their production.

More recently still, even more complex forms of 'diffuse industrialisation' (Van Hoogstraten & Jansen 1985) have evolved, in which nominally independent small firms become involved in the corporate production sector via sub-contracting relationships in which they provide specialised goods and services to the large firms as well as ironing out the peaks and troughs of production and demand. Pedersen (1985) has argued that such an hierarchical system of firms is associated with new and polarised demands for transport and communications. There is a dual polarisation, partly around a system of highly specialised long-distance networks devoted to the transport of bulk freight and highly standardised goods, and partly around local and short-distance communication and transport systems designed to carry smaller and more varied consignments.

We would contend that the growth of computer networking via advanced tele-communication linkages has been much more important, though less immediately visible, for the evolution of such complex forms of corporate spatial organisation, than recent improvements in freight transport. Although computer networking has, to some extent, provided an electronic substitute for other forms of communication - both in the physical movement of people and in intermediate inputs to the production process - it is also important to realise that entirely new forms of decentralised spatial organisation have been made possible which could not have developed without intra-corporate computer networking. As Hepworth (1985), Bakis (1985) and Gillespie and Hepworth (1986) have argued, computer networks have profound implications for the development prospects of peripheral or other-wise less favoured regions. Nor are the impacts of the new information technology revolution confined to corporate enterprise, for advanced telecommunications of-fer very real possibilities for helping small and medium sized firms in peripheral regions to overcome some of the disadvantages of remoteness, such as in access to markets and specialist external sources of information (Gillespie et al. 1984; Economist Informatics/CURDS 1985).

The growing importance of telecommunications for economic development re-flects major structural changes which Bell (1973) has described as the coming of the post-industrial society. In his terminology, the key 'transforming resources' are information and the computer networks which enable this information to be util-ised (Bell 1979). It can be argued that the quality of 'regional information envi-ronments' will emerge as the main factor differentiating one region from another. One of the principal components of the quality of a region's information environ-ment will be communication linkages - both within the region and between that region and the rest of the world. In the post-industrial economy, access to high-speed transport for people (particularly air transport) and access to advanced tele-communications in the form of integrated services digital networks (ISDNs) will be vital both for attracting the new industries and for retaining the competitiveness of the old. The significance of communications as a location factor will only dim-inish if the relevant infrastructure and services are eventually available in all re-gions. Transport and communications are consequently likely to remain important components of any strategy to encourage the economic development of less fa-voured regions, even if the emphasis changes from 'traditional' improvements in freight facilities towards measures involving the rapid movement of people and the communication of information electronically.

5.2. Transport

5.2.1. Introduction

The development of European Community policies for transport and communica-tion and the implementation of the Common Market in these areas envisaged in the Treaty of Rome have been beset with a number of major problems. The most obvious problem has been the integration of national and Community policy. Nat-ional policies towards transport and communication have moved at different speeds and, occasionally, in different directions from Community policy. Trans-port policy is decided by the Council of Ministers and only if their individual transport interests appear to coincide or if some sort of deal can be struck will the Council make new policy. The individual transport ministers remain under ob-ligation to their national parliaments. The Treaty of Rome called for majority vo-ting on issues related to land transport after 1970, but Ministers have not yet given up the practice of requiring unanimous agreement. The slow and piecemeal development of transport policies and the length of transitional time allowed for bringing agreed policies into effect has made Community transport policy difficult to integrate with the rather shorter-term regional-policy measures which either the Community or one of its member states might wish to follow. The transport policies of the individual member states of the Community have had a much greater impact on European transport development since 1958 than the exiguous Community policies, but have seldom been specifically related to policies for disadvantaged or peripheral regions. In May, 1985, the European Court of Justice asserted that the Council of Europe had infringed the Treaty of Rome by its failure to ensure that international transport services be freely supplied within the Common Market.

The second problem impeding Community policy on transport and telecommunications has been the failure of policy making to keep pace or direction with technological change. This problem has affected both national and Community policies. In the early days, policy makers and engineers moved in separate worlds. The spread of motorways, the development of bulk carriers at sea and major advances in telecommunication technology initially outstripped the capacity of policy makers to deal with them. It was almost a decade after the advent of bulk carriers had effected major changes in the hierarchy and regional significance of European ports that Community policy on ports began to emerge. The policies of the 1960s arose from essentially theoretical concepts of harmonisation and the establishment of free competition across the Market. It was not until the 1970s that attempts to apply these concepts to the real patterns of European transport provision led to more empirical approaches.

By the mid-seventies the third problem had emerged as national governments drastically cut back their plans for infrastructural investment which had been based on the indefinite projection of the growth rates of the 1960s, and began to make much more cautious appraisals of the costs and benefits of public investment in transport and telecommunications. These appraisals tended to support infrastructural investment along the main axes of Community development, where there were already major transport bottlenecks, but it became increasingly difficult to justify the use of scarce financial resources in peripheral regions where current demand for transport and communication services remained relatively low. This problem was exacerbated wherever deregulation allowed market forces, rather than perceived national priorities, to determine the direction of investment.

5.2.2. Harmonisation and regional development

The analysis of the problems surrounding the role of transport policy in regional development suggests that the Community policies which were rather tentatively pursued before 1973 did little to help the development of disadvantaged regions, and may have worked in the opposite direction. Early Community transport policy, as evidenced by Article 70 of the ECSC Treaty and Articles 3 and 74-84 of the EEC Treaty, was chiefly concerned with harmonisation. These articles involved the agreement of common international tariffs, the extension of tapering rates across frontiers, the removal of frontier formalities, comparability of vehicle dimensions and the establishment of common working and safety standards for transport employees. Such policies remove distortions in the Common Market which arise from the historical legislation of the individual member states. They also seek to minimise the use by member states of customs regulations, consumer standards and safety provisions in order to protect their own nationals and limit the penetration of foreign goods and transport operators within their territories.

The first guidelines for a Common Transport Policy appeared in the Schaus Memorandum (CEC 1961), which suggested that the introduction of competition across the Community transport market involved the five principles of: (1) equality of treatment for all operators, (2) financial autonomy including the regulation of cartels and monopolies, (3) freedom of movement, (4) freedom of consumer choice between public and private transport (involving the elimination of price discrimination and subsidies), and (5) the co-ordination of investment. None of these principles has a regional dimension in itself. Their implementation might help disadvantaged regions insofar as lower transport costs in general favour regional development. Harmonisation of tariffs which related transport changes directly to distance is unlikely, on balance, to favour peripheral regions.

Community legislation on working conditions in transport industries, which include raising welfare standards for workers in the poorer regions, may raise those costs which are directly attributable to distance and so weaken the compeittive position of the periphery. Community regulations on drivers' hours and the use of tachographs to enforce them have been vigorously resisted in Ireland and the UK because they are seen to impose distance thresholds at particular points on the transport netork.

Many observers (Aberle 1979, Cardia 1983, Oettle 1979, and Voigt 1979) consider, however, that differences in the economic geography of peripheral regions require that effective transport policies be specific to each area. What is good for the Isle of Lewis may be irrelevant for Rhodes; measures which bring Jutland more closely into the Common Market may not be equally effective for Calabria. The improvement of transport facilities to a peripheral region may destroy a 'protection of distance' which had been enjoyed by its own industries in local markets, or lead to the exploitation of its resources to the benefit of other regions. Cardia (CEC 1983) suggests that the improvement of transport infrastructure is not a privilege, but a precondition for the establishment of a proper competitive situation.

These views are reflected in transport policies pursued by many national governments since the beginning of the railway age, which were designed to give particular industries, groups of producers, regions or ports cheaper access to markets or a cheaper assemblage of raw materials. The most common measure was an increase in the distance taper (which normally reflects the real cost of shipping goods) beyond that suggested by the commercial judgement of transport operators. Transport companies often voluntarily cross-subsidised commodities and regions in order to develop new traffic, and governments, on occasion, enforced cross-subsidies through the imposition of maximum or minimum rates and gave direct subsidies to particular commodities or routes.

Some governments traditionally subsidised services either through the 'free' provision of public infrastructure upon which private services may be able to run a viable operation, or by direct subsidy to public transport services. Private companies may see no profit in operating where the population is too thinly scattered or poor to patronise a profitable service or because of uncertainties about the development of future traffic. In areas which only generate minimum traffic and are unlikely to be able to support competitive transport services, planned rationalisation of modal services has been undertaken to ensure that enough customers patronise one of the normally competing transport modes (usually the railway) to bring it to a theshold of commercial viability.

Of equal importance are national subsidies designed to cover the losses of new services during their initial years when custom is being built up. The development of new air services for business travellers provides a good example. Nationally subsidised services may serve as a substitute for trading, employment and consumption opportunities which are not available within the region, and so check the drift of population and industry away or even attract incomers. The maintenance of confidence in the continuity of a nationally supported regional transport system reduces uncertainty for immigrant firms who may be prepared to make long-term investments in particular regions. Government support for transport infrastructure and services can make an important contribution to the attractiveness of a region to investors. Publically financed services, for instance, may provide a standby service for firms and travellers who do not use them very often and, by their existence, ensure that private services cannot hold customers to ransom. Neither of these functions is likely to be financially profitable but they offer the promise of continuing transport opportunities within the region.

The governments of France, Germany and Italy in particular were reluctant to abandon transport policies which included elements of regional support. The development of road competition to rail and inland water transport probably contributed more to the development of a common transport market than the halting progress of harmonisation.

The Council of Ministers failed to agree on a suggested programme of action to implement the Schaus proposals (CEC 1962). Neither France, West Germany nor Italy were willing to allow long distance road haulage to develop too fast at the expense of their state railways, nor were they prepared to allow Duch hauliers to carry more than a very limited proportion of freight arising ouside the Netherlands. A measure of harmonisation of national customs procedures, axle weights and drivers' hours was achieved, however. The Transport Commission has favoured complementary rather than competitive development of individual transport modes, and has encouraged transport technologies such as containerisation, piggy back and roll-on, roll-off.

Whilst Article 70 of the Treaty of Rome forbids discrimination either in price or in conditions of transport based on the origin and destination of products, 'support tariffs' have been allowed provided they were temporary or conditional. Such tariffs have a limited effect on regional restructuring insofar as they are non-selective (reducing the effective distance cost for everyone) and non-transparent - it is not possible to quantify their benefits for each company. Support tariffs were, however, granted in favour of coal, ore or metal products associated with the smaller firms in the steel industry which were in process of reconversion or rationalisation. They have been invoked in the case of the Saarland, where rail rates into the Saar were reduced to meet the hypothetical rates which would have been charged on the Saar-Palatinate Canal if it had ever been built. They have also been allowed on traffic to the Zonenrandgebiet. Italian Railways were allowed special tariffs on some vegetable produce from and machinery to the Mezzogiorno. SNCF were allowed to retain tapering rates in favour of Brittany and the southern part of the Massif Central until 1984, when all support tariffs came to an end. Reduced tariffs have also been allowed where there have been time lags between the building of new routes and their full advantages being felt (Romus 1983).

The most important development of harmonisation policy was the adoption of the 40-tonne standard for lorries in 1984 (but not applied in Britain and Ireland before 1987). The Radius (Council of Europe 1971) and Mursch (CEC 1973) Reports had, however, heralded a retreat from policies designed to foster the freedom of private operators across the Market and of road transport in particular, in favour of infrastructural policies.

5.2.3. Infrastructure and regional development

After the energy crisis and the enlargement of the Community in 1973, more pragmatic policies were developed (Erdmenger 1983), which took more account of the actual operations of transport systems within the Community. Instead of seeking to minimise state intervention, Community policies have attempted to align state policies, considering for the first time issues of regional development, environmental deterioration, energy costs and social opportunity. Sea and air transport were added to the remit of the Transport Commission. The enlarged Community began to consider its transport policies in terms of a physical Community-wide infrastructure which would strengthen the links between its formerly separate economies. The adherence of the new members enhanced the significance of peripheral regions, bottlenecks appeared where investment in national infrastructure had petered out towards state frontiers, and also in Switzerland and Austria, which play such a vital role in long-distance Community transport flows. While the Community lacked funds to realise its subcontinental visions, its member states were losing their earlier enthusiasm for massive expenditure on transport infrastructure and became increasingly interested in the revenues which might help to offset it. Calls for cost-benefit analysis and public consultation delayed progress on schemes like London's Third Airport and the fixed links between the Danish islands. This situation left Community officials urging the merits of transport infrastructural investment which they could not themselves fund to national governments which were increasingly reluctant to spend their own revenues.

In October 1973, the Commission (CEC 1973) submitted an outline of a Common Transport Policy which envisaged the eventual development of new infrastructure and the harmonising of regulations as to the use of the infrastructure by transport operators and car owners. This concept was accepted by the European Parliament, but was neither discussed nor endorsed by the Council of Ministers.

Progress was still hampered by the conflicting political approaches of the member states insofar as some favoured a much greater degree of liberalisation than others. The enlargement of the Community exacerbated the situation. Three of the original six members pursued relatively dirigiste national transport policies with a fair degree of consistency over time and special concern for the interests of rail and inland water transport, and for nationalised shipping companies, road haulage firms and airlines. The Benelux countries and the new members, Denmark, Ireland and Britain, had been following a more liberal approach to road transport and to modal competition in general, because of political conviction, small area or insularity. They were more concerned that Market transport policy should allow freedom of movement for all their transport operators across the Community. Since 1979, it has become increasingly difficult to harmonise British transport policies with those of other Community members.

Expenditure on the major transport arteries of the Community may provide general benefits to disadvantaged regions that are relatively central. Their impact on peripheral regions will depend on the nature of the economy which emerges from greater accessibility to the core of the Market. Opinion in the regions themselves has generally supported such schemes as the Severn Bridge, and fixed links across the Great Belt and the Straits of Messina.

A resolution which proposed that a sector of the Community transport budget should be allocated to transport-infrastructure projects of Community interest was passed in 1976 and adopted by the Council in 1978. A Transport Infrastructure Committee was set up to survey the totality of national infrastructure programmes, identify Euroroutes and bottlenecks upon them and to produce Community-wide traffic forecasts.

Community-interest routes (Euroroutes) were defined in 1979 (CEC 1979) as the E-road network (European Declaration on the construction of main international traffic arteries of 1950) , major railways as defined by the International Railway Union in 1974, and waterways as the European Ministers of Transport category class IV (carrying barges of 1350 tonnes and over). It was suggested that nodal towns should be identified (including national and regional capitals, transport centres and other towns of over 750,000 population). The links of Community interest would be those between the nodal towns, plus links to similar towns outside the European Community, minus links carrying low traffic and/or of only intra-regional interest.

Bottlenecks (CEC 1980) arise at points of general traffic congestion, including customs posts and physical obstacles such as the Alpine crossings, sections of the long road to Greece and at the Straits of Messina, Danish Belts and English Channel. Some bottlenecks lie outside Community boundaries in Switzerland and Austria; others may be quite significant for transport in peripheral regions. Sicilian agriculture, for instance, is still severely hampered by traffic congestion on either side of the Strait of Messina. Klinkenborg (1981) found that delivery times of Sicilian produce to Hamburg in the 1930s could no longer be attained either by road or rail in the 1970s, and that Community aid funds designed to help Sicilian agriculture move into the more profitable irrigated fruit and vegetable crops were not fully effective as long as the ferry crossing was adding 19 per cent to the cost of Sicilian imports and exports and imposing waiting times of up to three days on road and rail traffic alike. On a more local scale, the alleviation of bottlenecks can allow a freer circulation of short-distance traffic among national frontier regions within the core of the Community.

Erdmenger (1983) suggests that one of the causes of the growth of long-distance road traffic has been the inability of the railways to guarantee delivery dates, most notably on traffic passing through their Alpine bottlenecks. Hence the importance of further investment in the major railway routes where road/rail combination traffic is most likely to be successful. The future of the railway in Europe therefore appears to be increasingly dependent on international agreement and international investment. The Klinkenborg Report (1983) regarded the development of such a modern railway network as central to the transport infrastructure policy of the Community and as a necessary prerequisite to any attempt to transfer traffic from road to rail in the interests of energy conservation or the reduction of investment in roads.

The same Report called for co-ordinated action between the administrators of transport funds and regional aid funds under the general guidance of the Commission and for the building of further international motorway links where they could be justified on regional-policy grounds. Such road building included schemes in Austria and Yugoslavia for the benefit of peripheral regions in Italy and Greece.

In 1980, the Transport Committee sent a proposal to the Council of Ministers (CEC 1979) for the improvement of international air traffic among non-metropolitan regions of the Community to fill gaps left by the main services operated by the major national airlines, and to halt or reverse trends towards larger planes serving fewer airports. Although this proposal was supported by the Economic and Social Committee, the European Regional Airlines Organisation and the European Parliament, it was opposed by the airline companies and the transport unions. The Council of Ministers failed to agree to it. The Transport Committee does not think that American-style deregulation would benefit European air transport, and still favour inter-airline co-operation based on bilateral negotiations between national governments (CEC 1984). Although the Committee favours the encouragement of direct flights between secondary airports it is not generally in favour of public subsidy to such routes.

Thomson (1976) makes the point that the historical development of European airlines and airports, under strict government control in most countries, has produced a network which is too heavily based on the pivot airports of London, Frankfurt, Paris, Madrid and Amsterdam. The operational superiority of air over railway services on long-distance links where the volume of traffic is small, such as inter-city business trips from one regional centre to another, has so far been neglected. It is these services which are regarded (CEC 1979) as most desirable from a Community point of view. Current British proposals for greater commercial freedom among European airways may further encourage a concentration of services on the most heavily used and profitable routes, and raise the relative cost of services to remoter and less used centres. In these circumstances, the interests of the regions would require a measure of protection and Community support for services to peripheral regions.

5.2.4. A European Transport Fund

Progress in setting up a fund to implement European transport policy has been slow. In 1981, after intervention by the European Parliament, the Council granted 10 million ECU to three projects: freightyard modernisation at the Domodossola customs station on the St. Gothard railway line, a road-improvement scheme in Greece and a series of preliminary studies of the Channel Tunnel, each representing a different type of Community transport interest. The transport infrastructure Committee proposed a list of projects along the Community routes which had been identified earlier. A computerised Transport Assessment System for the Community (TASC) was set up in order to ascertain priorities between projects. In the modal split of proposed expenditure on the initial list of projects, 53 per cent involved railways, 40 per cent roads and 7 per cent inland waterways. 90 per cent of the rail expenditure, and 2 per cent of the road expenditure was to be incurred in core areas of the Community. Almost half the proposed road expenditure in peripheral areas concerned routes linking Athens, Copenhagen, Belfast and Dublin to the core areas of the Community.

The most recent views of the Transport Commission (CEC 1984b) stress the importance of a relatively limited internodal network of Community interest where the present levels of service are below the average of services between Community centres, taking into account the volume and proportion of transit traffic, the importance of an international route for internal traffic, and socio-economic factors, which are not normally considered in cost-benefit analyses. Rather than use national investment criteria, the Committee favoured measures such as the degree of saturation of existing equipment and the time gained by users.

Looking to future Community transport policy, the Cardia Report (CEC 1983) called for improved incentives for competition between operators, co-ordination between modes and rationalisation of existing transport firms. A differential railway charging policy would be equitable if it applied to all member states equally and subsidies were justifiable in support of regional development. The Report called for a redefinition of the public service functions of transport with all public subsidies clearly transparent in the budgets of transport undertakings. Subsidies should, however, be limited to specific categories of passenger and freight over a defined period. While member states must provide the subsidies for the time being, the EC should shoulder part of this burden in the future. In some circumstances, special concessions and franchises for the movement of raw materials and manufactured goods would be preferable to subsidies.

The Transport Infrastructure Fund should be used for port and airport facilities, and social aid from the European Research and Development Fund should be extended to new maritime services. The Report echoed the Declaration of Tenerife of 9.4.81 calling for islands to be treated as if they were linked to the mainland by an overland route of the same length as the sea or air crossing. Technological innovation should be fostered, with special support for hovercraft and hydrofoil services in replacement of some unsuitable and obsolescent conventional ferries.

5.3. Telecommunications

5.3.1. The 'telecommunication revolution'

The technologically-driven revolution in telecommunications provides an essential context for understanding how policy is changing both at the European Community level and at the level of individual member states. Much more so than is the case for transport, telecommunication in Europe is in a state of flux, due to the inter-play of radical technological advances with changing competitive and regulatory regimes. The turbulence has been created by a series of technological develop-ments, beginning in the mid-1960s with the advent of computing, continuing in the 1970s as computer communication networks began to develop, and reaching a crescendo in the early 1980s as the technological convergence of computing and telecommunications became firmly established. That convergence, referred to by the French as 'télématique' and by the Americans as 'compunications', has arisen because on the one hand micro-electronics has so enhanced the power and flexibil-ity of computers that 'computing power' and the applications it can support can be distributed to a number of outlets through computer networking, thereby exten-ding the 'reach' of computer applications and its utility within organisations. In parellel, the advent of 'digitalisation' in telecommunication switching and trans-mission means that telecommunication now 'shares' so much core technology with computing that it is becoming increasingly difficult to tell where one starts and the other stops.

Following on from the new possibilities which the technological changes have afforded, large corporate consumers of telecommunication services are putting increasing pressure on the providers of such services to improve the quality and range of service, to reduce their costs and to permit or facilitate the development of intra-corporate computer networks. Increasingly, the new technologies - inclu-ding new technologies of data transmission, such as satellite communication, as well as computing and computerised switching, have eroded the so-called 'natural monopoly' in the provision of telecommunication service. In the US, the combina-tion of corporate pressure in the market place and an ideological conviction pre-disposed towards de-regulation has already resulted in the removal of the mono-poly for all telecommunication services except for the 'local loop' running from the network into individual homes and workplaces. Evidence drawn from the US experience suggests that de-regulation may well have profound implications in regional terms, as de-regulation appears not to be compatible with the continued provision of 'universal service' (that is, the same services available in all parts of the country at the same cost) which has been the hallmark of the provision of such services by a heavily state-protected monopoly in the US and by state-owned monopolies in all European countries. How the pressures which in the US have re-sulted in de-regulation are currently being faced by European member states and their telecommunication administrations provides one of the main features differ-entiating telecommunication policies in the various European countries. In many ways then, the present time may mark a water-shed in the development of tele-communication policy and, as we shall argue, in its regional impacts.

5.3.2. Regional disparities in the supply of telecommunication services

Without doubt the principal factor differentiating European regions, on the basis of the quality, range and price of the telecommunication services which are avail-able, is the ability of the member state within which they are situated to under-take the scale of investment required to modernise the national telecommunica-tion system. In the case of the UK, Cripps and Godley (1978) estimate that in-vestment in telecommunication equalled about 20 per cent of total manufacturing investment in the period 1963-78. Italian investment in telecommunications over the period 1985-90 is expected to be 19,000 m ECU (IRI 1985). Investments of that scale, sustained through many years, obviously impose a burden even on the most prosperous nations; for the poorer countries, constraints on the resources available for investment, competing claims from other forms of infrastructure provision (including transport), and the deleterious balance of payment implications of investment in telecommunication equipment, all serve to limit the ability of the telecommunication administrations to meet the demand expressed for existing services or to provide the quality and range of services which more prosperous countries are able to afford. One indication of the gap between supply capability and expressed demand can be seen in the waiting time between applying for a telephone line and being provided with the service: in Greece the average wait is almost six years, in Ireland it is 18 months, and in southern Italy it is 8 months (KMG Thomson McLintock 1985). Given the backlog of unmet demand for basic telephony, it is perhaps understandable that the poorer countries have given the introduction of new advanced services, such as data communication, videotex and the like, a relatively low priority. In Greece, for example, a packet-switched data service is planned, but its capacity when installed will only be 10 per cent of the demand forecast by the Greek PTT (OTE 1985).

Adding to the disadvantage imposed on enterprise in the poorer European countries by the limited availability of advanced services, the services that are available tend to be markedly more expensive than the (higher quality) services available in the more prosperous countries. A recent exercise undertaken to compare the telecommunication costs (fixed and variable) of a hypothetical 'Eurofirm' wishing to communicate with all other regions in Europe (weighted by their population size), for example, has demonstrated that Europe's less favoured regions have to bear the most expensive telecommunication costs (Gillespie et al. 1984). Luxemburg, Denmark and The Netherlands have an overall cost index (involving a combination of telephone, telex and data communication) only half that of Europe's most expensive location, the Republic of Ireland. Ireland and Greece have markedly higher cost indices than the remaining countries, with Germany, the UK and Italy also having above-average costs. These higher costs for the less favoured regions arise from a combination of geographical and technical/economic effects. The geograhical effect is because of the effect of transmission distance on the variable cost element; peripherally lcoated countries (which also in the case of Greece and Ireland happen to be the least prosperous) must, ceteris paribus, therefore set higher international tariffs to cover costs. The technical/economic effect arises from the less modern switching and transmission equipment, which for the reasons outlined above, the poorest nations in Europe rely on.

In terms of internal variations in levels of service and tariff levels within countries, there can be little doubt that public-sector monopoly provision in Europe has benefited peripheral and/or less favoured regions. Because of the acceptance of the notion of universal service provision within the terms of each national monopoly, economically disadvantaged, or remote, or sparsely populated regions and rural areas have received telephone services in advance of the provision that would have been made under more strictly profit-oriented service-supply policies. Although the principle of universality has been extended into the supply of new services, available evidence suggests that in practice there can be marked regional variations in the availability of new services arising from the phased stages by which investments are made and networks extended geographically.

To an appreciable degree, the extent of any such regional disparities in the provision of new services is an issue of public policy and consequently varies among European member states. The variation arises because of differences among them in their political commitment to the development of non-central regions and of differences in the extent to which telecommunication planning is perceived to be a regionally-relevant issue. In France, for example, telecommunication has been used as a positive tool of regional develpment. The modernisation of the French telecommunication system - which has taken it from one of Europe's most archaic systems in the 1960s to the most modern by the mid-1990s - has been seen as a way of reducing economic-development disparities between Paris and the rest of France. Similarly with the development of the packet-switched data service - Transpac -, which has location-independent connection and calling charges and a very dense network of access nodes from its inception, and, most recently, the introduction of the national videotex services (Teletel).

The development of new services which are being provided on a distance-independent charging basis, such as packet-switching and videotex services, raises questions concerning the regional implications of tariff policies adopted. As with some earlier transport services, peripheral and/or poorer regions appear to have benefited from cross-subsidisation within the framework of public-sector monopoly provision of telecommunication services. The cross-subsidisation arises from charging policies that are applied uniformly across space and are not related to the actual cost of providing services in different locations; peripheral and/or sparsely populated regions tend to have both higher investment costs and higher operating costs than equivalent services in core or densely populated regions . In particular, low population density results in longer subscriber loops and in lower subscriber-to-operating-staff ratios; the former increasing investment costs and the time and cost of line repair, while the latter directly increases operating costs. In spite of partially offsetting higher revenues per line, the effect of these higher costs of provision in peripheral regons can be illustrated by the example of Italy: in 1983, SIP (the telephone operating company) made a loss on all but one of its eight regions in the Mezzogiorno. The loss in these regions amounted to 46 per cent of the profit made in the rest of the Country, and represented a heavy regional cross-subsidy from North to South (KMG Thomson McLintock 1985).

A consistent pattern of cross-subsidisation is also apparent in the relationship between the cost to the operator of providing local and long-distance services and the charges made for these services. In those European countries for which evidence was available - the UK, Germany, Italy and France - the Deutsches Institut für Wirtschaftsforschung (1984) concluded that long-distance and international traffic was markedly more profitable than local services,and that the former were subsidising the latter to an appreciable extent. The regional implications of this pattern of subsidy are not, however, straightforward. On the one hand, it could be argued that subscribers in remote regions are placed at a disadvantage in paying an unrealistically high cost for communicating long distance with core-region subscribers. Against this, however, is the empirical observation, which holds in the UK at least, that companies located in the less favoured regions tend to have patterns of communication which are proportionately more local in their orientation than is the case for core-region companies (EIU/CURDS 1985). One important result of the cross-subsidisation of local calls by trunk and international calls (and by leased lines as well) has been the growing pressure by business users - particularly the larger ones with the most extensive corporate networks - to have tariffs brought more into line with the costs of providing the services, thereby reducing their costs of telecommunicating. The extent of existing cross-subsidisation has fuelled the demands of the corporations for de-regulation, both to permit them to 'bypass' the local loop and to enable competition on the trunk common-carrier markets, leading inevitably to more favourable tariff regimes as far as the large consumers of telecommunication services are concerned.

If pressures for de-regulation do make greater headway in Europe, what can we expect the regional implications to be ? Firstly, as the US experience has clearly shown following the break-up of the Ma Bell monopoly and the end to cross-subsidy from trunk to local services, substantial rises in local call charges can be expected. Secondly, competition for common carrier trunk traffic could be expected to reduce tariffs on the most heavily used trunk routes, which may well serve to disadvantage relatively peripheral or low-traffic regions. There is already some evidence from the UK, the only European country to have espoused de-regulation, that this will be the case. British Telecom introduced 'low-cost routes', heavily centred on the London market, as a competitive reaction to the licensing of Mercury Communications as a rival common carrier for the business market. As the Mercury example makes clear, however, a more disturbing impliction of de-regulation is likely to be the geographical differentiation in the availability of new services. Universality of service provision is inimical to de-regulation; consequently, although such provisions have been protected as far as basic telephony is concerned in the terms of BT's licence, universality will not apply for new advanced services offered either by BT or its competitor(s). In any developments towards genuinely de-regulated markets, we can expect to see major differentials between prosperous regions of the country and metropolitan areas on the one hand, which will be provided with a full range of low-cost services, and less prosperous parts of the country and rural areas which will receive a narrower range of higher-cost services. That effect is already evident in the more fully de-regulated market in the UK for value-added network services (VANS - which include electronic mail, message services, data-base services, and so on). Some 600 such services have now been licensed, although the geographical pattern of their supply and the demand at which they are aimed reveals a very pronounced London and the South East orientation. Given the importance of such services and networks for the emerging information economy, we can conclude that moves towards the de-regulation of telecommunications are likely to favour the economic development of prosperous core regions at the expense of less favoured peripheries.

5.3.3. The regional dimension to the development of the Community's telecommunication policies

The organisation of telecommunications in Europe has traditionally been seen by the EC as hindering the development of an integrated common market. Each national telecommunications administration has had its own technical standards and equipment-approval procedures, which have served to rigidly compartmentalise along national lines the European telecommunication networks. Early incursions by the EC into the telecommunications field attempted to encourage the development of common technical standards as a pre-requisite for the development of genuinely European-wide networks. Perhaps the best example of a successful initiative was EURONET, an international data-transmission network set up with financial support from the EEC and with the co-operation of national PTTs. Its importance was in leading to the harmonisation in Europe of technical standards for packet-switching networks (indeed many of the technical standards embodied - such as the X25 protocol - are now accepted worldwide). Its success is indicated by the fact that, having fulfilled its catalytic role, EURONET has now been phased out as inter-linking national packet-switched networks have taken over.

In the 1980s, the development of the Community's policy stance with respect to telecommunications has taken significant steps forward as the extent of the information-technology revolution has become appreciated and the competitive pressures upon European producers have become evident. Within the bleak scenario concerning Europe's position as a producer of information technology (McKinsey and Company 1983), telecommunication has been identified as a relative strength upon which to build. However, as one commentator starkly puts it:

"Telecommunications in Western Europe is a disaster waiting to happen. Europeans distressed by their failures in computers and chips have found consolation in their $ 2 billion trade surplus and handsome 25% share of the world's telecoms equipment market. They are kidding themselves. Americans and Japanese are hard at work knocking the props of that prosperity out from under Western Europe" (The Economist, November 1985, p. 24).

Faced with this scenario, the Information Technology and Telecommunications Task Force within the Commission instigated a number of in-depth studies of the problems facing European telecommunications and of the range of appropriate responses (see for example the influential Arthur D. Little report, 1983). At the end of 1983, a Senior Officials Group was established within the Commission to work closely with Ministers of Industry "with a view to determining the basis for proposing an action programme for the balanced development of the telecommunication sector" (Preamble to CEC, 1984d). Three broad objectives were set out in this action programme:

1. placing at the disposal of users, as quickly as possible and at the lowest cost, the equipment and services they require to ensure that they are sufficiently competitive;
2. stimulating European production of telecommunication equipment and services to create a climate in which the Community industry can maintain its strong position on the European market and stay in first place among world exporters;
3. allowing carriers to take up the technological and industrial challenges with which they will be faced (CEC 1984d, p. 16).

Importantly for regional considerations, hand in hand with the development of thinking within the Task Force, the Regional Policy Directorate of the Commission (DGXVI) had been addressing, by commissioning a research project, the issue of the likely regional consequences of new information technologies. The Final Report on this research to the Commission (CURDS 1983; see also Gillespie et al. 1984) drew attention to a range of deficiencies with respect to both the supply of and demand for telecommunications within the less favoured regions of Europe, and argued that, in the context of a developing European information economy, these deficiencies would both lead to growing regional disparities in economic well-being and, as importantly, hinder the attainment of a competitive European information economy. This line of argument was incorporated into the Action Plan which was proposed by the Commission in mid-1984 and accepted by the Council in December of that year. Four major handicaps were identified which "inhibit the development of telecommunications, and hinder the Community in taking full advantage of the opportunities offered by this development" (CEC 1984d, p. 16), these being:

- compartmentalised markets which stunt supply and demand;
- the uncertainty of carriers and companies over what development strategies to put in hand;
- weakness in the fundamental technologies of communications;
- backwardness of less favoured areas in respect of networks, equipment and advanced telecommunication services.

The Action Plan adopted addresses these handicaps in four ways:

- creation of a Community market for telecommunication equipment and terminals;
- implementation of infrastructure projects of common interest;
- launching of a development programme for the technologies required in the long term for the establishment of the future broadband networks (the Research in Advanced Communications in Europe - RACE - programme);
- co-ordination of negotiating positions within international organisations dealing with telecommunications.

In a comparatively short space of time, substantial progress has been made in defining the details and in beginning to implement the various elements of the Action Plan. Although the regional dimension to the Plan is not paramount, the incorporation of an explicit regional-policy objective within it (which we consider in the following section), clearly provides an important development in European policy thinking which could usefully be extended to other policy areas as well as to some of the member states which do not recognise the significance of the regional dimension to sectoral and technology policies, or the need to co-ordinate and integrate the development of sectoral and territorial policies.

5.4. Transport and telecommunications within the Community's regional policy

5.4.1. Introduction

In terms of direct Community spending, regional-policy budget lines are far more important than the limited expenditure under transport and telecommunication policy per se. In 1981, for example, the funds available for the Community's transport policy amounted to 10 m ECU, while expenditure on regional policy amounted to 2,400 m ECU. Since the objectives of the ERDF and Transport Funds are different, there has been no integration of spending in either schemes or areas. As noted in the section on harmonisation and regional development, proposed expenditure under the Transport Fund was roughly equally apportioned between the core and periphery of the Community. Regional-policy expenditure obviously concentrates on the less favoured regions, which are mainly on the Community's periphery. The differing geographical allocations reflect the contrasting objectives of the two policies, the Transport Fund being designed to further the integration of the Common Market and the Regional Development Fund to assist in solving problems of regional structural imbalance, low GDP and unemployment. Transport-Fund spending on the alleviation of bottlenecks is unlikely to relate directly to regional-development problems, although the supply of transport to peripheral areas may do so.

5.4.2. Investment in transport and telecommunication infrastructure

Three forms of regional policy aid are applicable to the funding of transport and telecommunication infrastructure in the designated less favoured regions of the Community. These are loans from the European Investment Bank (EIB), loans in the form of the New Community Instrument (NIC), and grants from the European Regional Development Fund (ERDF). In 1983, out of a total budget of 1256 million ECU, the ERDF dispersed 412 million ECU to transport infrastructure and a further 151 million ECU to telecommunications infrastructure.

Since the raising of the 70-percent threshold by the Council in 1983, three quarters of ERDF investment schemes have been devoted to infrastructure, notably in energy and transport. Between 1973 and 1983, 32 per cent of infrastructure assistance was given to transport schemes (amounting to 2,400 m ECU), and 9 per cent to telecommunication investment (714 million ECU; ERDF 1984). The share of investment in transport and telecommunications vis a vis energy and other infrastructural schemes has been declining, having been 36 per cent in 1982 and 22 per cent in 1983. Typical schemes have been the provision of the basic road network, as in Ireland and Brittany, the railway network in Greece, and telephone networks notably in Ireland, Crete and the Massif Central of France.

The ERDF is not, however, the largest Community instrument in terms of its contribution to funding transport and telecommunication investments in the less favoured regions. With respect to telecommunication investments, for example, over the 1981-83 period total resources provided by the Community amounted to an average of some 720 million ECU per year, of which approximately 70 per cent was provided by the lending instruments (mainly the EIB and the NIC) and 30 per cent by the budgetary instrument (the ERDF). This amount corresponds to approximately 5 per cent of total investment by telecommunication carriers in the Community (CEC 1984d). Although the total annual Community expenditure on telecommunication investments grew between 1981-83 and 1984, this was entirely due to an expansion in EIB loans from an average of 479 m ECU over the 1981-3 period to 564 m ECU in 1984, while ERDF grants fell from 162 m ECU to 157 m ECU. Some concern has been expressed about this shift in emphasis (KMG Thomson McLintock 1985, p. 46) on the basis that any increasing reliance on loans as opposed to grants would mean that regional aid would tend to concentrate on the 'safest' investment with the highest likelihood of financial return to the PTT, even though these might not be the most 'profitable' investments in terms of regional economic development.

5.4.3. The Special Telecommunications Action for Regional Development (the STAR Programme)

The Special Telecommunications Action for Regional Development (STAR) (CEC 1986) marks, in a number of respects, a new chapter in the development of European regional policy. In the 1985 revisions to the regulations governing the operation of the ERDF, the concept of a 'Community Programme' was introduced into the range of instruments available. The Community element of such programmes differs in two respects from the other instruments of the ERDF; firstly, they are initiated by a proposal from the Commission rather than from a member state; and secondly, "the purpose of the programmes is to provide a better link between the Community's regional develoment objectives and the objectives of oher Community policies. Whereas the specific measures under the former non-quota section of the ERDF were designed primarily to mitigate the adverse effects of other Community policies, Communiy programmes will concentrate more on enhancing in the less favoured regions the benefits that may result from implementation of those policies, including telecommunications policy" (CEC 1986).

The STAR programme is to be the first of the Community programmes. The thinking underlying the programme, which draws on the initial study of the impact of new informtion technology on the less favoured regions (CURDS 1983) and a second round of studies specifically on the situation with respect to telecommunications in certain less favoured regions(KMG Thomson McLintock 1985; IRI 1985; Consultel 1985; OTE 1985; Terrovitas 1985; Telecom Eirean 1985; Baltimore Technologies 1985; British Telecom Northern Ireland 1985; McLaughlin 1985), is set out in the explanatory memorandum which accompanies the proposal for a Council regulation instituting the STAR programme (CEC 1986):

"The prime aim of this particular programme is to foster the economic development of the least favoured regions of the Community by improving advanced telecommunications services in line with the Community's objectives in this field. The detailed studies carried out recently by the Commission have shown that these regions are lagging a long way behind the rest of the Community as regards both telecommunications equipment and the level of services on offer. There is the danger that the rapid change that has been taking place in this sector for several years, notably as a result of the expansion of new information technologies will accentuate the backwardness of the least favoured regions ... The Community cannot allow this to continue. The Commission takes the view that new technological developments instead of being allowed to ossify existing economic structures, must be the means whereby the less developed regions are able to participate in the qualitative improvements that Europe is making with regard to new technologies" (CEC 1986, p. 4).

The STAR programme consists of two main elements; firstly, the provision of the equipment needed to provide advanced telecommunication services, and, secondly, measures to promote the supply of and demand for advanced services. The bulk of the financial resources (some 85 per cent of the total proposed budget of 700 m ECU, covering the 1986-90 period) is earmarked for equipment - i.e. for telecommunication infrastructure. It differs from other financial provisions for funding infrastructure in the less favoured regions (under the ERDF, EIB and NIV) in that only certain pre-defined types of equipment necessary for providing advanced services will be eligible. These will include the infrastructure needed to integrate the less favoured regions in the new advanced telecommunication networks being set up across the Community, infrastructure for digitalisation with a view to the more rapid introduction of integrated-services digital networks (ISDN) and for specialist overlay networks - e.g. for high-speed data transmission - in the period before ISDN becomes a reality, and infrastructure to establish and develop cellular radio compatible with the development of a Community-wide system.

Perhaps the most innovative aspect of the STAR programme is the placing of these infrastructure measures into a broader development-focused package. As the explanatory memorandum to the proposal suggests:

> "The establishment of these different infrastructures is obviously a necessary but not sufficient condition for the development of advanced telecommunications services in the least-favoured regions. If proper use is to be made of these infrastructures, it is essential that appropriate back-up measures be taken to stimulate the supply of advanced services directly accessible to the productive sector on the one hand, and to encourage the demand for such services on the other" (CEC 1986, p. 3).

With respect to stimulating the supply of advanced services in the less favoured regions, the STAR programme will include support for:

-   technical and economic feasibility studies on the provision of new telecom services, notably to small and medium sized enterprises (SMEs);
-   the establishment and development of telecommunication service centres, outside the main urban areas, with a view to providing advanced services in sparsely populated areas and to providing common services shared by a number of SMEs;
-   the provision of regional services using computerised telecommunication facilities in the sphere of 'specialised information services'.

On the demand stimulation side, STAR will include:

-   measures to promote the use of advanced telecommunication services through publicity and information campaigns;
-   measures to demonstrate, by means of specific applications, the advantages of using advanced telecommunication services;
-   aid for SMEs or groups of SMEs to commission expert studies on the potential benefit of advanced telecommunications to them and, in instances where these studies provide justification, aid to enable the SMEs to purchase the equipment needed (for instance modems, terminals) to access advanced services.

Funding will be programme-based rather than on individual projects, and the intention will be to ensure that the programme designed for each eligible region is fully in tune with its development needs and objectives and is in accord with broader strategies for mobilising its indigenous development potential. The countries/regions which will be included in the STAR programme are the whole of

Greece and Ireland, the Italian Mezzogiorno, Northern Ireland in he UK, Corsica and the French overseas departments, and regions yet to be determined (at the time of writing) in Spain and Portugal.

While the impacts of the STAR programme will clearly not be measurable for some time to come - the programme has just, at the time of writing, been finally approved by Council - a number of its features make it an innovative and interesting development in the Community's regional policy: firstly, in its attempt to explicitly link a sectoral policy objective - concerning the development of telecommunications in Europe - with the Community's regional-policy objectives; secondly, in its recognition that infrastructure provision is not on its own sufficient to stimulate regional development, and that consequently the supply of infrastructure has to be accompanied by measures to ensure that the development potential of the infrastructure is realised and maximised; and thirdly by its adoption of a co-ordinated programmatic and above all positive approach to the issue it displays a firm commitment to the need to harness new technologies in such a way as to provide opportunities for less favoured areas, to help counter the threats that such technologies undoubtedly pose if allowed to develop in an un-regulated and un-planned economic context.

5.5. Conclusions

This review of the regional impact of European Community transport and tele-communication policy suggests a number of continuing problems for future policy makers. The first is the very slow development of policy in relation to the speed of technical innovation, especially in telecommunications. The basic political structure of the Community ensures that national policies have been and in the foreseeable future will be, more important than Community policies. Transport policy is decided by the Council of Ministers and only if their individual transport interests appear to coincide or if some sort of deal can be struck will the Council make new policy. The individual transport ministers remain under obligation to their national parliaments. The Treaty of Rome called for majority voting on issues related to land transport after 1970, but ministers have not yet given up the practice of requiring unanimous agreement. The slow and piecemeal development of transport policies and the length of transitional time allowed for bringing agreed policies into effect has made Community transport policy difficult to integrate with the rather shorter-term regional-policy measures which either the Community or one of its member states might wish to follow.

The second problem is the predominance of diverse national transport and tele-communication policies over those of the EC. Successive French governments have included telecommunication, motorways, high-speed passenger trains and regional air links among positive tools of regional development, associated with a planned hierarchy of settlements. West Germany has put more emphasis on transport corridors along which most transport modes are developed to a high density and quality. British governments have increasingly relied on market forces to steer the provision of new services and have, at the same time, virtually dismantled the regional policies of the 1960s. Britain has also been extremely reluctant to adopt Community harmonisation policies or to consider the regional effects of its proposals for the de-regulation of European air traffic.

The third problem lies in quantifying the contribution of transport and tele-communication investment to subsequent regional development and estimating the importance of telecommunication and transport services to contemporary regional prosperity. It has been difficult for advocates of spatial planning to defend their position against proponents of sectoral decision making and reliance on market forces. While almost all observers recognise a strong association between high levels of economic development and a substantial transport and telecommunication infrastructure, they are not agreed as to whether one depends on the other, whether there is a high level of interaction between the two or how to test these hypotheses. If certain levels of telecommunication and transport infrastructure and services are necessary (even if not sufficient) for the further economic development of problem regions, such services should not be removed when demand is no longer sufficient to support them: they should be provided even if the regional market is not large enough to justify them commercially. If Community funding, Community subsidy or modal cross-subsidy are ruled out, the regional policy is no longer one of development but of evacuation.

When the EC came into being, most regional policies had the divesification from agriculture toward manufacturing industry or from older to newer manufacturing industries as their main objectives. Supporting policies in the transport sector concerned the provision of better road and rail freight infrastructure and pricing policies designed to reduce the friction of distance. Almost thirty years later, the developments of service-dominated economies and multinational companies has greatly intensified the hierarchical organisation of economic life. Less developed regions are increasingly reliant on branch plants and subcontracts and help from national governments to win them. In these changed circumstances, good communication with financial and government centres is of prime importance, making telecommunciation, air and rapid railway services the main tools of regional policy in the transport field. Modern telecommunication technology has developed almost entirely during the years since the EC was established.

As telecommunication and transport services have become more sophisticated and varied, the gap between regions where demand has risen to support their commercial operation and regions which cannot afford such new development has grown. Even where governments have accepted responsibility for providing a virtually universal service, they have invested first in the routes offering the heaviest traffic, giving developed regions a critical lead during the often long drawn-out installation period. Where wide inter-regional variation of telecommunication and transport service have been avoided, the cost of service subsidies has risen very markedly. National funds for public investment are much harder to come by in the 1980s than in the early years of the EC and a growing tendency to favour consumer preference supported by a search for efficiency through intermodal competition has tempted governments to concentrate resources on the most heavily trafficked routes. Should an unremunerative transport service be cross-subsidised or provided from non-transport resources ? National policies conceived in modal terms may have unforeseen negative effects on disadvantaged regions. The Commission has pointed out the dangers of divorcing sectoral from territorial policies, notably in the field of telecommunications. Community policy on transparency and infrastructural investment would favour external funding rather than cross-subsidy, but Community funding of telecommunications and transport is as yet too small to make a significant regional impact. Policies to relieve bottlenecks arguably benefit peripheral regions but are of clear value to core regions. The effects of EC policies have been particularly small in member states which are actively pursuing deregulation and privatisation in the transport and telecommunication sectors. Given the unequal nature of inter-regional relationships in market economies, it can only be hoped that Community policies will be more adequately funded and pursued with vigour commensurate to the strength of the forces opposed to them.

5.6. References

Aberle, G. (1979), Transport and regional policy objectives in cost benefit analysis, in W.A. Blonk (ed.), Transport and Regional Development, Saxon House, Farnborough.

Bakis, H. (1985), Telecommunications and Organisation of Company Work Space, Centre National d'Etudes des Télécommunications, Paris.

Baltimore Technologies (1985), Economic Study for Ireland, Use of Telecommunications for Regional Development Project, Report of the Commission of the European Communities, Brussels, Baltimore Technologies Ltd., Dublin.

Bell, D. (1973), The Coming of Post-Industrial Society, Basic Books, New York.

Bell, D. (1973), The Social Framework of Information Society, in M. Dertouzar and J. Moses (eds.), The Computer Age: a Twenty Year View, MIT Press, Cambridge (Mass.).

Biehl, D. and others (1982), The Contribution of Infrastructure to Regional Development, Final Report of the Infrastructure Study Group, Commission of the European Communities, Brussels.

Bonnafous, A. (1979), Under-developed Regions and Structural Impacts of Transport Infrastructure, in W.A. Blonk (ed.), Transport and Regional Development, Saxon House, Farnborough.

BRD (1980), Federal Plan for Transportation Routes (Bundesverkehrswegeplan 80), Bonn.

British Telecom, Northern Ireland (1985), Technical Study on Northern Ireland, Use of Telecommunications for Regional Development Project, Report to the Commission of the European Communities, Brussels, BTNI, Belfast.

CEC (1961), Memorandum on the Guidelines for a Common Transport Policy (Schaus Memorandum), COM (61) 50, Brussels.

CEC (1962), Programme of Action on the Common Transport Policy, COM (62)88, Brussels.

CEC (1973a), Development of the Common Transport Policy (Mursch Report), COM (73) 850, Brussels.

CEC (1973b), Report to the Council from the Commission on the Development of Public Transport Policies, COM (73) 1725, Brussels.

CEC (1979a), Contribution of the European Communities to the Development of Air Transport Services, Bulletin of the European Commission, Supp. 5, Brussels.

CEC (1979b), The Role of the Community in the Development of Transport Infrastructure, COM (79) 550, Brussels.

CEC (1979c), A Transport Network for Europe, Bulletin of the European Commission, Supp. 8, Brussels.

CEC (1980), Report on Bottlenecks and Possible Modes of Finance, COM 80 (323), Brussels.

CEC (1981), Community Assistance for Transport Infrastructure: the Evaluation of "Community Interest" for Decision Making, COM (81) 507, Brussels.

CEC (1983), Report on Transport problems in the Peripheral Regions of the EC, DOC 1-755/83, Brussels.

CEC (1984a), Progress towards the Development of a Community Air Transport Policy, COM (84) 72, Brussels.

CEC (1984b), Broad Outlines of a Medium-Term Transport Infrastructure Policy, COM (84) 709, Brussels.

CEC (1984c), Ninth Report from the Commission to the Council on the European Regional Development Fund, COM (84) 532, Brussels.

CEC (1984d), Communication from the Commission to the Council on Telecommunications: Progress report on the thinking and work done in the field and initial proposals for an Action Programme, COM (84) 277 final, Brussels.

CEC (1986), Proposal for a Council Regulation (EEC) Instituting a Community Programme for the Development of Certain Less Favoured Regions of the Community by Improving Access to Advanced Telecommunications Services (STAR programme), COM (85) 836 final, Brussels.

CEMT (1975), Impact of Infrastructural Investment on Industrial Development (Conference of European Ministers of Transport), Round Table 25, Paris.

CEMT (1984), The Regionalisation of Transport and Regional Planning in Practice (Conference of European Ministers of Transport), Paris.

CURDS (1983), Study of the Effects of New Information Technology on the Less Favoured Regions of the Community, Final Report to the Directorate General for Regional Policy, Commission of the European Communities, (Centre for Urban and Regional Development Studies), University of Newcastle upon Tyne.

Clark (1975), The Spatial Impact of Telecommunication, in Impacts of Telecommunications on Planning and Transport, Research Report 24, Departments of the Environment and Transport, London.

Consultel (1985), Technical Study for Italy, Use of Telecommunications for Regional Development Project, Report to the Commission of the European Communities, Consultel, Rome.

Council of Europe (1971), Radius Report - Organisation of a European Network of Trunk Communications as Part of European Regional Planning, Doc 2903, Strasbourg.

Cripps, F.R., and Godley, W. (1978), The Planning of Telecommunications in the United Kingdom, Department of Applied Economics, University of Cambridge.

Deutsches Institut für Wirtschaftsforschung (1984), Economic Evaluation of the Impact of Telecommunications Investment in the Communities, Study on behalf of the Commission of the European Communities, DIW, Berlin.

Economist, The (1985), The World on the Line, Special feature, The Economist, November 23.

EI/CURDS (1985), Availability, Cost and Use of Telecommunications in the Northern Region, A Report for NECCA. Economist Informatics, London, and Centre for Urban and Regional Development Studies, University of Newcastle upon Tyne.

Erdmenger, J. (1983), The European Community Transport Policy, Gower, Aldershot.

Funck, R.H., and Blum, U. (1986), Regional Effects of Investments in the Transport Infra Structure, Papers of the Fourth International Transport Conference 1981, G. Konno and T. Okana (eds.), Tokyo.

Gillespie, A.E., Goddard, J.B., Robinson, J.F.R., Smith, I.J., and Thwaites, A.T. (1984), The Effects of New Information Technology on the Less-Favoured Regions of the Community, CEC Studies Collection, Regional Policy Series No. 23, Brussels.

Gillespie, A.E., and Hepworth, M.E. (1986), Telecommunications and Regional Development in the Information Economy, Working Paper no. 1, Newcastle Studies of the Information Economy, CURDS University of Newcastle upon Tyne.

Hepworth, M.E. (1986), The Geography of Technological Change in the Information Economy, Regional Studies, forthcoming.

Hoogstraten, P. van, and Jansen, B. (1985), New Forms of Industrialisation and Material Infrastructure in the Netherlands, Paper presented at the 25th European Congress of the Regional Science Association, Budapest, Hungary.

I R I (1985), Economic Study for Italy, Use of Telecommunications for Regional Development Project, Report to the Commission of the European Communities, Brussels. Instituto per la Ricostruzione Industriale, Rome.

Keeble, D., Owens, P.L., and Thompson, C. (1982), Regional Accessibility and Economic Potential in the European Community, Regional Studies XVI, 419-32.

Klinkenborg, J. (1981), The Role of the Community in the Development of Transport and Infrastructures, Official Journal C 144, 15 June.

Klinkenborg, J. (1983), Report on Transport Infrastructure Plannin in the Community, Commission Working Document 1/1347/83, Paris.

KMG Thomson McLintock (1985), The Use of Telecommunications for Regional Development Project, final report to the Commission of the European Communities, KMG Thomson McLintock, London.

Kraft, G., Meyer, J.R., and Valette, J.P. (1971), The Role of Transportation in Regional Economic Development, Lexington, Mass.

Lakshmanan, T.R. (1986), Information Systems for Infrastructure Planning, Paper prepared for the International Symposium on "Informatics and Regional Development", Delphi, Greece.

McLaughlin, R.A. (1985), Economic Study for Northern Ireland, Use of Telecommunications for Regional Development Project, Report to the Commission of the European Communities, Brussels.

Massey, D. (1984), Spatial Divisions of Labour, Macmillan, London.

Meadows, W.J., and Jackson, P.M. (1984), Infrastructue and Regional Development: Empirical Findings, Built Environment vol. 19, no. 4, pp. 270-281.

Oettle, K. (1979), Public Obligations and Transportation in Underdeveloped Regions, in W.A. Blonk (ed.), Transport and Regional Development, Saxon House, Farnborough.

O T E (1985), Technical Study for Greece, Use of Telecommunications for Regional Development Project, Report to the Commission of the European Communities, Brussels. Hellenic Telecommunications Organisation, Athens.

Pedersen, P.O. (1985), Communication and Spatial Inteaction in an Area of Advanced Technology with Special Emphasis on Goods Transport, Sydjysk Universitetscenter, Esbjerg, Denmark.

Pieda (1984), Transport Costs in Peripheral Areas, Final Report to the European Commission, Industry Department for Scotland and Department of Economic Development, Northern Ireland; ESU Research Paper no. 9, Edinburgh.

Romus, P. (1983), Economie Régionale Européenne, Brussels.

Telecom Eireann (1985), Technical Study for Ireland, Use of Telecommunications for Regional Development Project, Report to the Commission of the European Communities, Brussels. Telecom Eireann, Dublin.

Terrovitis, T.E. (1985), Economic Study for Greece, Use of Telecommunications for Regional Development Project, Report to the Commission of the European Communities, Brussels. Centre for Planning and Economic Research (KEPE), Athens.

Thomson, J.M. (1976), Towards a European Transport Strategy, in R. Lee and P.E. Ogden (eds.), Economy and Society in the European Economic Community, Saxon House, Farnborough.

Voigt, F. (1979), Transport and Regional Policy - some general aspects, in W.A. Blonk (ed.), Transport and Regional Development, Saxon House, Farnborough.

6 Labour Markets and Social Policies

W. STEINLE

6.1. Introduction

For the past 12 or 13 years, the situation on the labour market has deteriorated substantially in all member states of the European Community. The number of unemployed increased from about 2 million in 1970 to over 13 million in 1985. That steep rise was the result of various developments, both socio-economic and demographic.

The combined developments of demand and supply, as well as changing interactions between the two, led on the one hand to a noticeable rise in unemployment, and on the other hand to a change in the structure and problem content of unemployment and the labour market in general (Steinle 1983a). Various policy measures have been taken to remedy the situation, some of the demand-management type, others geared to improve the supply side (for instance, human capital). Yet others were intended to improve the workings of the labour market, or attenuate the negative social effects. The European Community has played an active part in this policy field, in particular through the European Social Fund. In this chapter we will go into the regional effects of these policies.

A first section will give a succinct introductory description of the problems and policies. The next one elaborates on some of the causes of regional trends and structures in the labour market. Against that background, the relevance and regional implications of European social policies, and especially of the European Social Fund, are examined. Finally, the regional impact of European social policy is discussed.

6.2. General description of problems and policy

6.2.1. Development of the European labour markets

While the growth of total population slowed down, the population of working age has continued to grow at rates more or less in line with those of the 1960s. Thus, the potentially employable population has increased in respect of total population (CEC 1981, 1984b). Moreover - despite the economic recession - female participation in the labour force has increased substantially, which has put additional pressure on the labour market. The general trends are displayed in Figure 6.1. On the demand side, the growth of employment in the service sector has been - and still is - insufficient to counterbalance the decreasing agricultural and manufacturing employment. These trends coincide with a reduced capacity to restructure declining industries and a lack of creation and establishment of new innovative economic activities (Empirica 1986).

Against the background of the unemployment situation in the Community, the present section presents an overview of European social policies. The relevant questions can be summarised as follows:
-To what extent has European social policy and have national policies adapted to the changing structure and content of labour-market problems ?
-What policy instruments have been brought to bear on the situation ?
With regard to social policies, a basic distinction is made between active and passive measures. Passive measures include all transfers to individuals designed to guarantee certain levels of income to those not gainfully employed (unemployment compensation, social-security benefits, etc.), or to those earning incomes below certain levels (housing or rent subsidies, education allowances, etc.). Active measures include transfers aimed at upgrading or developing skills to increase the employability of individuals and to create or maintain employment.

6.2.2. National policies in the area of training and employment

In all member states of the EEC, expenditures on social security represent a substantial proportion of GDP. Current expenditures range from 23 per cent of GDP in Ireland to 32 per cent in the Netherlands (1981). Moreover, as can be seen from Table 6.1, the cost of social security has increased considerably.

Table 6.1
Social-security expenditures in percentages of
GDP (market prices) in the countries of the EC, 1973, 1983

	1973	1983
Belgium	20.4	31.9
Denmark	21.3	30.2
FRG	23.2	28.9
Greece	9.6	-
France	19.8	28.8
Ireland	15.4	24.6
Italy	22.6	a) 27.3
Luxemburg	16.8	29.3
Netherlands	23.7	34.0
United Kingdom	17.1	23.7
Spain	-	-
Portugal	7.8	-

a) = 1975
Sources: EUROSTAT 1984, 1985b.

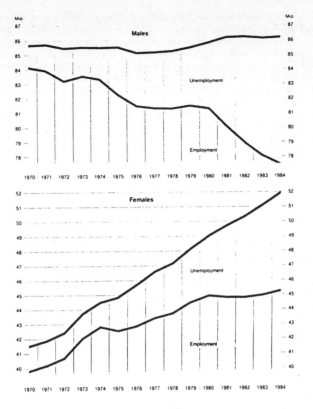

Figure 6.1
Overall labour-market trends in the EC, 1970-1984

However, in the framework of the present chapter, expenditures on social security are relevant only as far as they can be considered active components of social policy. An attempt at quantifying the proportion of active versus passive expenditures was made by Reissert/Schmid. On the basis of a fairly broad definition of active policies (labour exchange, retraining and rehabilitation, direct measures to maintain or create jobs), Reissert/Schmid conclude that expenditures for active policies are in the order of 30 to 40 per cent of total expenditure related to the labour market, with a tendency towards increasing passive contributions (Reisert/Schmid 1985, p. 4). Overall, apart from expenditures on social security for purposes not directly relevant to the labour market (for instance health, housing, etc.), active measures represent less than one per cent of GDP (Reissert/Schmid 1985, p. 4).

Apparently, on the level of national policies a small fraction of public funds is directed towards measures related to employment and training (total public expenditure, for instance, represents about 45 per cent of GDP in the EC). A look at the measures adopted by member states within the range of active social policies reveals that almost all these public funds are spent on traditional countercyclical measures in the area of training/retraining or employment.

Without going into further detail we may say that current national programmes have tried to alleviate unemployment by offering cost reductions to companies taking on or training different target groups, programmes for young people putting emphasis on the training components, and those for adults (usually over 25) concentrating on wage subsidies (with regard, for instance, to the long-term unemployed) or community work (for instance, the Community Programme in Great Britain, the TUC - Travaux à Utilité Collective - in France, or the Programm Arbeitslose Sozialhilfeempfänger in North-Rhine Westphalia, and similar programmes in other federal states in the Federal Republic of Germany). The common denominator of these programmes is the assumption that the rigidity of the labour market can be reduced through incentives to companies or training organisations. Such incentives are expected to increase the "absorptive capacity" of the economy (integration of unemployed), retain or increase the "employability" of unemployed persons (for instance, community programmes), or make available the skills needed in the labour market (for instance, programmes oriented to training or retraining).

Programmes for young unemployed people, for instance, aim at facilitating the training of the target group in companies or training centres through allowances or subsidies. Such programmes have been used in all member states. In Italy, for example, the Contratti Formazione Lavoro aim at increasing youth training and employment through reductions in the contributions employers have to make to social security; in France, the so-called Contrat Emploi/Formation (Employment/Training Contract) exempts companies from social-security contributions (for young people taken on), and accords hourly training subsidies to companies. The Youth Training or the New Workers Scheme in the United Kingdom has similar features, as have the youth employment plan in the Netherlands and related programmes in other countries (except the Federal Republic of Germany, where the dual system sets other preconditions). In general, up to 50 per cent of young people without gainful employment have participated in such programmes (for details, see Chronik 1986, pp. 1-4).

A wide variety of national policies and measures have direct or indirect effects on regional labour markets. Regulations with regard to hours worked, working conditions, equal opportunity, early retirement, collective bargaining, etc., are not neutral in regional terms. An analysis of the regional effects of early retirement, for instance, has indicated that - owing to demographic, participation, and sectorial factors - the depressed regions in Europe incur additional disadvantages (Steinle 1980). Although there is a substantial lack of empirical evidence, the regional effects of these and related policy measures should not be ignored.

6.2.3. European social policy: historical trends and present profile

European social policy is based on the European Social Fund (referred to as ESF), established in 1960. In 1986, this fund had a volume of over 2,500 million ECU (EC 12).

Originally, European social policy was not oriented to regional aspects. The Treaties of Rome, which define the orientation of European policies, state the following with regard to European activities and instruments of social policy: the "European Social Fund ... shall have the task of rendering the employment of workers easier and of increasing their geographical and occupational mobility within the Community." (Article 123, EEC 1973.) This task was to be accomplished by the following measures:
"a) ensuring productive re-employment of workers by means of
- vocational retraining;
- resettlement allowances;
b) granting aid for the benefit of workers whose employment is reduced or temporarily suspended, in whole or in part, as a result of the conversion of an undertaking to other production, in order that they may retain the same wage

level pending their full re-employment." (Article 125, EEC 1973.)
During the 1970s, regional considerations became more and more important. The reform of the European Social Fund in 1971 already contains regional elements. The council regulation of November 10, 1971 states, among other things, that the promotion of improved employment conditions in less developed regions is an objective of policy interventions (Article 3, CEC 1971).

The serious consideration of regional aspects began, however, only after the creation of the European Regional Development Fund (ERDF) in 1975. Initially established as a transfer mechanism to shift budgets across member states, after several revisions the ERDF has become a European instrument with relatively clearly stated development goals and measures (Giolitti 1983, Steinle 1983b).

In the late 1970s and early 1980s, the EEC Commission was working towards the increased coherence and co-ordination of European policies. That movement has given a new orientation to many policy instruments. With regard to regional aspects, the delimitation of European regions eligible for public aid implies, for instance, the reorientation of ESF to the regions. A large proportion of ESF support is reserved to priority regions. As can be seen from Table 6.2, in 1985 the commitment appropriations totalled roughly 2,200 million ECU, of which over a third were committed to less favoured regions.

Table 6.2
ESF-appropriations committed
(in million ECU)

Operations to assist young people under 25	
Less favoured regions	645
Other regions	967
Operations to assist people over 25	
Less favoured regions	186
Other regions	288
Specific operations	73
Total	2,159

Source: CEC 1986.

In its present form, the ESF gives high priority to operations for the training of young people. Following the reform of the Fund in 1983, 75 per cent of the total budget is spent on this group of population. Moreover, increasing importance is attached to vocational training for new technologies. All supported training schemes must contain at least 40 hours of training in new technology (1986 guidelines of the ESF).

By drawing a clear dividing line between active and passive social policies, the ESF is a policy mechanism that is geared to active measures. While article 125b (see above), which includes passive measures, has become less and less important (and by now represents an insignificant portion of ESF operations), article 125a has become a key element. Moreover, retraining and re-employment measures - which are the focal point of article 125a - have in practice been extended to include training and employment. The shift is particularly important to measures related to youth unemployment.

6.3. Regional labour markets in Europe: trends and structures

6.3.1. Introduction

In the light of the general trends described earlier, the following subsections examine the regional labour markets. Particular emphasis is laid on the content of regional problems. While an extensive investigation into those aspects would go beyond the scope of this chapter, the structure and nature of regional problems with regard to residents not gainfully employed is used to illustrate the workings and interactions of factors relevant to the lack of adaptability and dynamism of labour markets in a regional perspective.

The next subsection analyses the changing economic climate and regional trends in unemployment. Next, the regional (co-)incidence of unemployment and problem groups on the labour market is discussed. Finally, tendencies of regional cumulation and concentration of problem groups on the labour market are placed in a wider perspective.

6.3.2. The changing economic climate and regional trends in umemployment

During the 1950s and 1960s regional disparities of unemployment increased continuously. That general tendency was disrupted in the course of the 1970s. Similar changes have become apparent with regard to migration, GDP per head, and several other key indicators which are currently used to demonstrate the existence of regional problems.

The economic recession of the 1970s and early 1980s affected export-oriented industrial branches most. It may be assumed that in a situation of narrowing markets, unemployment tends to increase more in regions that are highly export-oriented than in regions not exposed to interregional competition. In addition, the presence of export-oriented sectors may be expected to make for more unemployment, because manufacturing industries are more likely to substitute capital for labour than, for example, services or agriculture. The general question then is whether those tendencies have weakened the adaptability of the more developed regions in respect of regions that depend heavily on basic industries.

To understand the regional evolution of unemployment, the response of various regions to changes in the economic climate must be examined (Borts 1960, Bassett/Hagget 1970, Harris/Thirlwall 1968). An examination of the regional evolution of unemployment with due consideration to overall cyclical movements produces the following results.

- By and large, the regional pattern during periods of recession was one of steep unemployment growth in export-oriented regions with traditionally low levels of unemployment.
- By contrast, the less developed sluggish areas with traditionally high levels of unemployment incurred but marginal increases during recession phases.
- However, as soon as the economy started to recover, the pattern was reversed. In recovery phases, the regions that had been deeply injured by periods of recession (in terms of unemployment) performed well, while the regions with small unemployment rises incurred above-average increases of unemployment afterwards.

Apparently, reduced regional disparities do not, in general, coincide with reduced regional problems. The regions that were worst hit by the recession phases were also those that recovered most easily (ceteris paribus, namely if the economic adaptability remained constant). Though these regions suffered steep increases of unemployment, they showed a high degree of economic dynamism, while in the depressed regions the labour market proved more intractable in the changing economic climate.

6.3.3. The structure of unemployment and problem groups on the labour market

A rough idea of the changing structure and problem content of unemployment can be obtained by looking at the evolution of the duration of unemployment. Table 6.3 displays the changing composition of unemployment by duration according to the labour-force surveys of 1975, 1979 and 1983 (Eurostat 1977, Eurostat 1981, Eurostat 1985a). Apparently, the share of long-term unemployment increased steadily between 1975 and 1983, while frictional unemployment became insignificant.

Table 6.3
Unemployment in the EEC by duration: 1975, 1979, 1983 (in %)

	1975		1979		1983	
Months	Men	Women	Men	Women	Men	Women
more than 1	13	16	10	10	6	7
1 - 2	21	20	14	13	9	9
3 - 5	23	21	17	15	14	14
6 - 11	23	25	22	24	23	24
12 and more	20	18	37	38	48	46

Sources: EUROSTAT 1977, 1981, 1985a.

As can be seen from Figure 6.2, unemployment rates vary greatly among member states and regions. With the notable exception of Greece, unemployment figures tend to be higher in the periphery than in the core regions. Most Belgian and Dutch regions are in an exceptional situation, too: unlike other central regions they register exceptionally high unemployment rates. However, the determinants of high unemployment rates are not homogeneous across the regions. The low unemployment rates in the Greek regions are basically due to the above-average rates of agricultural and self-employment, which imply that these regions are characterised by high under-employment rather than high unemployment (farmers and the self-employed do not register as unemployed). Similar tendencies can be observed in most Spanish and Portuguese regions (which are not represented in Figure 6.2 because in 1983, when the underlying data were collected, these two countries were not yet member states of the European Community). The labour-market problems in that type of region are marked by much unemployment as well as under-employment, with activity rates, generally speaking, below average. In highly industrialised regions, the problem content of unemployment is again different. In many Belgian regions, in Hamburg and Bremen in the Federal Republic of Germany, in Nord-Pas-de-Calais in France, and in the United Kingdom, for instance, both activity rates and unemployment are above average, while under-employment is below average. In these regions, high unemployment figures are the result of declining industries and lack of sectorial renovation. Nor is unemployment homogeneous; certain segments of the labour force are more affected by unemployment than others, and certain groups among the unemployed retain their unemployment status for a longer period than others. The segmentation of the labour-market coincides with severe rigidities in unemployment and a reduced capacity of the economy to integrate or reintegrate those without jobs into the working population.

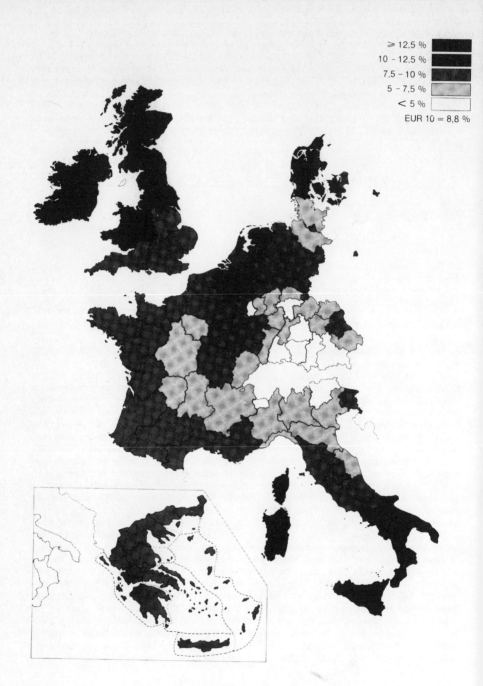

≥ 12,5 %
10 – 12,5 %
7.5 – 10 %
5 – 7,5 %
< 5 %
EUR 10 = 8,8 %

Figure 6.2
Unemployment Rate, total of 1983

118

In terms of numbers, younger people are more frequently affected by unemployment than older ones, the proportion of unemployed females exceeding that of males. While the volume of unemployment decreases with increasing age, the proportion of long-term unemployment is much larger among the elderly than among the young.

On the level of regions, there is a close correlation between youth and long-term unemployment. Apparently, depressed regions are marked by cumulation and concentration of labour-market problems. To some extent the unemployment of young people is identical with female unemployment; this is confirmed by a comparison of figures 6.3 and 6.4, which display the regional patterns of youth and female unemployment. There are, however, some significant structural differences in regional distribution. In the French and Danish regions, young females out of work determine the high rate of youth unemployment, while in Italy and parts of Ireland, high unemployment rates among young females make little impact on total youth unemployment, because females constitute but a low proportion of the labour force. Generally speaking, the problem of female unemployment is concentrated in regions with a weak service sector (the sector providing the majority of jobs demanded by women). These regions are, at the same time, highly dependent on declining industries. Weak agricultural regions also have a fairly high unemployment rate of females, but the share of females in total unemployment is quite low there (Steinle 1983a).

6.3.4. Regional cumulation and concentration of labour-market problems

While we cannot go into much more detail with regard to regional unemployment, to point out the main factors in the process of regional cumulation and concentration of labour-market problems is important in the light of the foregoing sections. These factors are displayed in Figure 6.5. The factors and interdependencies included have been derived from empirical analyses, to which readers interested in more details is referred (Steinle 1983a, Steinle 1983b).

As can be seen from Figure 6.5, regional labour-market problems are determined by a variety of often interdependent factors. To single out any mono-causal determinant is not possible. Rigidities in the labour market go together with a long list of regional characteristics, such as the lack of diversification of regional economies, traditionally high rates of employment in large companies (resulting in scarcity of managerial talents), absence of restructuring, lack of a wide fan of skills (declining industrial areas), underdeveloped economies, lack of market access, of socio-economic culture outside agro-product industries, etc., and of development of viable endogenous activities.

The above observations are relevant for the investigation of European policies with respect to training and employment. They suggest that such policies can have positive regional effects only if they take into account the given constellation of labour-market problems in depressed or backward regions.

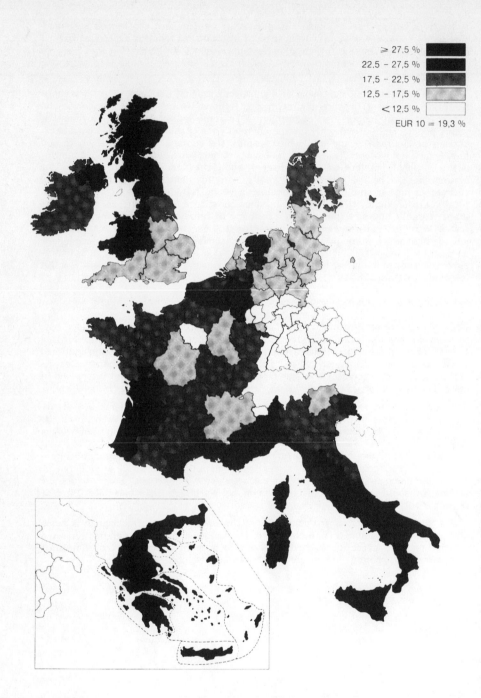

Figure 6.3
Unemployment rate for young people (under 25), 1983

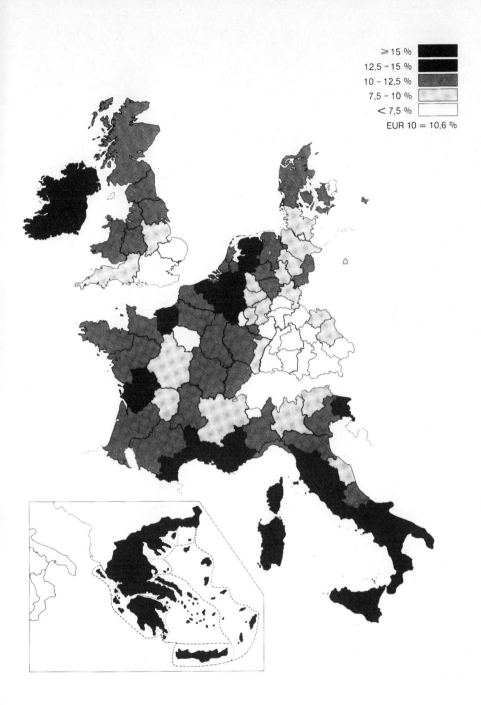

≥ 15 %
12,5 – 15 %
10 – 12,5 %
7,5 – 10 %
< 7,5 %
EUR 10 = 10,6 %

Figure 6.4
Unemployment rate for women, 1983

121

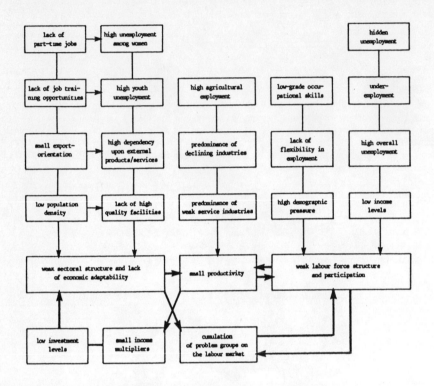

Figure 6.5
Factors in the process of cumulation and concentration
of regional labour-market problems

6.4. Regional impact of European social policy

6.4.1. EC practice

In the national reports on the activities of the ESF, which form part of the annual reports of the Commission of the European Communities, an attempt is made at assessing the impact of interventions by the European Social Fund. The outcome is disappointing, however. The Belgian report, for instance, states that "it is difficult to quantify the impact of the European Social Fund in terms of jobs created" (CEC 1984a, p. 3). The German report states that "the inaugural effect of the Social Fund of measures taken within the framework of labour market policy in the Federal Republic of Germany cannot be measured precisely" (CEC 1984a, p. 20). The French report says nothing about impact assessment; the others proceed along similar lines, present numbers of persons concerned in ESF operations, or describe examples of individual projects submitted to the ESF (for instance the UK report).

Such critical comments reflect to some extent the workings and structure of the ESF. The way it operates, the ESF cannot be expected to have significant regional impact or labour-market effects. Projects submitted to the Commission for ESF support are in general neither additional nor complementary to existing measures in the different member states. By far most projects submitted to the ESF by member states are envisaged within existing training or employment programmes. Even changing priorities and new guidelines for interventions of the European Social Fund cannot change that situation. The new priority of Social-Fund interventions for the training of young people, for instance, has on the whole not led to more young people being trained, but rather to member states submitting for ESF subsidies more projects within existing schemes.

An indication of the lack of additionality of ESF support to national measures is the fact that programmes submitted by member states and not supported by the ESF are often carried out anyway. Given the ESF and national-support mechanisms, that result is not at all surprising. Public organisations or ministries cannot work out new programmes, discuss them in government and parliament and vote for their execution, thus committing themselves, and then go on to say that they can be carried out only if the European Social Fund is willing to supports them. Either their commitment is so strong that they reserve the budget so that a new programme can be carried out even without ESF support, or they do not broadcast such programmes. If a new programme is positively evaluated, the public authority or ministry must reserve the money needed to implement it. If the ESF supports the programme, so much the better; if not, the programme is usually carried out even in the absence of ESF support.

The situation is somewhat different with regard to innovative projects, to which a small portion (about three per cent) of the total ESF budget is committed. The European Social Fund is not very clear about what is meant by "innovative" projects, for from the financial set-up of relevant measures, ESF support to innovative projects appears to be additional to currently available national funding mechanisms. In general, the projects involved are organised such that ESF money is used for activities that cannot be funded from available national or regional budgets (such as training allowances, compensations, enterprise allowances, etc.). The ESF funding share is normally used to cover salaries of project staff and training costs for participants not eligible on the basis of available programmes.

However, with respect to innovative projects most member states have built in control mechanisms to ensure that only project proposals agreed to by the national administration are submitted for ESF support. That means that in most member states the ESF cannot directly influence the selection of innovative measures.

In the light of the above observations, the ESF can hardly have any direct effects on the regional level. Its regional impact is mainly a function of how public institutions in the member states intend to spend the funds available for active social policy.

In terms of administrative procedure, ESF operations largely depend on national institutional and national political settings. The control mechanisms of most member states ensure that the qualitative impact of ESF operations - with the notable exception of some innovative projects - is only to a minimum extent influenced by 'European' instead of national considerations.

The rub, however, lies in the orientation of national and European policies to active measures. Training, retraining and employment are mostly treated in isolation, as disintegrate parts of labour-market policy. That general tendency is detrimental in view of regional cumulation and concentration of problem groups. In declining industrial or backward rural areas, training or retraining can generate positive labour-market effects only if embedded in strategies for the expansion of employment in viable industries, which in such regions are - at the least -

underrepresented.

The results achieved with training or employment measures are a function of the effectiveness of training institutions and the efficiency of companies in the regional economy. Schemes like the Youth Training Scheme in Great Britain, or the Contratti Formazione Lavoro, which are designed to facilitate the engaging and training of young people in companies, may be of use in diversified and dynamic regions, but not in depressed regions (the question whether dynamic regions need such schemes remaining for debate). Depressed regions hardly offer training and employment opportunities in viable industries.

6.4.2. Prospects of improvement

It is not impossible to change the labour-market situation in depressed regions. However, current schemes as mentioned above are unlikely to alleviate regional labour-market problems. To break the vicious circle of underdeveloped or mono-structural regional economies and cumulative concentration of problem groups on the labour market, training and employment schemes - or, more generally, active social policies - must be integrated in one framework (empirica 1986, Derenbach 1984, Prager 1977). Elements of such a framework must be, among others, the active development of economically viable projects generating employment, the activation and motivation of residents, the learning process of idea generation, social cohesion, an approach to regional bottlenecks and opportunities based on the active involvement of available human capital, development of managerial talents. These elements and processes cannot change regional situations overnight (or in an election interval), which may make it difficult to get wide support for them. Although at the beginning the Commission seemed inclined to work towards the integration of employment and training measures, in the recent past the ESF has tended to favour traditional types of vocational training.

In addition to measures directly aimed at the active development of regional labour markets, indirect measures should also be taken. New policy initiatives - early retirement, regulations of working hours, etc. - should be designed to maximise their contribution to the regional equilibrium in the EC.

Should procedures to monitor and assess regional implications of overall schemes or measures of national (or Community) social-policy initiatives be beyond the scope of the ESF, such procedures should be taken on at an early stage by other bodies, such as the Directorate General for Regional Policy, which should, if necessary, reorient policies so as to keep detrimental regional effects at a minimum. To develop appropriate methods of prospective regional analysis is not impossible. Data to simulate regional effects of early retirement, changing wage rates, etc., are available but to this date have not been exploited for the purpose.

6.5. Social policies in a regional framework - myth or reality ?

In recent years, policies geared to the creation of jobs have gained importance. A recent survey in the Federal Republic of Germany - where unemployment is still comparatively low by European standards - indicates that social matters rank as the population's greatest concern, significantly before the environment and defense. Against that background, social policies in the European Communities seem to lag behind the aspirations of citizens; neither the member states nor the EC Commission have developed consistent concepts to control the precarious situation we are facing.

Most regional labour-market problems spring from the cumulation and concentration of problem groups. At the moment, both the guidelines of the European Social Fund and the national policies are inclined towards separate measures for different problem groups on the labour market. To solve the problems and decrease the segmentation of employment and labour-market policy, the development of integrated policy concepts for the European Social Fund as well as national institutions, would be necessary.

In addition to active and direct measures of social policy, the prospective assessment of the regional impact of new social regulations could be a valuable mechanism to avoid adverse regional effects, or at least keep them at a minimum.

6.6. Bibliography

Bassett, K., and Haggett, P. (1970), Towards Short-Term Forecasting for Cyclical Behaviour in a Regional System of Cities, in Chisholm, Frey and Haggett (eds.), Regional Forecasting, Buttersworth, London, pp. 289 ff.

Borts. G.H. (1960), Regional Cycles of Manufacturing Employment in the United States 1914-1953, PUF, Princeton.

Cameron, G. (1981), Highly Qualified Manpower and Less Favoured Regions. Report, University of Cambridge, Cambridge.

Chronik (1986), Wissenschaftszentrum Berlin (ed.) , Arbeitslosenunterstützung reformiert,in Chronik nr 25, July 1986, pp. 1-4.

CEC (1981), Commission of the European Communities, The Regions of Europe. First Periodic Report on the Social and Economic Situation of the Regions of the Community, Brussels.

CEC (1971), Council Regulation of 10.11.1971 of the European Communities: New Guidelines for European Social Fund Intervention, Official Journal.

CEC (1973), Office for Official Publications of the European Communities (ed.), Treaties Establishing the European Communities - Treaties amending these Treaties - Documents concerning the Accession, Luxemburg.

CEC (1984a), Commission of the European Communities: Tenth Report on the Activities of the European Social Fund, Supplement, SEC (84) 486, Brussels, 23 March 1984.

CEC (1984b), Commission of the European Communities: The Regions of Europe. Second Periodic Report on the Social and Economic Situation of the Regions of the Community, Brussels.

CEC (1986), Commission of the European Communities (1986), Nineteenth General Report on the Activities of the European Communities 1985, Brussels, Luxemburg.

Derenbach, R. (1984), Berufliche Eingliederung der nachwachsenden Generation, Forschungen zur Raumentwicklung, Bundesforschungsanstalt für Landeskunde und Raumordnung, Bonn.

empirica (1986), Policy Instruments to Facilitate the Creation of Small and Medium-Sized Companies. Interim Report for the Commission of the European Communities, Bonn.

EUROSTAT (1977), Statistical Office of the European Communities, Labour Force Sample Survey 1975, Luxemburg.

EUROSTAT (1981), Statistical Office of the European Communities, Labour Force Sample Survey 1979, Luxemburg.

EUROSTAT (1984), Revue 1973-1982: Statistical Office of the European Communities, Luxemburg.

EUROSTAT (1985a), Statistical Office of the European Communities, Labour Force Sample Survey 1983, Luxemburg.

EUROSTAT (1985b), Revue 1975-1984: Statistical Office of the European Communities, Luxemburg.

Freiburghaus, B. (1978), Dynamik der Arbeitslosigkeit, Umschlagprozess und Dauerverteilung der Arbeitslosigkeit in der Bundesrepublik 1966-1977, Meisenheim am Glan.

Giolitti, A. (1983), Die Regionalpolitik der Europäischen Gemeinschaft, Raumforschung und Raumordnung, Heft 1-2, pp. 9-14.

Harris, C.P., and Thirlwall, A.B. (1968), Interregional Variations in Cyclical Sensitivity to Unemployment in the United Kingdom 1949-1964, Bulletin of Oxford University Institute of Economics and Statistics, vol. 30, nr 1, pp. 55 ff.

Prager, A. (1977), Job Creation in the Community. An Evaluation of Locally Initiated Employment Projects in Massachusetts, Abt Associates Inc., Cambridge, Massachusetts.

Reissert, B, Schmid, G. (1985), Finanzierung der Arbeitsmarktpolitik: ein internationaler Vergleich, in Wissenschaftszentrum Berlin (ed.), Chronik 22, Oktober.

Steinle, W.J. (1980), Regionale Folgewirkungen einer Herabsetzung des Ruhestandsalters in der Europäischen Gemeinschaft, Informationen zur Raumentwicklung, Heft 2, pp. 91-104.

Steinle, W.J. (1983a), Regional Labour Markets: Trends, Structure and Relevance from a European Perspective, Papers of the Reginal Science Association, vol. 52.

Steinle, W.J. (1983b), Europäische Regionalpolitik zwischen Mittelkonzentration, Koordination und Flexibilität, Raumforschung und Raumordnung, Heft 1-2, pp. 3-8.

7 Trade

J. BRÖCKER and K. PESCHEL

7.1. Introduction

Trade policy belongs to the hard core of EC policy making. Indeed, a customs union is at the basis of the European Community, and free trade among the partners was gradually established in the 1960s. Afterwards, the union was complemented by a common policy of trade with third countries. The present chapter studies the effects of the liberalisation of trade among the partners and of changed levels of protection vis-à-vis third countries on the European regions.

The chapter is organised as follows. First we briefly raise some policy and theoretical issues, describing the policy making of the EC with respect to internal and external trade, and relating the literature on economic integration to that on regional growth.

In the second section, several attempts at quantifying the relations between trade and the development of regions will be critically examined. As they are all unsatisfactory from a theoretical point of view, in the third section we propose a new approach, which we have tested with empirical data for Northern Europe. Some conclusions round off the chapter.

7.2. Trade policy and trade theory

7.2.1. Introduction

The economies of the EC member states are closely interwoven through trade relations. Therefore, changes in trade regimes tend to bear heavily on the national economies and consequently on their regional components. We will pay some attention to the degree of interweaving and to trade regimes, without pretending to give a detailed picture.

Proceeding to theoretical aspects next, we will try to relate the theory of integration - which refers to the changes of trade during the integration process - to interregional analysis.

7.2.2. EC internal and external trade policy

The treaty of Rome, by which the EC was created, codifies in article 9 the principles of the free trade of goods among partners as follows:
> "The Community shall be based upon a customs union which shall cover all trade in goods and which shall involve the prohibition between member states of customs duties on imports and exports and of all charges having equivalent effects, and the adoption of a common customs tariff in their relation with third countries."

The twelve-year period which the Rome Treaty foresaw for the complete abolition of tariffs, quotas, etc., could be shortened somewhat: in 1968 the last tariffs among the six original member countries were removed. At the same time the Common External Tariff (CET) was put into force. In accordance with the Treaty (and GATT rules) it was set equal to the arithmetical average of the existing tariffs of all member countries. Between 1961 and 1968, the differences among national tariffs in respect of the CET had gradually been levelled out. For industrial products the tariff was expressed in percentages of the value; for agricultural products variable levies were introduced to compensate for the difference between world-market and EC-guarantee prices. In this chapter, we will refer to manufactured goods alone.

The three countries that joined the EC in 1973 liberalised trade with the EC and have applied the CET since 1977. For the three south-European countries which joined recently, a transition period has been set.

The treaty of the EC also provides for a common commercial policy (artt. 110 - 116). Its basic principle is to "contribute to the harmonious development of world trade, the progressive abolition of restrictions on international trade and the lowering of customs barriers". After the transition period, the EC, not the member states, is responsible for carrying out this policy.

In line with the general principle of art. 9, the EC has agreed to lower its CET in three rounds of GATT negotiations. The CET of the EC is generally lower than that of the US or Japan. In principle, the EC is pledged to world free trade, but it maintains many protectionist measures. Apart from the CET, which is the equivalent of the most-famous-nation (MFN) treatment in GATT, the EC has negotiated preferential agreements with specific groups of countries, which have resulted in even lower customs duties. With the European Free Trade Area (EFTA), a free-trade agreement has been concluded, which has prevented the large trade diversions that might have occurred when the United Kingdom left EFTA to join the EC. With Mediterranean states, agreements have been concluded to give their manufactured products access to the EC markets. Products from ACP states (Africa, Caribbean, Pacific) may be imported into the EC free of duty; indeed the EC considers it has inherited a special responsibility from the former colonial powers. Within the framework of UNCTAD, agreements have been concluded for tariff quotas for developing countries. Finally, the EC has unilateral regulations regarding the countries of the East bloc, but negotiations to change that situation are in progress.

There are special agreements for certain commodities. The EC is a partner to the so-called Multifibre agreement; with respect to textile and other so-called sensitive sectors (shipbuilding, steel), the EC tends to be less "liberal" than with respect to other sectors.

7.2.3. Importance of trade flows

International trade is of outstanding importance to the economies of the member countries. In the period from 1958 to 1972 (the year of the extension), the share of exports in the GDP of the Six original member countries increased from 14 to 19 per cent, while in the decade 1972-1982 the share of exports in the GDP of the Nine increased from 18 to 29 per cent. Much of that proportion is internal EC trade: about half of total trade for the larger countries, as much as 70 per cent for smaller countries like Belgium and Ireland. As could be expected, the integration of the EC countries has brought about a shift in trade flows. In the period from 1958 to 1972 the exchange of goods among the six original member countries increased ninefold, while trade with the rest of the world multiplied by four. After 1972, trade between the three new member states and the six original ones has grown in importance in comparison to their total external trade. Nevertheless, in the early 1980s these countries were still more integrated with other countries than with the EC of the Six. Moreover, external trade is vital to all countries of the EC.

The impact of integration and the commercial relations the EC maintains with other highly industrialised countries are demonstrated in the dendrograms (figures 7.1 to 7.3). They present the results of a complete linkage procedure by which the OECD-countries were clustered according to normalised aggregate bilateral trade flows. The numbers in the dendrograms represent the critical values of the cluster analysis, which we have termed multilateral integration measures. They correspond to the smallest (normalised) trade flows between the integration areas identified, and vary between 0 and 100 according to the normalisation procedure. The trade matrices were normalised by the biproportional RAS-method (see Peschel, 1985), to eliminate the impact of differences in the volume of overall trade.

The first thing that hits the eye is the formation of the integration area of the EC of the Six, which was completed in 1977. We observe that in 1981, Denmark still belonged to the strong Scandinavian integration area, while the United Kingdom and Ireland, which had been tied with Scandinavia in an integration area, too, had developed a stronger connection with the USA and Canada than with the EC members. The dendrograms also reveal a comparatively strong trade relationship between the original EC members and Switzerland, Austria and Turkey.

7.2.4. Trade theory

The effect of trade barriers, such as tariffs, subsidies, quotas, and so on, has traditionally been the field of interest of the theory of international trade. Hence, preferential trading arrangements in connection with European economic integration have also received primary attention from international trade scientists. The greatest attention has been given to the national welfare implications of the customs union between the six member countries. The conjecture would be that the abolition of the trade barriers, as a movement towards free trade, would increase welfare. Viner, in his pioneering work "The Custom Union Issues" published in 1950, denied that. He pointed out that, while a union between some, not all, countries would create trade and thus have positive effects on welfare, trade diversion might offset these positive effects. Viner analysed trade creation and trade diversion in a neo-classical partial equilibrium model. That is, he considered the international market for one good on the generally accepted assumptions of neo-classical theory, which are, perfect competition, negligible transport costs, and so on. Besides, he assumed non-shifting supply and demand curves. Some of these restrictive assumptions were discarded in the subsequent discussion, and a trade-expansion effect was added to Viner's trade effects. Trade expansion arises from increasing demand caused be decreasing prices. Other authors have studied the effects of customs unions by general-equilibrium analysis (Vanek, 1965; Kemp, 1969).

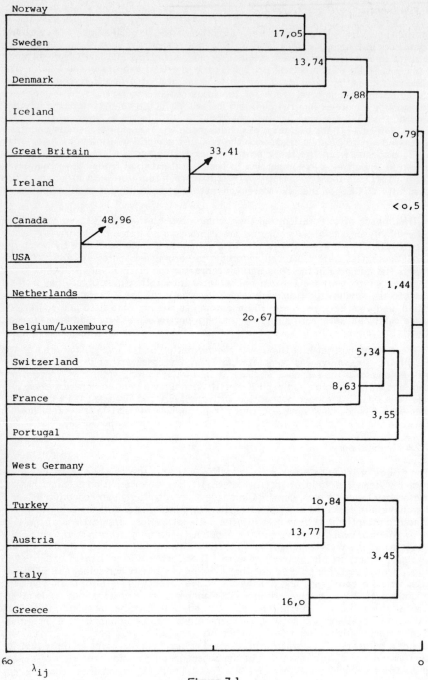

Figure 7.1
The spatial structure of OECD-trade in 1955

130

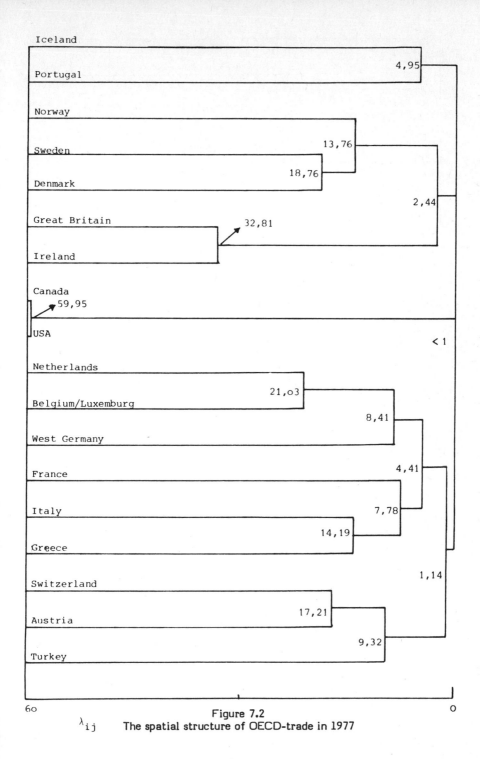

Figure 7.2
λ_{ij} The spatial structure of OECD-trade in 1977

131

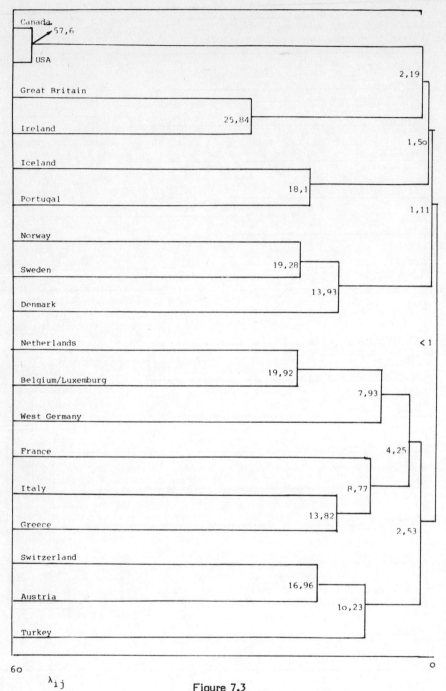

Figure 7.3
The spatial structure of OECD-trade in 1981

132

Lastly, the arguments were no longer strictly based on neoclassical assumptions. Instead, hypotheses were formed depending heavily on the assumptions of increasing returns to scale, and imperfect markets. Thus, to differentiate between static and dynamic effects of integration became common.

The term static effects of integration is used to characterise the trade effects (creation, diversion,and expansion) and their implications for welfare in the context of neo-classical, comparative-static equilibrium analysis. Static effects of integration develop from an improved allocation of available resources. They work within given production possibilities by changing the relative prices of goods and factors. If the reallocation of resources is related to changes in reinvestments, the effects are also termed "pseudo-dynamic". Dynamic effects of integration involve long-run changes of the national product; the most important are stronger competition and accelerated technological progress.

Apart from outriders like Giersch (1949/50), regional scientists started paying attention to the impacts of European economic integration in the early 1960s. If we are correct, none of them doubted that the formation of the European Common Market would increase the member countries' welfare; the question was whether regional disparities within one country would be widened by the integration process.

By neoclassical international trade theory applied to regions within nations, that cannot be true. In that case the principle of comparative advantage holds: each region specialises in the production of those goods which it can produce comparatively cheap. With the increasing international specialisation which follows integration, the international as well as the interregional division of labour changes. As a rule, every region will produce a higher valued output, since it is relatively superior to all others in the production of certain items; that advantage will become even greater with increasing specialisation. A region is favoured more, the greater its comparative advantage and the greater the increase in demand for its products as a result of integration.

Most regional scientists protested that the fundamental assumptions of this theory (such as complete factor immobility among regions, no agglomeration economies, the functioning of a balance-of-payments mechanism) do not hold in reality. However, even if only the assumption of factor immobility is replaced with that of (limited) factor mobility, integration may, in the case of regions varying considerably in production possibilities and efficiency, increase differences in wage rates as well as the over- or underemployment of productive factors, possibly in combination with a certain amount of migration. In that case, the principle of absolute advantage has to be substituted for that of comparative advantage. Moreover, such elements as agglomeration economies, transportation costs and regional accessibility, which are fundamental to regional economic theory, have to be taken into consideration. Regional scientists have argued that, the more important these elements are, the likelier the integration process will entail polarisation and increasing regional disparities. Their assumption was that polarisation tendencies would have a negative effect on peripheral regions, often already backward at the outset of the integration period, while favouring the existing industrial centres of the EC (see the review of the relevant literature by Vanhove and Klaassen, 1980, pp. 227). Thus, the discussion soon averted from comparative-static analysis, to focus on the dynamics of the integration process as a function of the location of industries. The discussion, which on the whole was based more on plausibility judgements and on critical statements than on stringent theoretical reasoning, was to some extent formalised by the potential approach of Clark, Wilson, and Bradly (CWB) (1969). The purpose of their study was "...to examine which regions in Western Europe are the most attractive to industry and the likely effect which an enlarged Customs Union and development in transport might have on the distribution of the most favored regions" (see CWB, 1969, p. 197). These authors formed the hypothesis that it is a region's capacity to act as a market and as a supplier of inputs which affects the location decision of industrial firms. From this they concluded that the regions most favoured by the integration process would be those that are densely populated and which are nearest to all possible markets, that is, those that are centrally situated.

One critical mark may conclude this review of theory. Somewhat amazingly, the hypothesis on the importance of market potentials for regional economic growth seems to have been accepted unquestioningly by regional scientists. Certainly, integration alters the spatial pattern of market potentials, because the abolition of artificial trade barriers has the same impact on prices as a decrease in distance costs. On the other hand, however, nothing is known about the relative importance of that effect when markets are imperfect. The calculations of CWB as well as those of Keeble, Owens, and Thompson (KOT) (1981, 1982) are based on assumptions, and not on estimates obtained from a well specified model. Moreover, not even the basic hypothesis of correlation between a region's economic development and its spatial position, or its market potentials, has so far been proved. These deficiencies will be discussed in full in the next section.

7.3. Concepts and some empirics

7.3.1. Introduction

In the following review we will concentrate on three approaches towards measuring the impacts of trading arrangements on the regional level. First, we will report the results of economic potential analysis. Second, we will summarise our own research work, aimed at measuring the effects of European economic integration on German regions by a residual approach. Third, we comment on studies addressing the regional impacts of the Community's external policy.

The procedure admittedly implies a somewhat narrow interpretation of our subject, because we dispense with the work of authors whose main focus was regional economic growth even if their models - FLEUR, REGIS, the Bröcker-Peschel-Reimers model - are potentially capable of inquiring into integration effects. On the other hand our procedure implies a broad interpretation of the subject, because in fact neither the potential analyses nor the studies of the Community's external policies have discarded the regional impacts of trading arrangements. Both analyses lack a measurement concept to separate the impacts of trade policy from other growth determinants.

7.3.2. Analysis of economic potential

Clark, Wilson, and Bradley (1969) were the first to apply the concept of economic regional potential to evaluate regional impacts of European Economic Integration. Their study has now been enlarged and updated by Keeble, Owens, and Thompson (1981, 1982) without any modification of the fundamental ideas and hypotheses. In the following we can, therefore, without loss concentrate on the KOT papers.

The fundamental hypothesis of both studies is that regional differences in relative regional accessibility play a major role in influencing investment decisions, and hence for the location and growth of economic activity.

Differences in regional accessibility are measured by the indicator 'regional economic potential', calculated by the following formula (KOT, 1982, p. 420):

$$P_i = \sum_{j=1}^{n} \frac{M_j}{D_{ij}}$$

where

P_i = the potential of region i,
M_j = a measure of the volume of economic activity in region j,
D_{ij} = a measure of distance, or cost of transport, between i and j.
(Relative accessibility is measured by relating each region's potential value to that of the highest value found that year).

In the KOT study, the mass or M_j-term is specified by values of regional gross domestic product (GDP) at current prices and exchange rates. The D_{ij}-term is measured by route distances, which are calculated by a shortest-route algorithm taking sea-ferry crossings into account. As in the CWB study, a measure of the barrier effects of tariffs is incorporated in the distance variable. According to the authors, this tariff barrier (the EC's common external tariff) was identified by a "logical procedure" (KOT, 1982, p. 425), which consisted of estimating an average EC tariff, translating it into road-distance equivalents (by comparing it with transport costs over a certain distance), and adding the value thus derived to the distance of the shortest path which joins the nodes across whichever Community boundary was in force for the year under consideration.

With the methodology just described, KOT computed values of regional economic potentials for the official level-II regions of the Community of the Six, and of the Community of the Nine, for several years in the period 1965-77, and for a hypothetical situation with the Community of the Twelve. Some major results are the following.

First, there is a clear trend towards widening regional disparities in relative accessibility within the Community of the Six during the 1965-73 period. The same trend is observed for the Community of the Nine between 1973 and 1977, but at a much slower rate than in the late 1960s and early 1970s (KOT, 1982, p. 428). In all these computations the distance pattern has been kept constant, so that the trends reflect only changes in the regional GDP pattern.

Second, computations were carried out to reveal the impact of the 1973 enlargement of the EC to nine members, on the assumption of a complete tariff removal in 1973 and a constant mass term. The outcome was that all regions of the new member countries record an increase in relative accessibility. Interestingly, the peripheral regions of the original Six benefit more than the central ones, measured in relative terms. Yet, in absolute terms a further widening of disparities in accessibility among the centre and periphery of the Six is registered.

We do not want to comment in detail on the KOT research. Their study certainly improves on the computations done by CWB; yet, among others, the following objections can be raised.

First, tariffs are the sole barrier effects taken into consideration. In the real world, however, national borders are strong impediments to trade even after the abolition of tariffs. That has been proved by an analysis of interregional trade flows of the Community of the Six by one of the authors. Bröcker (1984) estimates that the trade-impeding effects of national borders in the Community averaged the equivalent of a distance of about 300 km in 1970.

Second, the use of the distance function D_{ij}^{-1} seems open to criticism, because the denominator of the potential formula tends to infinity for D_{ij} tending to zero. Hence, the measurement results are highly sensitive to the, always arbitrary, way of incorporating internal distances. The unrealistically high potential values of Hamburg and Bremen are the outcome of that methodological deficiency. Additionally, the use of a distance exponent of unity may be seriously questioned. As the authors have illustrated (see Bröcker, Peschel, Reimers, 1983), the spatial pattern of economic potentials reacts much stronger to changing values of the distance exponent than to alternative specifications of the mass term. Hence, KOT's basing their approach on the statement that there is no clear theoretical justification for other values (1982, p.423) is highly unsatisfying. We think there is no escape from estimating the parameter values of the distance function in a model applied to data on interregional or international trade (see the corresponding estimation results in Bröcker, 1984, pp. 130, and Herrmann et al., 1982).

Apart from these critical aspects of the measurement problem, the question has to be raised what solution the computations of KOT provide for the true problem under consideration, namely, the regional impact of integration. For, the computations of economic potentials are relevant only if the rate and nature of economic development in different regions depend on regional accessibility. Moreover, a unique solution to the integration problem can only be found by running tests to prove that changes in the pattern of regional economic growth are induced by changes in the pattern of economic potentials springing from integration. The authors have not provided for such tests.

Certainly, in the Keeble report (KOT, 1981) relationships between economic potentials in 1977 and a series of economic indicators were tested. Yet, for the problem under consideration only those tests are of interest in which changes of economic variables (trends) are considered. For, a relation between the level of regional economic activity and regional accessibility may be the outcome of an earlier historical development process, which has no relevance at all for the present.

Furthermore, the fact must be stressed that the results of the relevant tests are by no means consistent with the basic hypothesis of CWB and KOT. Only the trends in Gross Domestic Product (GDP) (total, per capita, and per employee) were positively related to the economic potentials during 1970-73 and 1973-77, and that not always statistically significantly, and with R^2-values of less than 0.1. Besides, many results are not in line with their reasoning. The most important are the following. Total employment grew most in the peripheral regions and least in the central ones (see KOT, 1981, table 4.12, p. 105). Conversely, unemployment increased most in the central regions, and least in the peripheral ones (see KOT, 1981, table 4.35, p. 149). Admittedly, the peripheral regions lost the most manufacturing employment, on whose development CWB focused. On the other hand, the central regions lost more than the intermediate ones (see KOT, 1981, table 4.23, p. 125).

KOT's interpretation of these results is somewhat tricky. If they fit their picture, they take them as support for their hypotheses; if not, KOT look for explaining arguments. Thus, with respect to manufacturing employment, they argue: "However, central regions' job losses may be an indicator not of economic weakness but of increasing efficiency and labour productivity ..." (KOT, 1981, p. 111). They do not provide the reader with empirical evidence, however. Corresponding empirical results for the FRG, obtained by the present authors, clearly contradict the hypothesis of a positive relation between centrality and productivity (Peschel, 1983). Besides, extensive research into regional economic growth has not revealed any positive impact of economic potentials on the development of manufacturing employment in Scandinavian and German regions between 1960 and 1970 (see Bröcker, Peschel, Reimers, 1983).

Finally, we like to point out that the correct assessment of the impact of integration on regional economic growth presupposes an approach including all other candidate determinants of growth, that is to say, the construction of an empirical testable model of regional growth. Only then can the evident problems which KOT face in their report, be treated adequately. Presumably the most important of these are: first, to differentiate between the impacts of agglomeration, urbanisation, and accessibility. Second, to separate the impact of national and international determinants on regional ecnomic growth.

7.3.3. A residual approach

In several studies, a residual approach has been followed to determine the effects of integration on the national level. By such an approach, the effects of integration on trade flows are estimated by comparing the actual trade figures with hypothetical ones representing the expected development without integration.

In a major research project, we have applied such an approach to measure the effects of integration of the European Economic Community and the European Free Trade Association on the international trade and the industrial production of 58 German regions between 1960 and 1972 (see Peschel, Haass, Schnöring, 1979; Peschel, 1978, 1982). As a proxy for the hypothetical development of regional exports and imports to and from the EC, we used the development of actual trade flows between the German regions and the EFTA countries. Clearly, taking the EFTA countries as a control group is questionable. Admittedly, trade diversion, if caused by the creation of the EC and the EFTA, would have led to some overestimation of integration effects. Yet, only primary effects on international trade and production were counted, while secondary effects resulting from forward and backward linkages of the industries primarily effected, were excluded.

Our residual approach applied to exports can be described by the formula:

$$ix_{ir}^{1972} = x_{i r \mapsto EC}^{1960} [(\hat{x}_{i r \mapsto EC})^{12} - (\hat{x}_{i r \mapsto EFTA})^{12}]$$

with

ix_{ir}^{1972}	– 1972 exports of sector i of region r induced by integration measures
$x_{i r \mapsto EC}$	– export flow of sector i from the German region r to the EC
$x_{i r \mapsto EFTA}$	– export flow of sector i from the German region r tot the EFTA
$\hat{}$	– yearly growth factor of the log-linear trend

Figure 7.4 shows the export integration effects, aggregated over all 31 sectors of manufacturing industries, for the 58 German regions under study.

Are our empirical findings compatible with the basic hypothesis of the potential approach ? Several tests were done to answer the question, different measurement concepts for economic potentials being applied. In all of them the mass term was specified by population, and the distance function implemented with different values of the exponent. The results have led us to the conclusion that integration has in fact slightly favoured the more densely settled regions. Yet, there are important exceptions, such as the cities of Hamburg (region no. 4) and Berlin (region no. 58), which have had extremely small integration effects. More light is cast on the problem, if we look at the regional pattern of exports into the Community of the Six (in relation to total regional exports) in 1960 as an indicator of a region's chance to be favoured by integration effects. Our calculations reveal that the concentration of these chances on the more densely populated regions has been stronger than the factual concentration of integration effects. The main explanation might be that, contrary to what had been assumed by cumulative-causation theorists - agglomeration diseconomies in the broadest sense of the term (inclusive of labour-market shortages and environmental strains) prevailed in the densely settled regions of the FRG in the period under consideration (see Peschel, 1982).

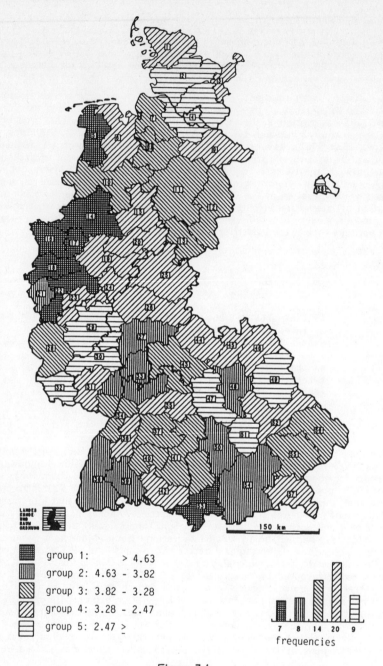

group 1:　　> 4.63
group 2: 4.63 - 3.82
group 3: 3.82 - 3.28
group 4: 3.28 - 2.47
group 5: 2.47 >

150 km

frequencies

Figure 7.4
The German regions ranked according to the effects of European
economic integration on exports of manufacturing industries
1972 (in % of total sales)

138

Another important result of our research is that integration has in fact favoured the German regions that are closest to the geographic centre of the EC. We cannot claim,however, that integration has been to the detriment of the periphery. There are even regions in or close to the Rhine-Main valley with integration effects weaker than those in peripheral regions (for example no. 29, Koblenz-Limburg). Moreover, the former argument also holds: the western regions were favoured less by integration than had been expected in consideration of their export activities in 1960.

To judge the residual approach, stress must be laid on the fact that the difficulty lies in the construction of the hypothetical figures. One possibility to avoid serious errors is to apply various approaches to obtain hypothetical estimates, and compare the results. That would no doubt be an expensive method. Yet, from our review, there appears to be no single procedure that can claim to be the appropriate method.

7.3.4. Indicators to monitor regional impacts of trade and trade policy

Various empirical studies have attempted to clarify how imports, exports and trade policies affect employment on the national level. The most common method uses accounting identities which lead to simple index numbers. No wonder then that the few approaches to tackle this sort of problem on the regional level, draw on such methods, too. That is especially true of the study THE REGIONAL IMPACT OF THE COMMUNITY'S EXTERNAL POLICY, ordered by the Commission of the European Communities (KEG, 1984), and a subsequent (unpublished) study of Begg and Cripps (1983). Because these authors claim to have achieved qualified success in developing a system of indicators for monitoring the regional impact of extra-Community trade, we must test their recommendations carefully. Moreover, one of the authors of the present paper has also used indicators, together with more elaborate methods, to reveal the impact of exports on German regions (Peschel, Schnöring, 1983).

The purpose of the former study was "to examine how the pattern of regional development within the European Community is affected by policies regarding the Community's trade with the rest of the world" (KEG, 1984, p. 1). Amazingly, and barely hidden by the authors' own conclusions, the question asked is not at all tackled by empirical investigation. It is rather replaced with the question how the change in the flow of trade (extra-EC trade and sales to intra-Community markets) in manufactures affected regional employment in each country during the second half of the 1960s and the first half of the 1970s.

The analysis started on the national level. First, the contributions of changes in extra-Community trade and in sales to intra-Community markets on the growth of output of each industry were calculated arithmetically, productivity changes being taken into account. The impacts of changes on the national level were then imputed to the regional level in proportion to the regions' shares of employment in each industry. The discrepancy between predicted and actual changes in regional employment in each industry was termed the "regional-shift" effect, and tabulated separately (KEG, 1984, p. 98). Readers familiar with the results of shift-share analyses of employment growth will not be surprised to hear that the values of the 'regional-shift effects' are in many cases even higher than the "market effects".

The authors of the report are no doubt aware that their approach does not reveal causal relations. Nevertheless, they believe to have discerned some characteristic patterns of change in extra-EC trade and regional employment (KEG 1984, p. 96). To discuss value judgements would certainly be sterile. It is somewhat amazing, however, that Begg and Cripps find the main disadvantages of the approach in the formula used, because of its "complexity and the arbitrariness of attributions between different components of change" (Begg and Cripss, 1983, part.

4.1(c)) rather than in the deficiencies of the index-number method.

The indicator which they regard as the most adequate to assess how important are the trade flows of one single industry's products for the country or region where the industry is located, is the so-called "composite trade (balance) indicator":

$$BE_{ij} = \frac{B_i}{Q_i} \frac{E_{ij}}{E_{Tj}}$$

where B_i is the trade balance (export less import) of industry i in one member country, Q_i denotes the value of output of industry i, E_{ij} denotes employment in industry i of region j, and E_{Tj} total employment in region j.

According to the authors, "the ratio of the trade balance to the value of domestic output provides a broad indicator of the strength or weakness of the trading position of an industry" (Begg and Cripps, 1983, part. 4.3), whereas the employment weight judges the significance of any particular industry for a region (Begg and Cripps, 1983, part. 4.4). Obviously, this indicator is a special version of the set of indicators constructed to reveal comparative advantages of a country's industry in international trade, generally termed RCA-indicators. Leaving aside that the formula of the composite trade indicator is less adequate than the generally applied formula of Balassa, we think that all the objections made to this type of indicator hold. Here we refer only to the most important ones: first, the RCA-values are highly sensitive to the choice of year and level of aggregation. Second, they describe the trade pattern of the past, which is the result of an unknown set of determinants, some of which are continually changing through time. Without specifying a model embodying the relations between the major explanatory variables, nothing can be inferred with respect to the behaviour of the RCA-values in time. That is, while we agree with the adherents to the indicator methodology that it may provide empirical evidence on questions under review, we also think that in any particular problem under discussion the validity of the chosen indicator has to be supported by additional theoretical and empirical findings. In that context, at least the key variables used in the index formula should be put together in a simple model to reveal its interrelationships and to cast light on the determinants that may have been omitted. Third, no need to say that the key properties of any index applied have to be examined in detail. The results of an analysis of the RCA indicator, carried out by Yeats, "show that the index, when used in the traditional manner, fails to serve as either a reliable cardinal or ordinal measure of a country's revealed comparative advantage (Yeats, 1985, p. 71).

As to the empirical results of Begg and Cripps, there are only case studies, which do not provide satisfying answers to the question under debate.

7.4. A new approach to measuring spatial integration effects

7.4.1. Introduction

This part summarises another study of ours, designed to quantify static regional integration effects for 73 regions in Scandinavia and the FRG. The study is concerned with effects of the foundation of the EFTA and the EC (of the Six) for 1970. Unlike the results presented hitherto, the estimates of this study are based on an explicit model of interregional trade that is theoretically consistent and empirically estimable with available data.

Following the partial equilibrium approach to integration theory, each branch of manufacturing industry is studied separately. The basic idea of partial equilibrium theory is, that - given the market of a certain commodity - tariff reductions will lead to price reductions on the demand side for imports from countries joining the common market. As a consequence, demand will shift towards those supply sources that become cheaper owing to tariff reductions. On the supply side, output will increase or decrease depending on whether a producer will gain from additional demand or suffer from increased foreign competition. If the price elasticity of supply is finite, supply prices will moreover increase or decrease, and this will again have a feedback effect on the demand side. After tariff reductions, the adjustment process will continue until a new equilibrium with respect to trade flows and prices is obtained. A comparison of the new equilibrium with the pre-integration equilibrium shows what are called the static effects of economic integration.

On the supply side, gains (or losses) from integration in a certain country or region result from increased (or decreased) demand for commodities from that country or region. On the demand side, gains and losses have also to be taken into account. While consumers gain from the chance of cheaper purchases in partner countries after integration, they also might suffer from the fact that supply prices increase through additional demand from foreign members of the common market[1].

The partial equilibrium approach as explained here, which originally was designed to study static effects of integration on a national scale, is in our approach applied to regions generally smaller than nations by the introduction of two straightforward modifications. First, while the original model specifies supply and demand functions for each nation of the system under study, we do it for each region; and second, while tariffs are the only impediments to trade in the original model, we also consider trade impediments resulting from geographic distance between regions. Therefore, in our model, there is in principle no difference between the impact of variations in tariffs and that of variations in transport cost on the pattern of prices and trade flows.

An extension of the partial equilibrium approach to regions shows that within each nation, integration effects may differ among regions, because the patterns of foreign trade also differ among regions. In our model, different foreign-trade patterns result from different locations implying different costs of transportation between the respective regions and foreign markets. For example, in one region sales may decline because consumers prefer a cheaper foreign producer after integration, while sales increase in another region owing to increased demand from a foreign country joining the common market.

Formally, static effects of integration are calculated by comparing, for each single industry, two equilibrium solutions of our model. One equilibrium is termed the 'benchmark equilibrium', and the other is termed the 'anti-monde-equilibrium'. The benchmark equilibrium describes the factual situation in 1970, which is the year under study. The anti-monde is the hypothetical world of 1970 constructed on the assumption of tariffs on the pre-integration level. If EFTA-effects are quantified, for example, pre-EFTA tariffs are inserted between EFTA-members instead of factual 1970 tariffs, to find the 'without-EFTA' anti-monde. Analogous definitions apply to the analysis of EC-effects and to joint EC-EFTA effects.

The model is based on the following <u>assumptions</u>:
1. Regional supply and demand are functionally related to prices in supply and demand regions, respectively. Prices to be paid by consumers exceed ex-factory prices by transportation costs and tariffs (in case of foreign supply). In that context, 'transportation costs' mean all costs which spring from geographic distance. Correspondingly, 'tariff' is understood to include monetary equivalents of non-tariff barriers.

2. Transportation costs are assumed to be proportional to distance. Among other advantages, this allows for a translation of tariffs into distance equivalents, which much simplifes the analysis.

3. With respect to regional supply, several assumptions concerning price

elasticity are tried, including zero elasticity (fixed supply quantity) as well as infinite elasticity (fixed supply prices). With respect to demand, we abstract from trade expansion, that is to say, total demand is assumed to be fixed. However, the split of demand by supply source reacts to price changes, such that after integration, demand shifts towards cheaper supply sources. Unlike theoretical models assuming homogeneous markets, the substitution among supply sources is modelled on the assumption of a non-homogeneous market. In accordance with empirical observations, the assumption is that consumers do not purchase exclusively from the cheapest source available; in other words, a finite elasticity of substitution among supply sources is supposed.

Clearly, this approach is subject to criticism as well. The most important objection is that it is confined to static effects (for the definition of static and dynamic effects, see the section on trade theory). Second, by using elasticities invariable among regions (and in addition partly set a priori), important reasons for spatially varying effects are excluded by assumption. A third criticism may be that the model implicitly accepts distance and international trade barriers as the only explanatory variables of interregional trade intensity. There is convincing empirical evidence of the dominant role of these variables in explaining trade patterns. An early demonstration for data on an aggregate level was given by Linnemann (1968), followed by Aitken (1973) and others. On the disaggregate level, distance has been shown to have a significant impact in 34 out of the 36 industries analysed in the study reported here. Dummies representing the effect of preference zones are not as important, but still significant for the majority of industries (Bröcker, 1984, Ch. III). Furthermore, among a large number of candidate variables explaining trade patterns, distance and preference dummies were proved in an empirical study (Herrmann et al., 1982) to be the key factors for trade in selected commodities as well as for aggregate trade flows. Admittedly, other things, such as traditional trade relations, might also be relevant (Peschel, 1981). Finally, our approach, like others, suffers from the fact that the partial analysis neglects secondary interindustry and income effects.

Readers not interested in methodological details may skip the following parts 2, 3 and 4, which describe the formal structure of the model.

7.4.2. The model

Consider n countries ($k,l = 1,...,n$), or groups of nations like the EC or EFTA, each country consisting of one or more regions. There are m regions in all ($r,s = 1,...,$ m $\geq$ n), each belonging to one country. Let x_{rs} be demand in s for products from r, and let x_s denote the demand vector in s, that is, $X_s = (x_{1s},...,x_{rs},...x_{ms})$. Moreover, let q_{rs} be the price - including transport costs and tariffs - which has to be paid in s for products from r, and let Q_s denote the vector of these m different prices in s, that is, $Q_s = (q_{1s}, ...,q_{rs},...,q_{ms})$. Then, demand is assumed to be a vector-valued function (V_s) of the price vector:

$$X_s = V_s(Q_s) \ \forall \ s \tag{7.1}$$

On the assumption that there is no price discrimination, the price in s for products from r equals ex-factory price in r (p_r) plus transport costs (d_{rs}) and tariffs (t_{kl}) by unit of commodity, if r belongs to country k and s to country l, and if country l levies tariffs on imports from k:

$$q_{rs} = p_r + d_{rs} + t_{kl} \ \forall \ r, s = r \in k, s \in l \tag{7.2}$$
$$t_{kl} = 0 \text{ for } k = l.$$

Regional supply functions (σ_r) assign a supply quantity S_r to the single supply price p_r for each region:

$$S_r = \sigma_r(p_r) \quad \forall\, r \tag{7.3}$$

Thus, producers are assumed to be price takers.

The model is completed by the demand = supply condition for equilibrium:

$$\sum_s x_{rs} = S_r \quad \forall\, r \tag{7.4}$$

The next step is to specify demand functions (7.1) and supply functions (7.3) in a form that is theoretically acceptable and still estimable with scarce regional data. Concerning <u>demand</u> we abstract from trade-expansion effects, in other words, total regional demand D_s - aggregated over supply regions - is assumed to be constant. The split of demand among supply regions, however, is log-linearly related to price differences, such that the share of region r decreases if its price - compared to other regions - increases:

$$x_{rs} = \frac{A_r \exp(-\beta q_{rs})}{\sum_r A_r \exp(-\beta q_{rs})} \cdot D_s \quad \forall\, r,s \tag{7.5}$$

A_r is a parameter measuring the attractiveness of r as a supply region, as far as it is not due to a low price. β is a parameter indicating the sensitivity of substitution among supply regions with respect to price differences. $\beta = 0$ means that prices are of no relevance at all, while in case of $\beta \to \infty$ the cheapest source (including transport costs and tariffs) will be chosen exclusively.

<u>Supply</u> is analogously supposed to be a log-linear function of price:

$$S_r = B_r \exp(\phi p) \quad \forall\, r \tag{7.6}$$

B_r and ϕ are parameters.

The model is completely specified by equations (7.2), (7.4), (7.5) and (7.6). S_r, x_{rs}, p_r, and q_{rs} are endogenous variables. t_{kl} is the exogenous variable, which has to be varied to study integration effects. A_r, B_r, D_s, d_{rs}, β and ϕ are exogenous variables and parameters held constant in comparative static analysis of integration.

As already mentioned, static effects of integration are analysed in this model by comparing the benchmark with an 'anti-monde' equilibrium. The next section summarises the equation system for the benchmark equilibrium, derived from this model. It is followed by a section showing how the 'anti-monde' equilibrium is calculated when the benchmark solution is already known.

7.4.3. The benchmark equilibrium

As can be shown, the benchmark equilibrium fulfils the following system of equations (in which the superscript ^{b} denotes benchmark quantities):

$$x^b_{rs} = A_r D^b_s \exp\{\beta(v^b_s - p^b_r - d^b_{rs} - t^b_{kl})\} \quad \forall\, r,s \tag{7.7}$$

$$\sum_s x^b_{rs} = S^b_r \quad \forall\, r; \quad x_{rs} = D^b_s \quad \forall\, s \tag{7.8}$$

$$\sum_{\substack{r \in k \\ s \in l}} x_{rs} = T^b_{kl} \quad \forall\, k,l; k = 1 \tag{7.9}$$

From this system a unique solution for the benchmark flows x^b_{rs} is obtained, if β and d_{rs} are known and if observed 1970 data are inserted for regional supply (S^b_r), total regional demand (D^b_s) and international trade (T^b_{kl}). The values of all other variables drop out of the solution of the system[2].

Equation (7.7) may be interpreted as a gravity formula describing interregional trade, which is negatively affected by transport costs and tariffs. Equations (7.8) are the standard constraints of a doubly constrained gravity model imposed on the interregional flows, stating that flows to (from) all regions have to add up to observed demand (supply).

Equation (7.9) is an additional constraint, stating that flows from regions in country k to regions in country l have to add up to the observed international trade flows from k to l (T_{kl}^b). Imposing this constraint allows calibration of the tariffs t_{kl} from observed data.

In addition to data on S_r^b, D_s^b, and T_{kl}^b, which partly have to be estimated under simplifying assumptions, estimates of β and d_{rs} are needed, as already mentioned. A little trick helps to get them:

If we assume that distance costs are proportional to distance, they can be measured in terms of 'kilometer' instead of 'DM per unit of commodity'. Furthermore, prices and tariffs can also be translated into distance equivalents by dividing them by the amount of money needed to transport one unit of commodity over a one-kilometer distance. Then, in equation (7.7), d_{rs} and t_{kl}^b are geographical and artificial trade impediments measured in terms of 'kilometer', and β is the standard distance parameter of a constrained gravity model with a log-linear distance term. We obtained sectoral estimates of β from a gravity analysis of international trade data (see Bröcker, 1984, Chapter III). Shortest routes (cross-sea links being taken into account) are inserted for d_{rs}.

7.4.4. The anti-monde equilibrium

Starting from benchmark flows, we can calculate anti-monde flows from the following system of equations derived from our basic model[3].

$$X_{rs}^a = x_{rs}^b \exp \{ \beta(\wedge p_r + \Delta t_{kl} - \Delta v_s)\} \quad \forall v,s$$

$$\sum_s x_{rs}^a = S_r^a \ \forall r; \sum_r x_{rs}^a = D_s^a \ \forall \ s \qquad (7.10)$$

$$S_r^a = S_r^b \exp(-\Phi \Delta p_r) \ \forall \ r$$

In addition to x_{rs}^b and β, which are already known from the benchmark solution, only the parameter Φ and the tariff changes Δt_{kl} are needed to solve equation system (7.10). Note that t_{kl} is the tariff on imports from country k to country l in the benchmark equilibrium minus the corresponding anti-monde figure, measured in distance equivalents. This means, for example, if the anti-monde is a world without EC, then for k = France and l = FRG, Δt_{kl} = - 1000 km means that the decline of trade impediments to imports of the FRG from France caused by EC-integration, is equivalent to a transport distance of 1,000 km. We use estimates of these distance equivalents, which are also obtained from the international trade study mentioned above.

Unfortunately, our approach does not permit a reliable estimation of the parameter Φ. Therefore, a series of results with different arbitrary values assigned to Φ (including from the extreme cases $\Phi = 0$ and $\Phi \to \infty$) have been produced.

Besides integration effects on trade flows, the solution of equation system (7.10) produces interesting results on the price effects of economic integration: Δp_r is the supply-price increase in region r caused by integration[4]. Like Δt_{kl}, it is measured as a distance equivalent in terms of kilometer. On the demand side, $\wedge v_s$ is an illuminating indicator, measuring the integration loss (that is to say, $- \Delta v_s$ measures the integration gain), again in terms of kilometer. For example, an estimated integration effect of $\wedge v_s$ -100 km means that the total integration gain of consumers in s corresponds to the amount of money needed to transport total regional demand over a 100 km distance. Or, roughly speaking: integration brings consumers in s 100 km closer to the market. The derivation of this indicator rests on Hotelling's (Hotelling, 1938) consumer's surplus indicator (for the derivation, see Bröcker, 1984, pp. 69-73). Traditionally, indicators of consumer's surplus are used to measure gains and losses from integration in economic-integration analysis.

7.4.5. Results

Detailed results of the estimated EC and EFTA effects in 36 manufacturing industries for 1970 have been published in Bröcker (1984, Chapter V). We confine ourselves here to the presentation of some aggregate figures. Table 7.1 and figures 7.5a to c show EC and EFTA effects (separate and joint effects) on regional sales (relative percentage change), aggregated over all branches of manufacturing industry. The calculations are based on the assumption of fixed supply prices (that is to say that supply is infinitely price-elastic). Table 7.2 gives corresponding results by country and industry, but aggregated over all regions of each country. A few important conclusions of general interest may be summarised here.

- Within each industry - with few exceptions - the variance of integration effects among the regions of each individual country is low. The reason is that the impact of distance on interregional trade, though always statistically significant, is not strong enough to induce large divergencies among regions with respect to their international trade orientation.
- No marked centre-periphery pattern can be observed with respect to estimated price or quantity effects of integration, neither on a sectoral nor on an aggregate level. The overall pattern differs among industries as well as between the supply and demand sides of each industry. Sometimes the periphery is gaining compared to the centre, sometimes the opposite is true. But often no centre-periphery pattern emerges at all. Thus the old conjecture that the periphery loses by integration seems to have no empirical justification.
- With regard to the integration effects on regional sales given in tables 1 and 2, Sweden and Denmark are evidently winners and Norway is a loser in the EFTA integration process. Furthermore, in Sweden there is a clearcut tendency towards larger gains in less agglomerated regions. Interestingly, the Malmoe-region, which is highly agglomerated and located closest to the rest of Europe, is the only loser on the supply side.
- In the FRG there is an approximate balance between gaining and losing regions. EC-effects in the FRG are slightly more favourable to agglomerated regions on the supply side - a result corresponding to the one obtained by completely different methods in the study referred to above (see the section on the residual approach[5]. As to the sectoral details, table 7.2 shows that in the FRG traditional industries like food, beverages, tobacco, textiles, clothes and shoes have had to reduce their output, while the output of investment goods, motor vehicles, etc., has increased owing to EC integration.
- Finally, it is interesting to note that effects of integration on non-member countries are generally negligible, with a few exceptions, such as basic-metal output in Norway. Obviously, basic-metal producers in Norway have severely suffered from the closure effect of the EC formation (see table 7.2, column 3).

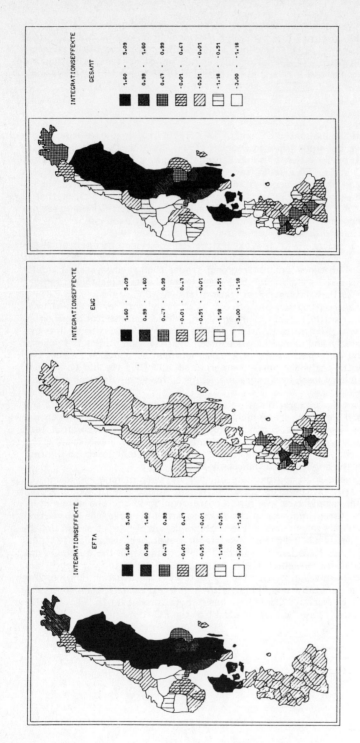

Figure 7.5
Regional integration effects 1970; relative % change of output

146

Reg. Nr.	Region	EEC	EFTA	Total
Bundesrepublik Deutschland				
11o1	Schl.-Holst.	-0,78	-0,13	-0,91
11o2	Hamburg	-0,73	-0,22	-0,95
11o3	Hannover	0,13	-0,22	-0,09
11o4	Hildesheim	-0,22	-0,15	-0,37
11o5	Lüneburg	0,67	-0,34	0,32
11o6	Stade	-1,78	-0,07	-1,86
11o7	Osnabrück	-1,08	-0,18	-1,26
11o8	Aurich	-0,60	-0,19	-0,79
11o9	Braunschweig	0,34	-0,17	0,17
111o	Oldenburg	-0,55	-0,13	-0,68
1111	Bremen	-0,47	-0,12	-0,59
1112	Düsseldorf	0,83	-0,14	0,69
1113	Köln	1,22	-0,19	1,03
1114	Aachen	0,42	-0,15	0,27
1115	Münster	-0,54	-0,20	-0,73
1116	Detmold	-0,07	-0,14	-0,21
1117	Arnsberg	1,05	-0,12	0,93
1118	Darmstadt	0,77	-0,15	0,61
1119	Kassel	-0,15	-0,20	-0,35
112o	Koblenz	0,19	-0,12	0,07
1121	Trier	-1,44	-0,09	-1,53
1122	Rheinland-Pfalz	0,13	-0,14	-0,02
1123	N.-Württemberg	1,06	-0,21	0,85
1124	Nord-Baden	0,73	-0,17	0,55
1125	Süd-Baden	0,34	-0,16	0,18
1126	S.-Württemberg	-0,10	-0,20	-0,29
1127	Oberbayern	0,21	-0,16	0,05
1128	Niederbayern	-1,17	-0,11	-1,27
1129	Oberpfalz	-0,38	-0,10	-0,48
113o	Oberfranken	-0,60	-0,18	-0,78
1131	Mittelfranken	0,52	-0,14	0,38
1132	Unterfranken	0,23	-0,14	0,09
1133	Schwaben	-0,45	-0,14	-0,59
1134	Saarland	1,02	-0,09	0,93
1135	Berlin (West)	0,44	-0,18	0,26
Dänemark				
17o1	Seeland	-0,26	2,00	1,73
17o2	Fünen	-0,28	1,95	1,66
17o3	Jütland	-0,30	2,80	2,49

Reg. Nr.	Region	EEC	EFTA	Total
Norwegen				
21o1	Oestfold	-0,26	0,87	0,61
21o2	Oslo	-0,19	-0,78	-0,97
21o4	Hedmark	-0,13	-2,87	-3,00
21o5	Oppland	-0,17	-1,93	-2,1o
21o6	Buskerud	-0,32	0,07	-0,25
21o8	Telemark	-0,28	0,38	0,1o
21o9	Aust-Agder	-0,58	-0,19	-0,77
211o	Vest-Agder	-1,01	0,20	-0,82
2111	Rogaland	-0,53	-0,46	-0,99
2112	Hordaland	-0,48	-1,67	-2,15
2114	Sogn, Fjord.	-1,24	-0,55	-1,79
2115	Moere, Romsdal	-0,47	-1,67	-2,15
2116	S.-Troendelag	-0,15	-0,39	-0,55
2117	N.-Troendelag	-0,15	-0,23	-0,39
2118	Nordland	-0,57	-0,61	-1,18
2119	Troms	-0,13	0,27	0,15
212o	Finmark	-0,13	1,11	0,98
Schweden				
22o1	Stockholm	-0,20	0,62	0,41
22o4	Oestergoetland	-0,28	1,54	1,25
22o5	Joenkoeping	-0,24	2,40	2,14
22o6	Kronoberg	-0,27	3,66	3,37
22o7	Kalmar	-0,24	3,25	2,99
22o8	Gotland	-0,09	0,19	0,09
22o9	Blekinge	-0,24	2,63	2,37
2211	Malmoehus	-0,18	-0,09	-0,28
2212	Goeteborg	-0,25	1,54	1,28
2215	Skaraborg	-0,22	2,09	1,86
2216	Vaermland	-0,34	4,oo	3,63
2217	Oerebro	-0,30	1,14	0,84
2219	Kopparberg	-0,30	1,84	1,54
222o	Gaevleborg	-0,35	3,31	2,94
2221	Vaesternorrland	-0,29	5,09	4,78
2222	Jaemtland	-0,12	3,05	2,92
2223	Vaesterbotten	-0,27	3,47	3,19
2224	Norrbotten	-0,30	3,71	3,39

Table 7.1

Regional integration effects 1970 - relative % change of output

147

Table 7.2
Sectoral integration effects 1970 - relative % change of output

	EC				EFTA			
	FRG	DK	N	S	FRG	DK	N	S
Agriculture	-3.54	-0.30	-0.06	-0.07	0.00	0.55	-0.39	0.44
Forestry	0.00	0.00	0.00	0.00	-0.01	-0.08	-20.51	5.12
Fishing	0.00	0.00	0.00	0.00	-0.01	1.01	0.83	-4.20
Other mining	0.00	0.00	0.00	0.00	-0.02	0.41	0.85	0.62
Food	-2.98	-0.38	-0.18	-0.04	-0.01	8.02	1.99	-1.35
Wine, spirits	-13.73	-0.24	-0.02	-0.01	-0.08	-4.25	-4.97	-9.18
Soft drinks	-0.21	-0.24	-0.04	0.00	0.00	0.82	-0.08	-0.52
Tobacco	1.21	-0.01	0.00	0.00	-0.02	6.43	-8.02	-8.08
Textiles	-4.82	-0.49	-0.15	-0.24	-0.63	8.36	-16.06	-7.07
Apparel	-1.70	-0.06	-0.01	-0.06	-0.08	4.42	-19.82	-6.78
Leather	-4.46	-0.36	-1.05	-0.29	-0.35	-3.74	-5.44	11.03
Shoes	-9.36	-0.09	-0.13	-0.34	-0.30	-7.02	-20.13	-9.34
Wood, cork	-0.31	-0.07	-0.01	-0.18	-0.11	-6.17	-2.80	5.51
Furniture	0.92	-0.16	-0.04	-0.16	-0.05	2.14	-4.49	5.33
Paper, pulp	0.20	-0.11	-0.36	-0.61	-0.20	-23.28	8.56	16.07
Printing, publishing	0.78	-0.01	0.00	-0.01	0.00	0.00	0.00	0.00
Chemicals	1.79	-0.50	-0.28	-0.24	-0.15	1.67	3.28	0.40
Petro-chemicals	-5.67	-0.09	-0.15	-0.09	-0.41	9.80	-8.14	-7.84
Rubber prods	-0.74	-0.25	-0.26	-0.13	-0.34	-7.54	-9.36	-4.50
Pottery	6.76	-0.20	-0.10	-0.12	-0.11	-2.96	-1.15	2.42
Glass	0.79	-0.39	-0.12	-0.35	-0.30	1.72	-1.29	0.98
Cement	2.01	-0.02	0.00	0.00	0.00	0.00	0.00	0.00
Minerals nec	-0.10	-0.05	-0.03	-0.02	-0.03	-0.01	-3.22	-1.32
Iron, steel	-0.07	-0.84	-1.18	-0.66	0.00	0.00	0.00	0.00
Non-ferrous metal	3.15	-0.44	-3.16	-0.62	0.00	0.00	0.00	0.00
Metal products	2.82	-0.22	-0.05	-0.21	-0.13	-0.61	-2.65	0.99
Machinery	4.11	-0.36	-0.23	-0.40	-0.13	1.01	-0.93	1.39
Elect.mach.	1.73	-0.32	-0.10	-0.21	-0.31	5.79	-0.67	2.08
Ships	-0.47	-0.05	-0.27	-0.02	0.00	0.00	0.00	0.00
Railroad eq.	3.57	-0.14	0.00	-0.10	0.00	0.00	0.00	0.00
Motor vehicles	4.07	-0.80	-0.20	-0.54	-0.60	-6.00	17.37	9.35
Motor cycles, bicycles	-0.43	0.00	0.00	-0.05	-1.11	-7.56	23.59	-12.34
Watches	1.08	-0.50	-0.06	-0.33	-0.50	-1.36	-11.96	8.21
Sports, music	7.11	-0.96	-0.31	-0.29	-0.37	2.27	0.58	1.29
Plastic prods	1.88	-0.17	-0.06	-0.08	-0.10	9.50	-2.11	-3.28
Electricity	0.00	0.00	0.00	0.00	0.00	8.11	1.04	-4.21

7.5. Conclusion

Without any doubt, a review of the debate on the impacts of free-trade policies, which has gone on since the beginning of the European integration process, shows significant scientific progress in the research field concerned. The debate started with certain theoretical conjectures - not testable in those days -, which were rather on the pessimistic side: free trade in Europe was claimed to initiate a relocation process in favour of the geographical centre of Europe, thus interfering with targets of regional policy. Those sceptical conjectures may have contributed to the establishment of a regional policy in its own right on the community level.

In the 1970s, sufficient experience had been gathered to test the theoretical hypotheses. Most empirical studies, however, bypassed the difficulties of quantifying integration effects. Potential countours for Western Europe, for example, may illustrate but do not prove the claim that integration enforces agglomeration. A similar objection can be made with respect to the trade-indicator approach. It does help to evaluate the trade performance of countries and regions; it does not tell us, however, how much is due to trade policy and what would have happened without free-trade agreements.

To a large extent, the difficulties of quantifying integration effects on a regional scale, spring from a lack of data. Information on prices, trade flows etc. is much harder to get for regions than for nations. Therefore, the most advanced methods, such as the empirical general-equilibrium modelling recently applied to the evaluation of trade policies on the international scale (Walsh, 1984), are not directly applicable on a regional scale. Nevertheless, the successful application of a partial equilibrium approach to the analysis of integration effects in Scandinavia and the FRG, which was presented in this chapter, shows that - on certain simplifying assumptions - considerable progress in that direction is possible.

Regarding the empirical results obtained so far, there is a lot of evidence to show that the adverse regional effects of integration feared at first have not emerged. Even though significant regional impacts of trade liberalisation have been observed to affect regions unequally, there is no sign of gains concentrating in the centres and losses in the periphery.

Some qualification of this conclusion is in order, however. It is not necessarily valid and must not be applied without modification to those parts of Europe which have not yet been studied. As regional inequalities are much more pronounced in countries like Greece, Turkey, Spain and Portugal than in North-European countries (Scandinavia, FRG), empirical results may well turn out considerably different once the South-European countries have also been investigated.

A further qualification concerns the exclusion of dynamic effects of integration from all empirical studies. Though nobody denies their existence, their measurement seems an impossible task. The authors have tried to assess integration effects in a regional growth model, but without finding a significant impact of integration on regional-growth differentials (Bröcker, Peschel, Reimers, 1983). One reason is that it is impossible to discriminate sufficiently between different sources of regional growth and decline.

The policy conclusion to be drawn from the empirical research are more on the optimistic side as far as the centre-periphery problem is concerned. Unfortunately, in the context of changing patterns of international specialisation under the pressure of a less protectionist EC foreign-trade policy, the rapid decline of old industrialised agglomerations has become a new regional problem.

Ironically, industrial decline has in particular affected such regions as Lorraine or the Rhine-Ruhr agglomeration, which allegedly would gain most from European integration owing to their central geographic location. Obviously, that geographic advantage does not outweigh the disadvantage of the regions' specialisation in declining sectors. The fact that trade liberalisation accelerates the adjustment process, has led to the manifestation of regional interests in the shape of increasing protectionism. While in the past the interests of backward peripheral areas seemed to contradict policies favouring free trade, now the desire of old centres to be protected from industrial decline is getting into conflict with the targets of trade policy. Up to now, regional policies have responded with ad hoc support programmes, whereas systematic revision of tools and targets of regional policy would be required.

Designing such a policy concept requires a thorough understanding of causes and consequences of the regional restructuring process, which cannot be obtained any more by looking at the individual European countries as isolated entities. Though the EC is far from being a fully intregated economy, integration has nevertheless gone far enough to require an analysis of the causes of regional growth and decline from an international point of view.

7.6. Notes

1. On the national scale, tariff receipts are also among the losses of integration.
2. In fact, not all of them are uniquely derived. For example, A_r and p_r^b are not obtained separately, but only the term $A_r \exp(-\beta p_r)$, up to an arbitrary multiplicative constant. That need not concern us here, however, as we are not interested in interpreting either A_r or p_r^b.
3. Superscript ^{a} denotes anti-monde quantities. Note that, by assumption, $D_s^a = D_s^b$. Δ means benchmark minus anti-monde, that is, $\wedge p_r = p_r^b - p_r^a$ for example.
4. Unlike for p_r^b, a unique solution is obtained for p_r as well as v_s.
5. Note, however, that figure 7.4 shows export effects only, while figure 7.5 and table 7.1 show total effects, including import effects.

7.7. References

Aitken, N.D. (1973). The Effect of the EEC and EFTA on European Trade: A Temporal Cross-Section Analysis, American Economic Review, vol. 63, pp. 881-891.

Begg, I., and Cripps, F. (1983), Indicators for Monitoring the Regional Impact of Extra-Community Trade, Department of Applied Economics, University of Cambridge, unpublished.

Bröcker, J., Peschel, K., Reimers, W. (1983), Regionales Wachstum und ökonomische Integration. Eine empirische Modellstudie für Skandinavien und die Bundesrepublik Deutschland. Schriften des Instituts für Regionalforschung der Universität Kiel, Bd. 5, Florentz, München.

Bröcker, J. (1984), Interregionaler Handel und ökonomische Integration, Schriften des Instituts für Regionalforschung der Universität Kiel, Bd. 6, Florentz, München.

Bröcker, J. (1984), How Do International Trade Barriers Affect Interregional Trade ? in A.E. Andersson, W. Isard, T. Puu (eds.), Regional and Industrial Development Theories, Models and Empirical Evidence, North Holland, Amsterdam, pp. 219-239.

Clark, C., Wilson, F., and Bradley, J. (CWB) (1969), Industrial Location and Economic Potential in Western Europe, Regional Studies, vol. 3, pp. 197-212.

Giersch, H. (1949/1950), Economic Union of Nations and the Location of Industries, The Review of Economic Studies 17, pp. 87-97.

Herrmann, H., Schmidtke, W.D., Bröcker, J., and Peschel, K. (1982), Kommunikationskosten und internationaler Handel, Schriften des Instituts für Regionalforschung der Universität Kiel, Bd. 4, Florentz, München.

Keeble, D., Owens, P.L., and Thompson, C. (KOT) (1981), The Influence of Peripheral and Central Locations on the Relative Development of Regions, Final Report, Cambridge.

Keeble, D., Owens, P.L., and Thompson, C. (KOT) (1982), Regional Accessibility and Economic Potential in the European Community, Regional Studies, vol. 16, pp. 419-432.

Kemp, M.C. (1969), A Contribution to the General Equilibrium Theory of Preferential Trading, North Holland, Amsterdam.

KEG, Kommission der Europäischen Gemeinschaften (1984), Studie der regionalen Auswirkungen der gemeinsamen Handelspolitik, Sammlung Studien, Reihe Regionalpolitik, Luxemburg.

Kemp, M.C. (1969), A Contribution to the General Equilibrium Theory of Preferential Trading, North Holland, Amsterdam.

Linnemann, H.(1968), An Econometric Study of International Trade Flows, North Holland, Amsterdam.

Peschel, K. (1978), Auswirkungen der europäischen Integration auf die grossräumige Entwicklung im Bundesgebiet, in Informationen zur Raumentwicklung, Heft 11/12, pp. 963-976.

Peschel, K., Haass, J.M., and Schnöring, Th. (1979), Auswirkungen der europäischen Integration auf die grossräumige Entwicklung in der Bundesrepublik Deutschland, Schriftenreihe "Raumordnung" des Bundesministers für Raumordnung, Bauwesen und Städtebau, Bad Godesberg 1979.

Peschel, K. (1981), On the Impact of Geographic Distance on the Interregional Patterns of Production and Trade, Environment and Planning A, vol. 13, pp. 605-622.

Peschel, K. (1982), International Trade, Integration, and Industrial Location, Regional Science and Urban Economics, vol. 12, pp. 247-269.

Peschel, K. (1983), Der strukturelle Wandel der Industrie in den Regionen der Bundesrepublik Deutschland 1960-1976, in Determinanten der räumlichen Entwicklung, Schriften des Vereins für Socialpolitik, Gesellschaft für Wirtschafts- und Sozialwissenschaften, Neue Folge Band 131, Duncker und Humblot, Berlin.

Peschel, K., and Schnöring, Th. (1983), Analyse der Exporte der Bundesrepublik Deutschland unter regionalem Gesichtspunkt, Studie im Auftrag der Kommission der Europäischen Gemeinschaften, Beitrag Nr. 3 des Instituts für Regionalforschung der Universität Kiel, Kiel.

Peschel, K. (1985), Spatial Structures in International Trade: An Analysis of Long Term Developments, Papers of the Regional Science Association, vol. 58, pp. 97-111.

Vanek, J. (1965), General Equilibrium of International Discrimination, Harvard University Press, Cambridge, Mass.

Vanhove, N., and Klaassen, L. (1980), Regional Policy, A European Approach, Saxon House, Farnborough.

Viner, J. (1950), The Customs Union Issue, Carnegie Endowment for International Peace, New York.

Yeats, A.J. (1985), On the Appropriate Interpretation of the Revealed Comparative Advantage Index: Implications of a Methodology Based on Industry Sector Analysis, Weltwirtschaftliches Archiv, Bd. 121, pp. 61-73.

8 Macro-economic and Monetary Control

R. BRANCATI

8.1. Introduction

The need for integration of macroeconomic and regional policies has recently been a theme of growing importance. On the one hand, regional policy had lost much of its effect in a rapidly changing macroeconomic environment where macroeconomic policy instruments were used intensively. On the other hand, the changing pattern of regional development, with a differentiated evolution of the labour market, technical innovation, accumulation and overall growth - in other words, the structural aspects of the economy - has made macroeconomic policy appreciably less effective.

This chapter analyses some interdependences between macroeconomic and regional policies, in terms of both instruments and objectives, in a context of international co-operation.

After a brief presentation of the European context of economic co-operation and a general introduction into the relations between the two institutional levels considered, we will go deeper into the impacts of monetary policy. In particular we will present a model of credit rationing on the regional level, and some empirical evidence for Italy.

8.2. International co-operation in macroeconomic and monetary control

8.2.1. The need for macroeconomic integration

It is worth noting that domestic macroeconomic policies have largely been governed by the dynamics of international conditions and the agreements that European countries entered into in the second half of the 1970s. These agreements sprang from the wish to realise the co-ordination of economic policies and the convergence of the individual economic dynamics (objectives already included in the Rome Treaty), and were fostered by the economic debate emphasising the actual advantages of co-ordination and convergence (see Meade, 1951; Steinherr, 1980; Blanchard-Dornbusch, 1983; Canzoneri-Gray, 1983). The argument was that a convergence process - while not in itself representing an objective of domestic economic policy - makes for economic efficiency without imposing significant constraints on each country's autonomy. Such constraints, and hence restrictions on the choice of internal economic policies, seem to follow unavoidably from the international openness and the interdependence of the economies. An open economy constrains macroeconomic policy in that it reduces the effective control of instruments (for instance, the monetary aggregates in conditions of fixed exchange rates) and the influence on final objectives (for instance, production levels), and leads to changed expectations and thus to increasing uncertainty about the link between instruments and objectives (Basevi-Calzolari, 1982). Policy co-ordination, to the contrary, would lead to a stabler and more efficient economy.

In neo-classical hypotheses (see Vaubel 1983), policy co-ordination is considered useless, because flexible exchange rates, prices and wages, and the self-clearing ability of the markets, should be able to achieve maximum "world welfare"; however, lagging tendencies modify the situation substantially. For example, even with flexible exchange rates, unco-ordinated monetary policies cause overshooting of exchange rates, that is, temporary revaluations or devaluations which create excessive and undesirable fluctuations of internal production (Dornbusch 1976).

Apart from co-ordinating as much as possible the monetary policies of member states (especially as far as monetary control and exchange rates are concerned), the co-ordination of macro-economic policies remains important to limit the structural differences among EC member states, in particular differences in public expenditure and tax policies.

8.2.2. Co-ordination of EC macropolicies

In spite of the concrete importance of an overall macroeconomic policy for the European countries, the EC has not, so far, conducted such a policy, in part because of the different attitudes of member states, and partly for lack of instruments on the supranational level.

Direct intervention of the EC in macroeconomic policy is practically negligible at present. The EC cannot pursue budgetary policies of its own, as article 199 of the Rome Treaty explicitly states that the outlays and receipts of the EC budget need to be in balance. If the EC's own resources (see chapter 1) are not sufficient, the member states have to put up the money; unlike the EC, they have recourse to (international) loans or tax ressources. And even if the obstacle of art. 199 could be overcome, the Community budget (a little over one per cent of the member states' overall GDP) would render such a strategy almost ineffective. Fiscal policy, too, is practically excluded. Although the EC derives part of its financial means from its own (para)fiscal sources, they all spring from other policy measures (such as import duties on trade) and cannot be used for demand management.

Indirect intervention has also been very troublesome. The co-ordination of macroeconomic policies has in fact been largely assigned to various committees with a mainly consultative task. At least four such committees can be mentioned:
- the committee of governors of central banks;
- the monetary committee;
- the committee for economic policy;
- the co-ordination group of financial and economic policies.
The committee of central-bank governors meets regularly, normally in Basle, in connection with the monthly meetings of the Bank for International Settlements. All problems of external or domestic monetary policy are discussed, and there is a continuous flow of information about market developments and intervention activities.

The monetary committee is one of the few Community bodies set up by the Treaty of Rome. It is referred to in almost all treaty articles dealing with capital movements, the balance of payments and monetary aspects, and thus given an institutional role. This role has become even more important since the extension of Community legislation and the development of its machinery. For instance, no community loans to member states for balance-of-payment motives can be granted by the ECO/FIN council without the prior formal approvement of the committee. The committee's activities include also the surveillance over the economic and financial developments in, and the international monetary relations of, the member states, as well as decisions regarding the ECU. Nevertheless, with respect to policy co-ordination its role remains a consulting one.

The economic-policy committee is subdivided into three groups (reflecting the previous existence of three separate committees):
- one dealing with medium-term policies
- one dealing with budgetary policies;
- one dealing with cyclical policies.
The specific purpose of the committee is to give general assistance to the Commission by preparing reports covering the relevant fields.

The last committee, the co-ordination group of financial and economic policies, meets mainly to examine the annual economic report of the Commission.

The road towards the Economic and Monetary Union, especially that towards the co-ordination of monetary policies, has been paved with a multitude of measures, but still has not led to satisfactory results. The monetary committee and the committee of central-bank governors were established as early as 1958 and 1964. In addition, after the end of the 1960s, the Barre Plan and the Werner Report marked an orientation towards an independent monetary organisation on the European level, as the Bretton Woods regime began to collapse. Among the concrete measures taken were the agreements of central banks on a system of short-term monetary support (1970) and the introduction of medium-term financial aids (1972). Subsequent agreements aimed at narrowing the margins between, and the joint floating of, the currencies of EC countries. In various forms ('snake in the tunnel' and, after 1973, 'snake outside the tunnel') that situation lasted till 1979.

The launching, that year, of the European Monetary System (EMS) represented undoubtedly the most important single step towards a progressive monetary integration. The evaluation of EMS experience points out some aspects that are not wholly consistent. For one thing, the numerous parity changes since 1979 inspire little confidence in an agreement presented as defining a system of 'stable' exchange rates (Table 8.1, taken from Padoa Schioppa 1984; see also Ungerer et al. 1983). On the other hand, many analysts are agreed that short-run exchange rates have been kept well in hand (CEC 1984), and that parity changes have taken place in a co-operative context, and not been unilaterally decided on by weak-currency countries (Padoa Schioppa 1984). Moreover, the fact that most of these changes did not cover entirely the inflation differences among countries has constantly drawn the governments' attention to the need for internal adjustment.

In view of the above analysis it is not surprising that, while the monetary policies in EC countries have in recent years shown a tendency to converge (tables 8.2 and 8.3, from Padoa Schioppa 1984); in a deflationary direction, the structural constraints in each member country have caused most of their fiscal policies to diverge (table 8.4).

The conclusion is that among macroeconomic policies, monetary policy has been the main weapon used in a co-ordinate manner by EMS member countries, as well as the main instrument for inflation control.

Table 8.1
Nominal exchange-rate variability

	MEAN ABSOLUTE PERCENTAGE CHANGE (MAP)				EFFECTIVE EXCHANGE RATES (VEER) (1)				EFFECTIVE VARIATION (EV) (2)			
	before EMS (3)		after EMS (4)		before EMS (3)		after EMS (4)		before EMS (3)		after EMS (4)	
	daily	monthly	daily	monthly	daily	monthly	daily	monthly	daily	monthly	daily	monthly
NON-EMS CURRENCIES												
Against major currencies (5)												
US Dollar	.21	1.01	.36	1.51	.32	1.33	.51	1.86	.47	1.99	.64	2.30
Yen	.29	1.52	.41	1.88	.47	1.97	.58	2.52	.53	2.43	.69	2.90
Pound sterling	.27	1.56	.35	1.53	.43	1.68	.52	2.04	.55	2.17	.63	2.46
EMS CURRENCIES												
Against major currencies (5)												
D.Mark	.19	1.00	.14	.80	.29	1.41	.22	.88	.45	1.87	.38	1.41
Lira	.23	1.38	.10	.58	.46	2.00	.20	.65	.56	2.37	.36	1.32
F.Franc	.21	1.00	.14	.70	.34	1.40	.28	.98	.47	1.97	.40	1.44
Against EMS currencies												
D.Mark	.20	1.04	.11	.57	.30	1.42	.22	.75	.41	1.76	.31	1.09
Lira	.26	1.52	.11	.55	.48	2.13	.21	.69	.55	2.36	.31	1.08
F.Franc	.21	1.03	.12	.57	.34	1.44	.26	.89	.44	1.88	.34	1.16

(1) Standard deviation of percentage changes of the trade weighted effective exchange rate.

(2) Measured by the weighted average of standard deviation of percentage changes of bilateral exchange rates, with weights equal to foreign trade shares.

(3) March'73 - March'79.

(4) March'79 - March'84.

(5) Major 14 currencies.

Table 8.2
Correlation between monetary aggregates in the EMS countries

Countries	Nominal growth rate						Real growth rate (1)					
	FRG		IT		UK		FRG		IT		UK	
	before EMS (2)	after EMS (3)	before EMS (2)	after EMS (3)	before EMS (2)	after EMS (3)	before EMS (2)	after EMS (3)	before EMS (2)	after EMS (3)	before EMS (2)	after EMS (3)
	M1						**M1**					
France	.24	.70	.17	-.40	.07	.36	.19	.45	.57	.32	.34	.79
Germany	-	-	-.36	.46	.69	.58	-	-	-.06	.60	.47	.69
Italy	-	-	-	-	.08	.24	-	-	-	-	.68	.25
	M2						**M2**					
France	.27	-.05	-.25	-.30	.12	-.17	.05	.12	.18	.09	.50	-.84
Germany	-	-	-.44	.06	.11	-.20	-	-	-.30	.66	.10	-.21
Italy	-	-	-	-	.05	-.79	-	-	-	-	-.37	-.30

1) Real growth rates are calculated on the basis of consumer price changes.

2) Correlation before the EMS: 1973 II – 1979 I.

3) Correlation after the EMS: 1979 II – 1983 III.

Table 8.3
Correlation between interest rates in the EMS countries

Countries	Nominal interest rate						Real interest rate (1))					
	FRG		IT		UK		FRG		IT		UK	
	before EMS (2)	after EMS (3)	before EMS (2)	after EMS (3)	before EMS (2)	after EMS (3)	before EMS (2)	after EMS (3)	before EMS (2)	after EMS (3)	before EMS (2)	after EMS (3)
short term												
France	.56	.62	.37	.79	.29	.11	.69	.08	.19	.65	.54	.67
Germany	–	–	-.33	.38	.24	.57	–	–	-.11	-.03	.65	-.27
Italy	–	–	–	–	.23	-.15	–	–	–	–	.42	.75
long term												
France	.32	.73	.14	.94	.59	.31	-.33	.55	.60	.66	.30	.82
Germany	–	–	-.79	.68	.28	.69	–	–	-.05	.58	.37	.70
Italy	–	–	–	–	.25	.24	–	–	–	–	.31	.80

1) Nominal interest rates deflated by changes in the consumer price index.

2) Correlation before the EMS: March 1973-March 1979.

3) Correlation after the EMS: April 1979-Febr. 1984.

Table 8.4
Correlation matrix between net public investment
as a percentage of GDP in the European countries

1971-78

	B	FRG	F	I	N	D	UK
B	1.00						
FRG	0.62	1.00					
F	0.82	0.84	1.00				
I	0.77	0.90	0.93	1.00			
N	0.75	0.94	0.86	0.85	1.00		
D	0.77	0.89	0.92	0.82	0.92	1.00	
UK	0.61	0.81	0.53	0.65	0.46	0.56	1.00

1979-83

	B	FRG	F	I	N	D	UK
B	1.00						
FRG	0.58	1.00					
F	0.66	-0.17	1.00				
I	0.79	0.17	0.93	1.00			
N	0.86	0.21	0.86	0.86	1.00		
D	0.88	0.33	0.74	0.75	0.98	1.00	
UK	-0.47	-0.52	-0.34	-0.57	-0.56	-0.55	1.00

Source: Steinherr, 1984.

8.3. Theory and concepts

8.3.1. Analysis of the interdependence between macroeconomic policies and regional structures

The analysis of the regional impacts of macroeconomic and monetary policies meets with some major methodological problems. The existing literature is poor, and lacking in relevant references; in particular, it presents:

(i)   an inadequate framework for analysing the relations between regional and national economic structures, especially with reference to problems of economic policy (Marelli, 1985);

(ii) a poor specification of the policy instruments and the transmission mechanisms associated with them;

(iii) a somewhat aggregate view of the regional economic systems, in which these systems react more or less according to "top down" approaches (Bartels et al. 1982; Cappellin 1980).

It seems necessary, therefore, to single out more carefully the typical preliminary steps of the analysis, which are usually the following (Bartels et al. 1982):

(i)   to choose the policy instruments and objectives which can usefully be studied;

(ii)   to get a qualitative insight into the working of the instruments (their enforcement, the way they affect both the microeconomic and the sectorial level, and so on);

(iii)   to develop a theoretical framework representing the relations between various economic and social quantities, as well as the links between instruments and objectives;

(iv)   to select the policy effects that are, and those that are not, significant in the proposed methodological approach;

(v)   to choose which quantitative results can usefully be obtained;

(vi)   to collect the data and analyse their limits.

The few attempts at analysis made until now, by different methods (Keynesian-type econometric models, input-output and integrated models, etc.) have been beset with many difficulties concerning the specification and the time lag, the choice of adequate 'proxies' of the instruments and objectives, the correct evaluation of the indirect impact, the selection of relevant variables, and the quality of the data.

The present study represents an effort to analyse how, in a field marked by the lack of useful references, the relations between the national economic framework and the regional structures are - often implicitly - dealt with. A bottom-up approach is adopted, in an attempt, first, to link macroeconomic with regional policies, and second, to consider the impact of macroeconomic policy on the regional level.

The first problem, then, is to make clear how the two sets of policies hang together, at a time when the debate on economic policy is focused on such macroeconomic variables as the amount of money the public sector needs to borrow, the external deficit, and the type of monetary control that is worth aiming for, given the domestic and international dynamics. Indeed, the increasing awareness of many economic 'trade-offs' (employment vs inflation, internal growth vs the equilibrium of the balance of payments, reduction of interest rates to guarantee the productive sector's growth vs the necessity of satisfying the public sector's need for loans and avoiding negative effects on international capital flows, etc.) seems to keep the debate from dealing with far-reaching programmes.

On the other hand it can be argued that, facing an economic policy constrained both by international conditions and by a sticky internal supply structure, the only way for a single country to get through reasonably - apart from actions undertaken on the supranational level - is to intervene in the internal supply structure.

8.3.2. Regional constraints on economic development

To support the above basic choice, first of all the significance must be shown of the supply structure, in all its parts, with respect to the great aggregate equilibria, that have, or seem to have, priority on the national level.

Next, 'paths' must be pointed out, linking together the different levels of economic policy, in terms of short- and long-run objectives and the instruments of policy. Within that framework, the particular objectives of macroeconomic policy can be connected with the presence of comparatively backward regional areas. From that point of view, for purposes of economic policy the most important thing is the set of constraints operating on the national economy system; consequently, the main concerns are the public budget and deficit, the balance of payments, inflation, and the labour market (Magnifico 1985).

Not on all the topics mentioned above is evidence permitting careful evaluation available, but some important links can anyhow be pointed out, in particular as far as the Italian case is concerned.

With respect to budgetary policy - apart from the problems of the distribution of taxation and fiscal equity - most criticism has been directed against the management of public expenditure. The almost general complaint is that a budget consisting mainly of transfer payments is very difficult to manage, and that public expenditure which is dominated by the dynamics of its current-account component (that is, wages and salaries, and social-security expenditure), is sticky to handle.

The way these criticism are connected with, and partly dependent on, regional problems, can be summarised as follows. On the one hand there is the minor problem of the cost of regional policies in the narrow sense pushing up the absolute level of expenditure. On the other hand, there is the more serious problem of the disproportionate share taken up by transfer payments intended to level incomes (in the form of pensions, unemployment benefits, or unnecessary employment in the public administration), payments that are not directly and explicitly included in re-equilibrium policies (Molle 1986), and increase the stickiness of the expenditure, at the same time straining its composition (over-expenditure in current account, increasing consumption expenditure as opposed to investment).

The few empirical analyses available (Boccella 1982; Brancati 1985) emphasise that, even if, calculated pro capita, public expenditure directed to the regions of southern Italy does not exceed the national average, its incidence with respect to the regional product is higher. So, the economy of southern Italy depends heavily on public disbursements, which in turn increases the proportion of public expenditure with respect to GDP on the national level.

This last point is also important for the analysis of the relations between the public budget and inflation. If indeed 'bottlenecks' in production impose a constraint on the ability of aggregate supply to expand sufficiently for the overall quantity of unemployed resources to be used up on the national level, demand-pull inflationary pressures would be fostered. Moreover, differences in productivity levels combined with even wage levels may set in motion accelerating mechanisms in the dynamics of prices. (Indeed, these differences also tend to weaken the effectiveness of 'income policies' built on average wages and productivities.)

As far as regional disequilibria and the balance of payments are concerned, three areas of interdependence can be singled out. The first relates to the dynamics of internal prices (given the international dynamics); the second concerns the sectorial specialisation of the economy; finally, there is the problem of different productivity levels.

On the one hand, different inflation levels affect the competitiveness of exports and imports, and/or the exchange-rate dynamics; on the other hand, the international economic recession has emphasised specific difficulties in some industries marked by low demand levels and worsening terms of trade. Where the industrial problem comes on top of the regional one, the causes of recession are multiplied. In fact, the social costs prohibit proposing the abandonment of productive activities in areas which already suffer from high unemployment rates. At the same time, the possibility of industrial reorganisation and in general of growth are reduced when the productive structure is weak and badly integrated. Recall that, apart from the crisis in particular industries, many analyses of Italian external trade emphasise the precariousness of a productive structure featuring increasing import penetration as well as peculiar export specialisation. The regional implications of import penetration become very clear if one considers that it follows from phenomena already investigated, namely, the weakness of agricultural and chemical production and of some innovative industries, and the inability of some productive systems to adjust their supply structure to the quantitative and qualitative dynamics of internal demand.

In the Italian case, for instance, the export data available show that the contribution of the southern regions is still very feeble (Brancati 1985). From 1968 to

1980 their share in the national export decreased from 6.4 to 6.1 per cent; afterwards it increased to 7.4 per cent in 1983. So, despite the low starting level the total change in fifteen years was small; even the ratio of exports to value added denotes a degree of external openness much lower than that of other Italian regions. Moreover, the sectorial specialisation of Italian exports seems to be connected with the specific features of the regional productive systems.

In fact, the optimism or pessimism that different studies (Onida 1986) show about the national pattern of specialisation seems to follow strictly from their evaluation of the strengths of the productive systems. The better the firms' international competitive position, productivity levels and investment rates, the more probable are conditions warranting positive evaluation, the sectorial dimension being left out of consideration. By contrast, the lower and less dynamic are productivity and investment, the more probable is the marginality of the firms, their survival depending on price competition and either devaluation of the exchange rate or a drastic cutting-down of labour cost.

Even so, the statistical information available shows no homogeneous picture for the various regions of Italy. In view of the changes in profitability and productivity, southern firms behave worse than the national average; worse still is the dynamics of investments (Brancati 1985).

If it is true that the international competitiveness of Italian firms depends more and more on their ability to innovate and grow up, the weaker regions have the greatest poblems on that score, but also great potentialities of increasing their share in world trade.

To summarise, my argument is that regional performances tend to affect a country's balance of payments both indirectly (through the general dynamics of the economy, with particular reference to production and prices) and directly. For the direct influence, two phenomena are relevant:
(i)   import penetration, which may be connected with the weakness of industries with specific regional features and with local productive systems not always able to adjust to changes in internal demand;
(ii)   the dynamics and outlook of exports, which may be determined by the efficiency and the overall degree of development of the regional economic structures.

8.3.3. The regional impact of macroeconomic policies

A similar argument is possible about the regional impact of macroeconomic policies. Failing the special analyses needed for a complete picture, my arguments are based on a sort of 'economist's common sense'. According to the usual analytical plans, the three basic areas of macroeconomic policy can be perceived even on the regional level. Regional economies respond differently to monetary policy measures taken on the national level. (This is a field in which quite some analytical efforts have been made: Fishkind 1977, Garrison, Chang 1979, Roberts and Fishkind 1979, De Felice 1982, Deiss 1978, Miller 1978, Mathur and Stein 1980, 1983, Scott 1955, Niccoli 1980). In fact, given a monetary policy decision that is supposed to be 'neutral' (for instance, a national change in the interest rate), the expansion of real income in the various regions will depend on their structural features, or, in other words, on the different regional elasticities of the product with respect to the interest rates.

As far as fiscal policy is concerned, remarks similar to those made above about monetary policy can be made; on the other hand, some special phenomena can be pointed out which follow from the operative conditions of this kind of policy. Fiscal policy is in fact, almost by definition, not 'neutral' in that it changes particular items of expenditure and revenue which are not homogeneously distributed on the local level. Moreover, the regional differences ensuing will be fostered by the wide variance of regional income multipliers that springs from the regions' widely different propensity to import (in turn following from different degrees of completeness of the local productive systems).

Finally, built-in stabilisers - apart from their normal working in the course of national economic cycles - can be argued to have different spatial effects. In fact, the lower the income of households and firms, the lower will be the regional fiscal revenues; on the other hand, the higher the regional unemployment rate, the higher will be the level of aids involved. In an evaluation of the effects of policies aiming at an equilibrium in the balance of payments, the argument has been put forward that an exchange-rate devaluation, for instance, tends to support regions that are comparatively open (manifest in a higher ratio of exports to the regional product) or specialised in products with a highish price elasticity of demand. As far as imports are concerned, the same devaluation favours the areas producing goods with, once again, a high price elasticity, or goods subject to quantitative ceilings on the national level.

Some more details can be given with respect to financial markets and monetary policies on the regional level, for which some tradition in economic analysis exists.

8.3.4. Financial markets and regional structures

Despite various analyses of credit institutions and financial markets on a sub-national level, the role of the finance sector in regional economic development remains relatively unexplored. The rare studies available in international literature mostly relate to experience in the United States[1]. Moreover, the majority of analytical studies are of an applied nature and do not provide a coherent theoretical framework for the study of financial markets on the regional level. Furthermore, the consideration of capital as a commodity practically without transportation costs traded on highly transparent markets, has always resulted in theories that leave little room for regional analysis. The various lines taken in the scarce available literature can be sub-divided, for the sake of clarity, into two groups.

1. The first group, which analyses the <u>adjustment process connected with regional development</u>, is fairly general and tends to concentrate on the connections between monetary and financial sectors and the development of the real economy in limited zones within one country. In such appraisals, regions are taken as "small open economies" operating within a fixed exchange-rate regime (Deiss 1978; Goodhart 1975; Gnesutta 1971; Cutilli 1978). In such situations, development is limited by regional balance-of-payments constraints and, given an exogenous level of exportation, in particular by each region's propensity to import. Beyond that general theory, the existence of a consistent surplus or deficit in international trade, even for long periods, is not in doubt[2]. The fact that connected problems are not explicitly considered, springs from the ease with which disequilibria in the balance of payments can always be financed with appropriate sales or acquisitions of financial claims on national markets. On these markets, individual regions are supposed not to meet any quantitative limits. The level of interest rates is exogenously determined, and equilibrium income is linked to national interest rates rather than to the propensity to import, as is the case of small open national economies.

The continual state of indebtedness of regions in deficit, if not compensated by the transfer of public funds, tends nevertheless to produce wealth effects that influence the level of effective demand and that of regional income (Deiss 1978). That mechanism is explained by the hypothesis that financial markets function perfectly with extremely mobile interregional flows, and that financial assets can be perfectly substituted[3].

If imbalances between demand and supply occur on a regional level, linked in particular to differences in the growth rate of the real economy, then interest rates may increase compared with the national average. The process of arbitrage would set compensatory flows of capital in motion in such a way as to restabilise the equilibrium on financial markets and to allow sustained levels of growth.

Similar impulses arising from operations on the open market, given a territorial distribution of dealers and stocks or bonds held, can create variations in the monetary bases of the regions. Because interregional financial markets are marked by mobility and substitutability, prices and relative interest rates are not so much affected as the balance of payments[4].

In spite of the possibility of growth associated with the movement of capital, the hypothesis that commercial banks play a specific role in the development of productive activity applies. In his discussion of the role of banks and money in the development process, Minsky (1965), for example, refers back to models of regional growth of the 'export-base' type. He maintains that "the essential role of commercial banks in the growth process is that they supply 'loan' capital to (a) those local enterprises which must grow at least at the same rate as the local economy, and (b) those export enterprises which are too small, and perhaps too new, to be able to generate nationally acceptable liabilities". A relative extension of the available monetary base (through exports) on the regional level depends on the success of those companies. This in turn brings about an increase in deposits and reserves at local banks which facilitates further development (Dreese 1974; Minsky 1965).

2. The second line of study concentrates more directly on specific characteristics of financial assets in order to analyse the workings of individual markets. Even in an analysis of interreginal capital flows it is not always possible to consider in the same light assets and liabilities displaying widely differentiated characteristics, in terms of interregional mobility as well as of the links with the dynamics of 'real' economic variables.

While the definition of regional financial markets for public bonds or dealings involving large companies may hardly seem relevant, the diversity among areas within one country does increase through the activity associated with small companies or deposit dealings of restricted mobility[5]. By reconstructing disaggregated financial accounts we can evaluate the relative importance attributed to them by region (undoubtedly relevant to the type of monetary control adopted) as well as identify models of dealer behaviour on subnational markets[6].

The difficulties involved in obtaining the necessary information (different from one country to the next) are far outweighed by the interesting nature of this type of analysis. The only attempts known to the author refer to the United Kingdom, where they are primarily concerned with the reconstruction of data, and Italy, where they provide some interesting explanatory points but are limited to individual regions[7].

8.3.5. Impact of changes in monetary policy

Another analytical approach developed in the literature concerns the specific reactions of the regional economic system to changes in monetary policy. It can be subdivided into four separate approaches.

The first approach, which we can call one of Open Market System Accounts, rests on the assumption that the acquisition and sale of bonds is not homogeneously distributed among the various dealers involved. The existence of both specially differentiated results and simple delays in transmission can then be assumed. Particularly worth noting are the specific characteristics that determine delays in the contraction (or expansion) of the monetary base in the various regions as regards the place where dealings are actually carried out[8]. Temporal lags are connected to the spatial diffusion of impulses and, in the final analysis, to the imperfection of markets. Even when the variations in the monetary base are the same, the effects on regional economies vary (from the monetary point of view) where different money multipliers are in evidence[9]. In fairly transparent markets, it is the balance of payments rather than prices or interest rates that is affected, as has already been pointed out. When the bonds purchased by monetary authorities come from areas characterised by a high multiplier, growth is faster than average with an expansion of income and a deficit in the balance of payments. Contrary considerations are naturally associated with the sale of bonds.

The second approach relates monetary policy to business cycles on the regional level. It specifies the nature of actual lags in the transmission of effects of monetary policy (lags that are not always connected to the open-market operations mentioned previously), and emphasises the differing impacts of central monetary policy on business cycles, which occasionally lead to leads and lags among regions (Jamsa et al. 1984; Scott 1955; McPheters 1976). In both cases, the main cause of the differences lies in the degree of development and the specificity of regional productive structures. On the one hand, the real economy reacts at various speeds to changes in monetary variables. The expected differences, verified in the few studies that have been carried out[10], show an elasticity which depends on specialisation in the various sectors of the regional economy; the greater the specialisation in consumer durables and investments, the greater the effect of monetary policy. On the other hand, the higher the quota of primary and tertiary activity, the lower are the cyclical fluctuations associated with measures of monetary policy. According to at least some empirical studies (Jamsa et al. 1984; Scott 1955; McPheters 1976). however, the temporal phase displacements of the cycle are more significant than simple delays in the diffusion of impacts of monetary policy due to structural causes. Different cyclical phases are accompanied by different reactions rendering measures more or less effective, and significantly influencing the width and depth of the national cycle itself. Thus, expansionary monetary policy is supposed to stimulate growth with relatively more effect in regions at the low turning point of the cycle and about to enter a phase of rapid growth, than in regions at the high turning point and tending towards a slower rate of development. Once again, the opposite is true of restrictive measures.

The third approach is in some respects related to the second: it concentrates on the differing reactions of different regional economic structures to variations in monetary policy through theoretical and empirical analysis[11]. According to studies following this approach, each regional market and each financial asset has an equilibrium between demand and supply constrained by the conditions prevailing on the national level. Small differences in interest rates from region to region do sometimes exist (owing to the cost of information) in spite of the relative mobility of capital, but these are generally negligible. The basic hypothesis is that information costs demarcate a band of fluctuation within which the rates are determined by local supply and demand (figure 8.1). The more isolated the region, with correspondingly high information costs, the greater is the distance to the national rate within the possible band of fluctuation. That aspect, which in some way represents the possibility of differentiation of regional financial markets, is specific to each financial asset.

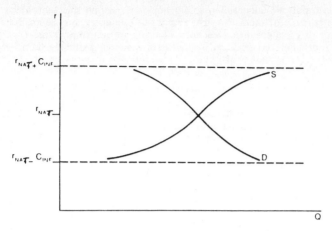

r_{NAT} = National interest rate C_{INF} = Information cost
S   = supply   D   = demand

Figure 8.1
Fluctuation margin of regional interest rates

With reference to capital flows in aggregate terms, an analytical plan based on IS-LM curves is generally adopted. In that case the LM curve is considered to be parallel to the axis of abscissae and is determined by the level of rates on the national market. On that level, regional operators can obtain any amount of money. The IS curve shows degrees of elasticity in the various regions depending on their structural characteristics[12]. In the hypothetical example of regions A and B (Figure 8.2), where the IS curve is relatively elastic for A and inelastic for B, the implications of a restrictive (or expansionary) monetary measure are trivial: with a rise of the national rates and a shift of the LM curve from LM_1 to LM_2, the decline (or growth) of the product is much more noticeable for region A than for region B. Within this diagram, the interest rate is exogenous to the region, and any variability is cancelled out by the process of arbitrage (Moore-Hill 1982).

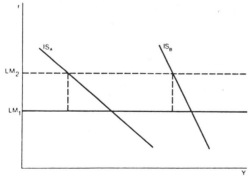

LM = money demand/supply equilibrium   IS = investment/savings equilibrium

Figure 8.2
Different regional reactions to monetary policies

165

Most empirical analyses undertaken so far have focused on this theoretical hypothesis for the purpose of measuring the impact of monetary, and sometimes fiscal, policy in terms of aggregate elasticity of regional economic systems. These studies, which moreover use reduced monetarist models[13], clearly demonstrate the significantly differentiated effects of macroeconomic policies on different regions.

The fourth and final approach is that based on geographical variation in interest rates. Lösch (1954), in his well known and seminal study of location theory, already analysed the territorial distribution of interest rates in the USA. In the 1920s and 1930s, the lowest interest rates were recorded on the New York market, while higher rates were found in areas far from the financial centre of the country. A type of spatial regularity was simultaneously discovered, by which the interest rate increased with the distance from New York City (between 1919 and 1925 the rate on commercial credit rose by about 0.5 percentage points for every 1000 miles of distance). This seminal work already attributed such differences to imbalances between demand and supply in different geographical areas: in fact, in the western regions demand rose rapidly owing to faster rates of growth than in the rest of the country, and the national interest rate was not able to guarantee the balance between the demand for and the supply of financial assets. Lösch's view has since been expanded and developed in new studies, but its logical structure has not been substantially modified.

From such studies, the following general framework can be put together:
- Stable differences in interest rates reflect persistent imbalances between supply and demand on regional markets.
- Given these differences in interest rates, capital appears to flow towards areas with relatively higher rates. Compensatory flows of capital, however, do not entirely cover the financial requirements of areas of rapid growth at the national interest rate. The differentials in the cost of money remain, albeit proportionally reduced[14].
- These differentials are associated with information costs, which tend to reduce the perfect mobility of capital and depend on the size of firms and the typology of financial assets in question[15].

Along with the above factors, the following limitations should be pointed out: administrative constraints, dealer behaviour, and also elements of uncertainty which prevent the free circulation of finance.

A final factor to explain the differentials among regional interest rates is the microeconomic efficiency of banks and the different strategies they adopt. Given the generally accepted hypothesis that scale economies are significant in this sector, the importance of the financial agents involved is particularly relevant (Meyer 1967).

8.4. A case study of differences in regional interest rate and credit conditions in Italy

8.4.1. Introduction

If logical frameworks of the type described above have always proved valid enough when applied to the USA (where there is a steady flow of finance towards the west, consistent with the territorial structure of interest rates), analogous studies of European countries are completely lacking, at least to the author's knowledge. Moreover, the Italian case, about which much has been written, does not appear to conform to the above format. Actually, it is precisely in the slow-growing areas that the higher interest rates are registered, and where the indicators available reveal a relative abundant supply of financial assets. Nor is the system of interest rates coherent: remunerations below the national level for deposits are found in the very regions where credit rates are higher than average. Given the fact that the interpretative formats most common in international literature are not immediately relevant to the Italian experience, an analysis of Italy's situation, marked by regional imbalances, would seem particularly pertinent. We will undertake it by first offering some theoretical and factual explanations of differential interest rates and general credit conditions, building, on that foundation, a model of credit rationing, and finally, giving some empirical results of this model.

8.4.2. Common explanations of different interest rates

The explanation of lasting differences in the regional structure of interest rates, through long periods, without compensatory movements, can be found in the non-homogeneity (and non-substitutability) of financial assets in different regions. This non-homogenity is the result of the imperfect (or costly) information and differentiated economic structures on which studies of the Italian situation have focused[16]. These studies describe the determination of interest rates and apply it to existing regional structures.

Given the same credit conditions, the determination of interest rates is based on the following elements:
1. cost of 'raw material' (the central bank's advance and discount rate, and, more importantly, the interest rates on deposits, both of which depend on the guide rates on public bonds);
2. cost of production (depending on the efficiency and the range of operations of the bank, and on the presence of compulsory reserves in addition to the bank's own policies);
3. the individual banks' evaluation of the loan risk.

There are, on the other hand, significant differences among regional structures, such as the type of banking system and particular features of the local economy. We may assume that the larger banks, which operate without geographical constraints, enjoy scale economies based principally on a choice of profitable investments, and far less on their efficiency. The smaller banks, which operate only on a regional, or even local, level, need to concentrate on less risky and less profitable assets, such as public bonds or interbank loans, once the possibilities of the local market have been exhausted. Such banks therefore resort to lower interest rates on deposits or higher rates on loans (or some combination of the two). Multiregional banks have a greater range of investment possibilities (in terms of both geography and range of operations). They therefore enjoy a higher level of optimisation than smaller banks. That tendency is accentuated during periods when monetary authorities impose a quantitative ceiling on each bank's overall credit, as was the case in Italy from 1976 to 1983. The fact that banks of different size are unevenly distributed can therefore influence the level of regional rates in the ways mentioned above.

On the other hand, different rates are determined by different criteria in the 'real' sector. In fact, the loan risk varied appreciably from one region to another in the period 1981-1982, the risk being higher in southern Italy. If we base an (even purely subjective) approximation of the degree of risk on the ratio of uncollectable to total loans, the 1981-1982 average reveals regional groupings in Italy. (The Bank of Italy considers 'incollectable' those loans which have been made to borrowers acknowledged to be insolvent by the courts.) The national value of this ratio being taken as equal to 100, the north-west area showed a value of 79, the north-east 88, and central Italy 118, while in the south the figures were 144 for the continental area and 235 for the islands. These factors account quite satisfactorily for geographical differences in the level of interest rates and for the gap between loan and deposit rates. (The only additional factor to clarify the last point is the small size of deposits, and consequently low remuneration, in depressed areas; Marchesini 1982; Marzano 1983; Tamagna-Qualeatti 1978.) They fail to explain, however, the cyclical nature of these differences, which seem to be connected with monetary policy; nor do they provide a basis for analysing such aspects as the quantitative credit rationing, which deeply influences the relation between the 'real' and the financial sector.

For a regional analysis, therefore, it seems appropriate to consider a credit-market model that deals explicitly with the possibility of a stable disequilibrium between the supply of and the demand for credit[17].

8.4.3. A credit-rationing model

Any initial hypothesis must take into account a banking system characterised by oligopoly (and price determination based on a mark-up process), and an objective function in which both profit maximation and risk minimation, through constraints imposed on the variance of expected profits, are important. The structure of the model can be expressed by three equations, referring to, respectively: (1) demand, (2) the credit supply (with an equation expression the mark-up process which determines the bank's lending rates), (3) constraints on profit variance.

$$D = f(\overset{+}{Y}, \ \overset{-}{r}) \tag{8.1}$$

$$r = f \ (\overset{+}{q}, \ \overset{+}{r}t, \ \overset{+}{R}K, \ \overset{+}{A}S) \tag{8.2}$$

$$VP = f \ (\overset{+}{P}F, \ M\overset{-}{O}N) \tag{8.3}$$

where:
D = credit demand;
Y = income level (the relation between income and credit demand depends on the specific economic structure);
r = interest rate on loans;
rt = interest rate on alternative 'guide assets' (treasury bills);
q = mark-up;
RK = risk evaluation
AS = insurance against insolvency, increasing from a certain level of credit;
VP = variance of bank's profits;
PF = profitability of bankruptcy, or insolvency;
MON= degree of restriction (on quantity, prices, or both) imposed by monetary authority;
(+ and - are the expected signs of the coefficients).

The demand for credit is affected positively by the growth of the 'real' sector (particularly by investment plans), and negatively by interest rates. The rate on bank loans is determined by a mark-up function based on the opportunity cost of lending (usually regarded as the rate on treasury bills). This function includes an evaluation of the borrower's risk and insurance against insolvency, which increases with the amount of money lent.

The variance of profit constraint in relation to the borrower's probability of bankruptcy is expressed by a curve which is the locus of the points with equal probability of bankruptcy. This curve will shift according to the monetary policy pursued (the more restrictive the policy, the tighter the constraint). If we suppose that, ceteris paribus, the probability of bankruptcy is positively related to the amount of money to be repaid both as capital (Q) and as interests (r) (Niccoli 1979), this constraint can be represented on a plane defined by cartesian axes, the vertical axis representing the interest rate, the horizontal axis the quantity of credit. Figure 8.3 reproduces for bank customer A a position of equilibrium where the supply of and demand for credit are consistent with the VP constraint, while a rationed situation ($\overline{C_{BR}C_B}$) is obtained for customer B. The risk evaluation of the borrower is the same in both cases (same curve), but the quantity of money requested by B overtakes the VP constraint.

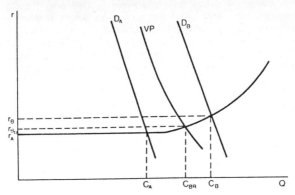

Figure 8.3
Constrained credit supply and demand

The risk discrimination of the customer is represented by a shortening of the horizontal segment of the credit-supply curve and a subsequently steeper curve for less confident borrowers, while for primary customers a longer horizontal segment is maintained. However, the curve slopes positively from a certain level of credit onwards, although it is flatter than for the riskier customers.

Assuming that loans to less developed areas are riskier than others, we can apply the above analysis to two firms (A and B) located in regions at different stages of development (A being more developed than B), also taking into account a change in monetary policy, as in figure 8.4.

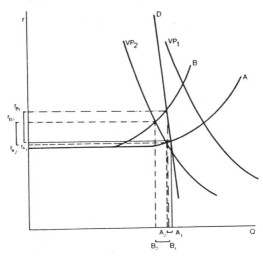

Figure 8.4
Regional impact of a restrictive monetary policy

Under the relatively expansionary monetary policy reflected in the variance-of-profits curve VP1 with a credit-demand curve D, neither A nor B are rationed, while the different risk evaluation determines a high difference in interest rates ($R_{B1}R_{A1}$). When monetary policy becomes more restrictive, it determines an increase in the interest rate and a shortage of 'money base'. This increase results in an upward shift of the supply curve, with a change in the relative positions of primary and non-primary borrowers, which in turn reduces the interest-rate differential. The shortage of 'money base', on the other hand, induces the bank to discriminate more carefully against risky customers in order to achieve a less risky composition of the asset portfolio. To that end, controls on loans become stricter and the guarantees required greater. This in turn shifts the VP curve towards the origin of the axes (VP_2). If the demand curve is stable, a quantitative rationing will result for both firms. In the figure, the rationing for A is given by the segment $\overline{A_1A_2}$, and for B by the segment $\overline{B_1B_2}$. The difference between the interest rates is also appreciably reduced. If the demand curve is inelastic (as we can reasonably assume from econometric estimations on the national level), the credit rationing will be greater for risky borrowers ($A_2A_1 > B_2B_1$).

We can thus put forward the hypothesis that, given a certain economic structure, it is possible to identify the impact of monetary policy on a regional level. If, for example, low-risk firms tend to be concentrated in the more developed regions while high-risk firms are found in depressed areas, the following assumptions can be made:
(a) in the case of an expansionary monetary policy, credit flows will be relatively abundant for all, but interest rates will differ widely according to the relative prosperity of the geographical areas;
(b) a restrictive policy, on the other hand, will reduce differences in interest rate, but also entail an increase in quantitative rationing and in the guarantees in depressed areas. In addition, the marginal efficiency of capital (MEC) in the various regions and the level of investment for each given interest rate can be considered to determine the credit-demand function.

Two hypotheses seem reasonable for the MEC. The first relates to the position of the curve, the second to its inclination. Lower overall efficiency in the less developed areas determines a curve closer to the origin of the axes than in other regions, while the wide differences in efficiency on an infraregional level typical of the first case sustain the hypothesis of a particularly inelastic curve.

In fact, analyses of the Italian situation based on large-scale examples[18] emphasise that in depressed regions there is not only less efficiency but also greater variability.

While the efficiency of leading firms in rich and poor regions differs but little, a much greater difference is revealed by a comparison of marginal firms. That being so, the demand curve in the capital market can reasonably be expected to be unresponsive to a variation in rates: an increase in interest rates cannot affect the plans of the more efficient firms, while a decrease rarely satisfies the requirements of the marginal firms.

The proposed model confirms the conclusions: the more inelastic the demand curve for depressed areas, the greater the mobility of interest rates, and the wider the quantitative rationing.

8.4.4. Empirical evidence; a shift-share approach

A first empirical test of the model should take into account three variables for the twenty Italian regions:

(1) interest rates (credit rates and the difference between credit and deposit rates);
(2) an indicator of quantitative rationing (the ratio of actually used credit to utilisable credit, defined as 'utilisation rate');
(3) the proportion of total credit that is 'secured' (that is, credit provided on the basis of 'real' guarantees from the borrower).

The interregional analysis seems to corroborate the hypotheses mentioned above. Other studies have outlined the persistence of regional differences in interest rates and their cyclical movement following changes in monetary policy[19]. Our analysis, while less aggregate (we have considered 20 regions rather than five areas), confirms the previous results and is perfectly consistent with the model (see table 8.5).

Between 1974 and 1982, every increase in interest rates on the national level was followed by a marked decrease in the differences among regions. In all southern regions the rates rose towards the average (national) value, while the opposite occurred during expansionary periods. The north-western regions (Piemonte, Lombardia and Liguria), on the other hand, displayed the opposite trend, while in the north-eastern regions values remained close to the average.

'Secured' credit (table 8.6) is the second variable to be considered. An analysis of the ratio of 'secured' to total credit still gives the expected results. If the national ratio is taken to be 100, the index values in 1982 are particularly high for the whole Mezzogiorno (except Campania) and for other areas where there are many small and medium-sized firms (Veneto, Emilia, Umbria and Marche). The indexes from 1974-75 onwards, however, show that the trends were quite different in the two cases. While in Veneto, Emilia, Umbria and the Marche the difference between regional and national value was appreciably reduced, indexes continued to rise in the southern regions, particularly in Calabria, Sicilia and Sardegna. Puglia and the Abruzzi, however, displayed the same trend as the north-eastern area[20].

Why the ratio of actually used to utilisable credit of banking institutions should be a significant indicator of market tensions and a proxy of credit rationing, can be briefly explained as follows. This ratio can be useful in solving some well known problems involved in identifying supply and demand curves with credit data. It is assumed that the two variables in the ratio have slightly different determinants. Utilisable credit arises from negotiations between bank and client, while the actual value of available funds is linked to the needs and particular conditions of the firm making the request, that is, the demand for credit. The higher the amount of actually used with respect to utilisable credit, the more probably it is that limits to the expansion of loans are imposed by the supply side (that is, credit rationing).

The analysis of the 'utilisation rate' reveals the expected picture (see table 8.7). High levels occur in (a) the less developed regions (in the Mezzogiorno values are nearly always above average, and particularly high in Calabria, Molise, Basilicata and Sicilia), (b) some north-eastern regions (Trentino, Friuli, Toscana and Umbria), and (c) Lazio. From 1975 to 1980 in particular (the period of the greatest quantitative monetary restrictions), four out of six regions whose indexes increased (Val d'Aosta, Lazio, Basilicata, Calabria, Sicilia and Sardegna) were among the weakest regions of the Mezzogiorno. The same pattern can result, however, from the dynamics of specific economic sectors rather than regional differences. Applying a shift-share analysis in a static formulation, we have tested that point by separating the 'compositon effect' from the geographical effect (differential). The following formulation of the S/S is proposed:

$$\frac{UT_{tr}}{ACC_{tr}} - \frac{UT_{tn}}{ACC_{tn}} = \sum_{i=1}^{30} \frac{UT_{ir}}{UT_{tr}} \left[\frac{UT_{in}}{ACC_{in}} - \frac{UT_{tn}}{ACC_{tn}} \right] + \sum_{i=1}^{30} \frac{UT_{ir}}{UT_{tr}} \left[\frac{UT_{ir}}{ACC_{ir}} - \frac{UT_{in}}{ACC_{in}} \right]$$

Total shift   Structural effect   differential effect
where: (MIX)   (DIF)

UT = utilised credit
ACC = overall utilisable
i   = sectors 1 to 30
t   = total
r   = regional values
n   = national values

The figures clearly indicate the relevance of the specific regional structure (particularly for 1981) for both negative (sign +) and positive (sign -) performances (see table 8.8). Mark that positive differential shifts (sign -) with a lower rationing are evident only in northern Italy. The significance of DIF effects confirms the validity of a regional approach in any analysis of the banking system.

In 1981, there were particularly high levels in the following regions: Calabria (TOT +100.1, DIF + 99.2), Basilicata (TOT + 40.9, DIF + 41.1), Sardegna (TOT + 23.6, DIF + 22), Val d'Aosta (TOT + 16.5, DIF + 7), and Sicilia (TOT + 15.7, DIF + 13.8). Negative levels resulted in Emilia (TOT - 6.8, DIF - 5.5), the Marche (TOT - 6.3, DIF - 4.9), and Veneto (TOT - 3.1, DIF - 2.8).

Deviations from the mean are also consistent with the model: in 1973, a year of relatively expansionary policy, they were negligible (data not recorded); in 1977, a year of moderate restriction, they were significant, and in 1981, a year of severe monetary restriction, they were high.

8.4.5. Empirical evidence: a test of the model

The attempt to put the whole model to an empirical test is based on one of the fundamental mechanisms discussed earlier. The objective is to evaluate the influence of the discussed factors on regional differences in interest rates. We have considered in particular the three variables previously analysed: the relative severity of monetary policy on the national level, the quantitative rationing of credit, and the accessorial condition (given by the ratio of 'secured' to total credit).

Data being available only for a relatively short period (1974-1983), a system of 'data pooling' (cross section/time series) had to be adopted for a significant estimation of parameters[21]. The uni-equational model estimated with OLS can be expressed in the following linear form:

$$TR = a + b R_n + cRU + dGAR + u$$

where:
TR   =   active regional interest rates expressed as indexes against the national average (taken as 100);
R   =   growth rate of interest rates on the national level (as proxy of the strictness of monetary control);
RU   =   ratio of regional credit utilisation (Italian index = 100);
GAR   =   ratio of 'real' guarantees given to total credit (Italian index = 100).

The regions were divided into five groups by any similarity in parameters revealed by a preliminary estimate as well as similarities which had emerged in the preceding descriptive analysis. The five groups are:

172

A.   developed regions (at least in terms of the financial market. In these regions
      there are many medium-size to large firms and many links established with
      credit institutions (Piemonte, Lombardia, Liguria and Lazio);
B.   developing regions (first group). In these north-eastern areas, a notable de-
      velopment in the system of production has been accompanied by improved
      relations with the local banking structure (Emilia Romagna, Toscana, Um-
      bria and the Marche);
C.   developing regions (second group). These regions, mostly in the north east,
      have slightly less impressive economic records than those in the previous
      group, and less positive relations with credit institutions in spite of interest
      rates that are generally in line with the national average;
D.   the more developed southern areas. These are the regions in the Mezzogior-
      no with a somewhat consolidated, or at least developing, productive struc-
      ture (the Abruzzi, Molise, Campania and Puglia);
E.   the backward southern areas. These are the weakest regions of the country,
      at least with reference to the bulk of credit data (Basilicata, Calabria,
      Sicilia and Sardegna).

The estimates (see table 8.9) would seem to confirm the initial hypotheses. Apart
from the conformity of estimated to observed values, which appears to be exceptionally high but is closely connected with reduced fluctuations of the dependent
variable, the signs of the parameters, their values and their importance are as expected.

The regions of group E show an extremely high value for both coefficients. With
each increase in quantitative rationing and each credit squeeze on interest rates,
the gap between the rates in these regions and the national average is reduced.
The request for 'real' guarantees has relatively little effect on the dependent variable, and seems to follow rather than go against the fluctuations in the differences among rates.

Analogous characteristics can be found for the other southern areas (group D),
even though the extent and importance of the parameters are considerably reduced. They can also be found in areas classified as developing regions (group C)
with, however, a further reduction in the value of the parameters and the statistical tests for RU and GAR; in such regions, the differences in regional rate seem
to be prevalently linked to fluctuations in the general level of rates.

In the regions of group B, the other two variables play a significant role (positive for the utilisation rate; where investments and non-financial activities are
highly dynamic, this can be explained by a shift in the curve of credit demand
rather than in the supply curve; and negative for the real guarantees), while the
movements of the national interest rate are relatively less important.

Neither the GAR variable nor the parameter for the utilisation rate are particularly significant in the regions defined as 'strong', while the coefficient relating
to the national rate remains high. Recall that a positive parameter is to be expected for areas with interest rates appreciably lower than average (a rise in national
rates entails a rise in the index, which brings it closer to the average).

8.5. Conclusions

To draw conclusions about the many themes dealt with in this chapter is difficult.
In any case there is no doubt as to the lack of a general framework capable of relating macroeconomic to regional policies, in particular as regards their specific
objectives and instruments. We hardly know how far regional economic performance contributes to the achievement of important policy objectives on the national level (such as the inflation rate or the equilibrium of the balance of payments). And we know even less about the effects of instruments peculiar to

macroeconomic policy on each regional economy. That lack of knowledge is serious on the national level and perhaps even more so on that of the EC. Because objections to the co-operation of macroeconomic policy tend to be based on the different structural features of single economies (and particularly their differentiated reactions), adequate knowledge of the structural and regional consequences arising from each policy measure may lead to a more meaningful debate.

Acceptance of the generalisation of the model presented in this paper necessarily implies agreement on the fact that institutional changes such as the EMS have had important effects on the regional level. Even if we leave the effects of a stabler exchange rate out of consideration, such changes have had macroeconomic consequences. On the one hand, EMS member states have converged towards a tighter monetary policy, even if subjected to short-term fluctuations. On the other hand, the less developed areas may have suffered from either higher interest rates or a lack of credit availability. These may in turn have led to the freezing of prospects of regional development, new unemployment and further constraints on overall national growth.

Even if the autonomy of centralised monetary policies is not in discussion, from a regional point of view the addition of specific measures to attenuate their unbalancing effects would be useful. Unfortunately, such measures are not very reliable. If, for instance, the credit market is oligopolistic, and the degree of oligopoly can be reduced only in the long run, and the 'real' sector cannot be balanced within a few years, the constraints on the overall national growth and the economic disequilibria seem hard to get rid off. On the other hand, the use of instruments tending to reinforce such phenomena - such as ceilings on bank credit (Niccoli 1980) - might be drastically limited, while other measures, possibly promoted on the EC level, might be introduced. In that manner, the stability of the banking system might be made consistent with the financing of entrepreneurial activities characterised by a high degree of technological innovation and at the same time highly important to the economic development of specific regional areas. That goal can be achieved, for instance, by creating - apart from ERDF intervention - consortia for money-back guarantees with participation of public bodies, or particular forms of financial innovations designed for the purpose. The policy aiming at a higher degree of bank competition in EC member countries works, of course, in the same direction.

Table 8.5
Active interest rates by region (Index: Italy = 1) and national interest rates

	1974	1975	1976	1977	1978	1979	1980	1981	1982
Piemonte	1,01	0,97	1,01	1,00	0,99	0,99	0,99	0,98	0,97
Valle d'Aosta	1,02	1,12	1,05	1,06	1,05	1,06	1,03	1,00	1,00
Lombardia	1,00	0,96	0,99	0,98	0,98	0,98	0,99	0,98	0,98
Liguria	1,01	0,95	1,01	1,00	0,98	0,98	1,00	1,00	0,99
Trentino	1,02	1,05	0,97	0,95	0,99	1,01	0,98	1,02	1,02
Veneto	1,02	1,05	1,00	1,02	1,03	0,99	1,01	1,00	1,01
Friuli	1,01	1,01	0,99	0,99	0,98	0,99	0,97	0,99	0,99
Emilia	1,01	1,02	1,02	1,00	1,00	1,01	1,01	1,03	1,02
Toscana	1,00	1,02	1,02	1,03	1,02	1,02	1,02	1,02	1,04
Umbria	1,01	0,99	1,04	1,06	1,04	1,05	1,03	1,02	1,03
Marche	1,01	1,08	1,04	1,09	1,09	1,09	1,06	1,07	1,09
Lazio	0,96	0,95	0,97	0,97	0,95	0,98	0,99	1,01	0,99
Abruzzi	1,00	1,16	1,04	1,09	1,13	1,10	1,06	1,05	1,07
Molise	1,09	1,11	1,04	1,07	1,13	1,10	1,07	1,06	0,98
Campania	1,10	1,14	1,05	1,08	1,09	1,10	1,06	1,02	0,97
Puglia	1,08	1,23	1,08	1,10	1,12	1,10	1,06	1,05	1,07
Basilicata	1,08	1,39	1,07	1,13	1,20	1,17	1,09	1,04	1,06
Calabria	1,08	1,28	1,09	1,15	1,15	1,15	1,08	1,06	1,11
Sicilia	1,10	1,26	1,08	1,10	1,14	1,10	1,04	1,02	1,08
Sardegna	1,02	1,14	0,96	1,01	1,02	1,01	0,93	0,94	1,00
Tassi nazionali	+7,52	−5,23	+7,92	−1,93	−2,15	+0,83	+4,82	+2,10	−1,06
Varianza	15,8	150,2	14,99	31,9	51,5	36,7	17,5	10,4	18,6

Fonte: Elaborazioni su dati Banca d'Italia.

Table 8.6
Ratio of credit covered by real guarantee on
total credit (Index: Italy = 100)

Table 8.6
Ratio of credit covered by real guarantee on total credit (Index: Italy = 100)

	1974	1975	1976	1977	1978	1979	1980	1981	1982
Piemonte	86,70	61,50	72,00	66,70	79,20	59,10	54,40	50,00	76,20
Valle d'Aosta	56,70	61,50	56,00	62,50	25,00	59,10	63,60	59,10	47,60
Lombardia	106,70	115,40	104,00	104,20	87,50	100,00	95,50	95,50	104,80
Liguria	73,30	73,10	88,00	91,70	87,50	104,50	104,50	100,00	85,70
Trentino	40,00	61,50	48,00	58,30	66,70	54,50	54,50	54,50	47,60
Veneto	120,00	123,10	120,00	112,50	125,00	131,80	104,50	104,50	128,60
Friuli	113,30	100,00	92,00	104,20	116,70	131,80	113,60	100,00	76,20
Emilia	200,00	203,80	192,00	170,80	170,80	172,80	172,30	163,60	161,90
Toscana	116,70	115,40	108,00	100,00	91,70	86,41	85,0	72,70	80,90
Umbria	173,30	211,50	172,00	195,80	175,00	172,70	150,00	131,80	152,40
Marche	270,00	261,50	232,00	229,20	212,50	190,90	195,50	159,10	152,40
Lazio	73,30	69,20	72,00	70,80	79,20	68,20	59,10	95,50	71,40
Abruzzi	180,00	200,00	188,00	191,70	179,20	181,80	154,50	131,80	142,90
Molise	70,00	126,90	120,00	154,20	220,80	172,70	204,50	277,30	166,70
Campania	56,70	61,50	64,00	91,70	75,00	95,50	118,20	86,40	66,70
Puglia	186,70	207,70	192,00	212,50	212,50	172,70	186,40	168,20	133,30
Basilicata	493,30	450,00	304,00	337,50	291,70	463,60	486,40	381,80	304,80
Calabria	90,00	88,50	88,00	91,70	120,80	122,70	136,40	113,60	114,30
Sicilia	90,00	93,20	88,00	83,30	79,20	100,00	104,50	122,70	114,30
Sardegna	63,30	61,50	68,00	66,70	66,70	81,80	81,80	104,50	114,30

Fonte: Banca d'Italia, Centrale dei rischi.

Table 8.7
Utilisation rate by region (index: Italy = 100)

	1974	1975	1976	1977	1978	1979	1980	1981	1982
Piemonte	102,80	101,40	101,30	99,50	100,40	101,50	99,40	101,30	102,50
Valle d'Aosta	103,00	101,50	103,50	108,30	105,50	95,80	103,00	118,10	116,00
Lombardia	95,10	93,80	97,10	97,00	99,30	98,90	97,40	100,10	99,70
Liguria	103,70	102,30	101,70	102,60	100,10	98,70	97,00	97,80	98,20
Trentino	104,10	102,70	102,00	103,10	104,60	105,90	100,80	110,60	112,00
Veneto	97,30	95,90	94,60	94,80	97,90	97,30	93,90	99,30	100,60
Friuli	101,30	99,90	95,60	93,30	97,80	95,90	96,30	104,20	105,90
Emilia	90,10	88,80	91,00	90,70	92,20	90,90	87,00	93,60	94,60
Toscana	99,50	98,10	103,50	100,90	102,50	104,90	100,00	107,70	109,80
Umbria	95,60	94,30	97,10	100,30	104,50	103,70	100,10	108,40	106,90
Marche	92,10	90,90	94,00	94,10	95,00	92,10	89,10	95,10	97,20
Lazio	108,60	107,10	105,90	105,10	104,80	108,90	107,20	111,00	108,90
Abruzzi	101,30	99,80	97,20	98,00	97,50	93,20	95,40	102,50	104,50
Molise	99,10	97,70	98,90	99,50	103,60	96,10	96,50	109,70	119,00
Campania	106,10	105,00	113,10	123,70	108,70	106,00	100,10	111,10	109,10
Puglia	107,50	106,40	111,50	119,20	105,00	100,60	102,40	107,40	107,20
Basilicata	109,10	108,00	86,60	96,80	114,60	119,00	125,90	123,70	117,40
Calabria	104,40	103,30	105,80	116,40	107,60	129,40	135,80	142,00	139,10
Sicilia	97,40	96,40	110,10	109,40	111,50	111,30	112,60	118,10	114,60
Sardegna	100,40	99,40	104,00	109,10	120,40	141,80	126,60	124,30	107,80

Fonte: **Banca d'Italia, Centrale dei rischi.**

Table 8.8
Total shift, sectoral composition effect (COMP),
differential effect (DIF), in the utilisation rate
by sector and region - total credit

| | 1977 | | | 1981 | | |
	Tot	Dif	Comp	Tot	Dif	Comp
Piemonte	3.1	-1.7	4.8	.7	-3.2	3.9
Val d'Aosta	10.7	.2	10.5	16.5	7.0	9.5
Lombardia	-1.0	-	-1.0	1.8	2.2	-.4
Liguria	6.6	2.4	4.2	-.4	-1.6	1.2
Trentino	5.8	2.4	3.4	8.9	4.1	4.8
Veneto	-1.5	-.7	-.8	-3.1	-2.8	-.3
Friuli	-1.1	-1.7	.6	1.3	1.4	-.1
Emilia	-6.4	-5.4	-1.0	-6.8	-6.5	-.3
Toscana	1.5	1.2	.3	3.1	3.4	-.3
Umbria	2.5	3.3	-.8	6.7	7.3	-.6
Marche	8.0	9.7	-1.7	-6.3	-4.9	-1.4
Lazio	.6	-1.0	.4	3.8	2.0	1.8
Abruzzi	-.2	1.3	-1.5	-.4	1.2	-1.6
Molise	2.3	1.5	.8	6.8	6.3	.5
Campania	10.5	11.2	-.7	7.2	6.5	.7
Puglia	8.0	9.4	-1.4	2.2	2.9	-.7
Basilicata	10.0	10.3	-.3	40.9	41.1	-.2
Calabria	13.4	13.5	-.1	100.1	99.2	.8
Sicilia	12.1	10.8	1.3	15.7	13.8	1.9
Sardegna	9.9	9.1	.8	23.6	22.0	1.6

Source: Bank of Italy

Table 8.9

Estimation results of the regional interest-rate model

Regioni	Parametri relativi a:									
	Stime con pooling (gruppi di 4 regioni: 1974-1983)									
	a	(t)	ΔR_N	(t)	RU	(t)	GAR	t	$\bar{R}^2$	DW
GRUPPO 1										
Piemonte	86,4	(7,1)	0,22	(4,1)	0,12	(0,99)	–	–	0,999	1,4
Lombardia	86,0	(7,2)	–	–	–	–	–	–	–	–
Liguria	86,7	(7,2)	–	–	–	–	–	–	–	–
Lazio	84,4	(6,5)	–	–	–	–	–	–	–	–
GRUPPO 3										
Valle d'Aosta	117,2	(12,8)	-0,23	(2,4)	-0,11	(1,3)	-0,02	(0,6)	0,999	1,4
Trentino	112,9	(12,5)	–	–	–	–	–	–	–	–
Veneto	114,6	(12,2)	–	–	–	–	–	–	–	–
Friuli	112,3	(12,1)	–	–	–	–	–	–	–	–
GRUPPO 2										
Emilia	92,6	(11,7)	-0,15	(2,3)	0,13	(1,7)	-0,02	(1,7)	0,999	1,9
Toscana	90,5	(10,8)	–	–	–	–	–	–	–	–
Umbria	92,8	(10,7)	–	–	–	–	–	–	–	–
Marche	98,5	(11,9)	–	–	–	–	–	–	–	–
GRUPPO 4										
Abruzzi	123,2	(11,3)	-0,55	(3,3)	-0,16	(1,6)	0,01	(0,5)	0,999	1,4
Molise	124,0	(10,9)	–	–	–	–	–	–	–	–
Campania	124,5	(10,7)	–	–	–	–	–	–	–	–
Puglia	126,4	(10,8)	–	–	–	–	–	–	–	–
GRUPPO 5										
Basilicata	125,2	(17,1)	-1,20	(6,2)	-0,24	(3,6)	0,04	(2,6)	0,999	1,8
Calabria	139,5	(14,4)	–	–	–	–	–	–	–	–
Sicilia	134,4	(18,0)	–	–	–	–	–	–	–	–
Sardegna	126,6	(16,4)	–	–	–	–	–	–	–	–

8.6. Notes

1. Along with these studies, numerous contributions from other countries, particularly Italy, should be mentioned, although their circulation is limited to the country in question. They focus on the intensive use of monetary policy for economies marked by persistent regional imbalances.
2. Even in the absence of direct findings, there is a lot of supporting information available: from the differences between the formation and use of resources to migratory flows, not to mention the estimates of interregional capital flows: Occhiuto-Sarcinelli (1962), Tamagna-Qualeatti (1978).
3. Elaborating on this theme, one supposes a degree of substitutability differentiated by type of financial asset under consideration: even if the substitutability for deposits is taken as minimum, and for bonds as maximum, these studies reveal an average that is high enough to characterise the financial market as almost perfect.
4. Miller proposes this monetary approach to the balance of payments in his model (1978).
5. The mobility and limitations of deposits are discussed at length in Moore-Hill (1982).
6. See Onado-Pedani (1984) for a description.
7. Short-Nicholas (1981), Onado-Pedani (1984), Istituto Bancario S. Paolo di Torino (1983).
8. This place is always taken to be New York in studies of American experience.
9. This is particularly true where monetary authorities can apply differentiated reserve coefficients to different areas within a country.
10. These differences can also be deduced from the studies of Garrison-Chang (1979).
11. The analyses referred to are: Lösch (1954), Mathur-Stein (1980-83), Garrison-Chang (1979), Fishkind (1977), Roberts-Fishkind (1979), Jamsa (1984).
12. Explicit references are made in: Roberts-Fishkind (1979).
13. Despite the significant results of these analyses, the authors themselves have emphasised the numerous problems involved in using such simplified analytical frameworks. Three points stand out:
    (a) Monetary manoeuvres can also be carried out to balance variations in exogenous variables not taken into consideration within reduced formulations.
    (b) Policy makers can use monetary policy to stabilise monetary variables (interest rates).
    (c) The variables of the model can be correlated to exogenous variables. This is particularly probable when reduced formulations are used.
    See Mathur-Stein (1983).
14. While there are many analyses of interreginal differences in interest rates, nearly all, at least those pertaining to the USA, emphasise the relative unimportance of such differences. See Meyer (1967), Davis-Banks (1965).
15. See Dreese (1974) and occasional references in Minsky (1965).
16. See Tamagna-Qualeatti (1978), Marchesini (1982), Marzano et al. (183), Busetta (1983), De Felice (1982).
17. On a national level, see Carosio (1975), Jaffee-Modigliani (1969), Niccoli (1979).
18. Further discussion of this point can be found in M. Crivellini (1979).
19. The studies taken into consideration are: De Felice (1982), Tamagna-Qualeatti (1978), Busetta (1983), Marzano et al. (1983).
20. The relatively low index values for Campania can be explained by particular circumstances: the index rose sharply until 1980, to decrease rapidly afterwards, probably because of aid provided to the region following the earthquake of November 1980.
21. For a detailed analysis of the method of pooling adopted, see Maddala (1971, 1977).

8.7. References

Bartels, C.B., W.R. Nicol, and J. van Duijn (1982), Estimating the Impact of Regional Policy: a Review of Applied Research Methods, Reginal Science and Urban Economics, no. 1.

Basevi, G., and M. Calzolari (1982), Multilateral Exchange Rate Determination: a Model for the Analysis of the European Monetary System, in Bilson and Marston (eds.), Exchange Rate Theory and Practice, NBED, Chicago.

Blanchard, O., and R. Dornbursch (1983), U.S. Deficits, the Dollar and Europe, Economic Papers no. 24, Commission of the European Communities.

Boccella, N. (1982), Il Mezzogiorno sussidiato, Franco Angeli editore, Milan.

Brancati, R. (1985), Politiche regionali e politiche macroeconomiche, Franco Angeli editore, Milan.

Busetta, R. (1983), Evoluzione dei tassi: il caso della Sicilia, Delta no. 3.

Canzonieri, M., and J. Gray (1982), Monetary policy Games and the Consequences on Cooperative Behavior, Federal Reserve Board, Washington.

Cappellin, R. (1980), Un approccio alla costruzione di un modello di sviluppo interregionale per l'economia italiana, in Ith Conference of the Italian Section of RSA, Rome.

Carosio, G. (1975), Discriminazione dei clienti e controlli selettivi del mercato dei prestiti bancari, Contributi alla ricerca economica, Banca d'Italia.

Cebula, R.J., and M. Zaharoff (1974), Interregional Capital Transfer and Interest Rate Differentials: an Empirical Note. The Annuals of Regional Science, no. 8.

CEC (1984), Five Years of Monetary Cooperation in Europe, COM (84) 125 Find, Brussels.

Crivellini, M. (1979), I divari di produttività come misura del fattore organizzativo imprenditoriale, in Lo sviluppo dei fattori imprenditivi e organizzativi dell'industria italiana, ISTAO, Ancona.

Cutilli, B. (1978), Aspetti moonetari dell'economia regionale, Quaderni sardi di Economia, no. 4.

Davis, R.G., and L. Banks (1965), Interregional Interest Rate Differentials, Federal Reserve Bank of New York, Monthly Review, August.

De Felice, G.(1982), Gli effetti regionali delle politiche di stabilizzazione, III Conferenza Italiana di Scienze Regionali, Venice (mimeo).

Deiss, J. (1978), The Regional Adjustment Process and Regional Monetary Policy, paper presented at the XVIIIth European Congress of the Regional Science Association, Rivista Internazionale di Scienze Economiche e Commerciali, October.

Dreese, G.R. (1974), Banks and Regional Economic Development, Southern Economic Journal, April.

Dornbusch, R. (1976), Expectations and Exchange Rate Dynamics, Journal of Political Economy, no. 6.

Fishkind, H.H. (1977), The Regional Impact of Monetary Policy: an Economic Simulation Study of Indiana 1958-1973, Journal of Regional Science, no. 1.

Garrison, C.B., and H.S. Chang (1979), The Effect of Monetary and Fiscal Policies on Regional Business Cycles, International Regional Science Review, vol. 4, no.2.

Gnesutta, C. (1971), Sulla rilevanza di una definizione della base monetaria a livello regionale, Quaderni sardi di economia, February.

Goodhart, C.A.E. (1975), Money information and uncertainty, MacMillan, London.

Instituto Bancario San Paolo di Torino (1983), Aspetti regionali dei flussi finanziari: il caso del Piemonte, Thema no. 8.

Jaffee, D.M., Modigliani, F. (1969), A Theory and Test of Credit Rationing, American Economic Review.

Jamsa, J., Kananen, J., Toiviainen, E. (Year 1984), On the Transmission of the Effects of Monetary Policy to the Regions, paper presented at the XXIV European Congress of the Regional Science Association.

Lösch, A., (1954), The Economics of Location, Yale University Press, New Haven.

Maddala, G.S. (1971), The Use of Variance Components Models in Pooling Cross Section and Time Series Data, Econometrica, vol. 32, March.

Maddala, G.S. (1977), Econometrics, McGraw-Hill, New York.

Magnifico, G. (1985), Regional Imbalances and National Economic Performance, Commission of the European Communities, Brussels.

Marchesini, G. (1982), La variabilità geografica dei tassi bancari, Delta, no. 1.

Marelli, E. (1985), Economic Policies and their Effects upon Regional Economies, Papers of the Regional Science Association, vol. 58.

Marzano, F., Del Monte, A., Fabroni, M., Martina, R. (1983), Il sistema bncario meridionale, lo sviluppo del Mezzogiorno e l'ingresso delle banche estere in Italia, Economia Italiana, no. 1.

Mathur, V.K., and S. Stein (1980), Regional Impact of Monetary and Fiscal Policy: an Investigation into the Reduced Form Approach, Journal of Regional Science, vol. 20.

Mathur, V.K. and S. Stein (1983), Regional Impact of Monetary and Fiscal Policy: a Reply, Journal of Regional Science, vol. 23, no. 2.

McPheters, L.R. (1976), Banking System Diffusion of Open Market Operations, Southern Economic Journal, 43.

Meade, J.E. (1951), The Balance of Payments, Oxford University Press, London.

Meyer, P.A. (1967), Price Discrimination, Regional Loan Rates and the Structure of Banking Industry, Journal of Finance, vol. 22, March.

Miller, R.J. (1978), The Regional Impact of Monetary Policy in the United States, Lexington Books, Massachusetts.

Minsky, H. (ed.) (1965), California Banking in a Growing Economy, Berkeley University of California, Printing Department.

Molle, W.T.M. (1986), Regional Impact of Welfare Policies in the EC, in J.H.P. Paelinck (ed.), Human Behaviour in Geographical Space, Gower, Aldershot.

Moore, C.L., Hill, J.M. (1982), Interregional Arbitrage and the Supply of Loanable Funds, Journal of Regional Science, vol. 22, no. 4.

Niccoli, A. (1979), Razionamento del credito e allocazione delle risorse, Il Mulino, Bologna.

Niccoli, A. (1980), I massimali di crescita: effetti territoriali e sulla struttura del sistema bancario, Moneta e Credito, settembre.

Occhiuto, A., Sarcinelli, M. (1962), Flussi monetari Nord-Sud, Bollettino Banca d'Italia, no. 3.

Onida, F. (1986), Vincolo estero, strutture industriale e credito all'exportazione, Il Mulino, Bologna.

Onado, M., Pedani, D.P. (1984), I conti finanziari dell'Emilia-Romagna, Federazione delle Casse di Risparmio e delle banche del Monte dell'Emilia Romagna, Il Mulino, Bologna.

Padoa Schioppa, T. (1984), Policy Cooperation and the EMS Experience, Paper prepared for the NBER-CEPR Conference on the International Coordination of Economic Policy, London, June 28-29.

Roberts, B.R., and H. Fishkind (1979), The Role of Monetary Forces in Regional Economic Actiity: an Econometric Simulation Analysis, Journal of Regional Science, no. 1.

Scott, O. (1955), The Regional Impact of Monetary Policy, Quarterly Journal of Economics, no. 69.

Steinherr, A. (1980), Convergenze e Coordinamento delle politiche macroeconomiche: alcuni problemi fondamentali, Economia Europea no. 20, Brussels.

Tamagna, F., and D. Qualeatti (1978), Sviluppo economico e intermediazione finanziaria nel Mezzogiorno d'Italia, 1951-1972, F. Angeli, Milan.

Ungerer, H. Evans, O., Nyberg, P. (1983), The European Monetary System: the Experience, 1979-1982, Occasional Paper no. 19, International Monetary Fund, Washington D.C.

Vaubel, R. (1983), International Coordination or Competition of Macroeconomic Policies, Kiel.

9 Conclusions

R. CAPPELLIN and W. MOLLE

9.1. Introduction

The object of this book was to give a state of the art as to the regional impact of EC policies. Now that we have come to the end of this collective effort[1], in which several experts have treated their specific subjects in some depth, let us survey the general picture that emerges from the case studies.

From the thorough analysis of Community and national policies and regional development in the previous chapters, they are closely and intricately linked together; the relationships are fluent, for the scope, instruments and objectives of policy have gradually changed during the last few decades.

In this final chapter, putting aside much of the complexity revealed by the analyses, we will first discuss the methods used to analyse the impact of policies on regions and regional disparities. Next we will make some general remarks about the role of regional policy in the entire policy context. Ironically, measures of regional policy, not explicitly demanded in the treaties instituting the European Community, have been designed and implemented in the course of the years and adapted as the economic and social problems in the European countries and the role of Community institutions evolved, while other policies provided for in the treaty, like transport policy, have failed to develop as expected. Finally, we will suggest some changes in European policy making.

9.2. Survey of the previous chapters

9.2.1. Agriculture

The objectives of the common agricultural policy are to stabilise the European agricultural markets and protect European productions from external competition. As is well known, this policy has put the European Community to high expenses, thus reducing the possibility of undertaking other Community policies.

Strijker and de Veer have indicated in their contribution, that the benefits from these high outlays are not equally distributed among the European countries and regions. The price-support policy favours the richer countries. The structural measures of the common agricultural policy have a direct regional impact, as they aim to modernise agricultural production, especially in regions where the structure is less efficient owing to natural conditions, lower integration of the agricultural sector with industry and services, and less easy access to modern technology. However, by increasing productivity, structural policies have also boosted aggregate production on the Community level. Therefore, regional structural measures should be designed to avoid contradictory effects on the national and Community levels.

Increased productivity of workers will reduce employment in agriculture and make it necessary to expand employment in manufacturing industry and services in the less developed regions. To bring about that transformation, public intervention schemes such as already used by the European Community in the case of other declining sectors, will be needed. The multifacet character of agriculture calls for a tight co-ordination of agricultural policies with environmental, industrial and social policies.

9.2.2. Industry and services

A future-oriented development of manufacturing industry and services is crucial to European integration. Community industrial policy has aimed not only at a homogeneous market and sound competition but also at the modernisation of European industry and improved competitiveness of European production on international markets. Traditionally, industrial policy has given much attention to the restructuring of declining sectors, but recent programmes have been addressed to the development of modern sectors.

Industrial policy has clear regional consequences, since declining as well as growing sectors are often concentrated in particular regions. Even if there is no such concentration, specific regional factors may still explain why the same sectors in different regions show the wide disparity in development which Molle has pointed out in his chapter.

Indeed, the sectoral reconversion of individual regional economies from less to more productive sectors, and the adoption of process and product innovations in particular regions, depend on specific local factors which affect horizontally all the sectors of a regional economy and may promote its endogenous development or its innovation potential.

Regional policy measures, too, can affect the objectives of national industrial policies and the development of national sectoral productions, as is illustrated by the industrialisation policy of the Mezzogiorno area in Italy. Specific regional policies can foster macro growth by removing local bottlenecks which prevent the birth of new small and medium-size firms and job creation. Community programmes to promote R&D institutes, innovation-diffusion centres, and professional and training facilities in the various regions, can contribute to macro growth.

9.2.3. Energy

The energy policies of the Member States and of the European Community aim at national objectives and assign minor roles to regional objectives. As indicated by the contribution of Bourgeois, energy policies have tried to cut down the energy bill, promote energy saving, diversify energy sources, reduce dependency on oil, maintain or increase the relative shares of natural gas and solid fuels, increase the share of renewable energies and, at least in the past, to increase the contribution of nuclear energy.

Energy policies and overall changes in the world energy market make heavy impacts on regional economies. Energy is crucial to the industrial development of some peripheral regions. The unit cost of energy supply and distribution differ widely among areas, dependent on accessibility and economies of scale. Subsidies to the price of energy and tariff equalisation have been used to attract new industries to peripheral regions.

The acknowledgement that the pursuit of the Community's energy objectives may have specific direct or indirect effects on certain regions may lead either to attempts at allowing regional considerations to influence the definition of the objectives, or to specific measures to compensate for the changes most harmful to certain regions. The EC has chosen the latter strategy by encouraging specific investment projects in the regions structurally most vulnerable in their energy supply, and promoting energy saving and the exploitation of potential alternative and renewable energies. Such 'software measures' as regional energy studies and technological transfers serve the express purpose of better equipping the less favoured regions for evaluating and deciding on new investments, and developing their endogenous energy potential.

9.2.4. Transport and communications

Transport and communication policies aim at reducing the friction of distance. The role of transport and communication is important because the competitiveness of manufacturing firms often depends on the efficiency and scope of distribution.

As indicated in the contribution by Fullerton and Gillespie, national and community policies have emphasised such specific national or international objectives as the harmonisation of the different national transportation and communication systems, the co-operative development of new technologies, the decrease of costs, the improvement of quality and the introduction of new services. National policies differ widely in their objectives and strategies, ranging from deregulation to dirigist co-ordination. Deregulation strategies clearly enhance the advantages of the most central regions, while the provision of an universal service implies (cross) subsidy from the more to the less developed regions.

National and Community policies make an impact on regional growth. Improved transportation and communication clearly stimulate the spatial diffusion of industries, the access of peripheral areas to specialised information, and the regional development potential. However, the impact of particular infrastructure projects varies according to the development phase and the sectoral structure of the regions concerned. Projects not oriented to the relief of actual bottlenecks, may have but minor effects.

Transport and communication represent a complementary or necessary but not sufficient condition for regional development. Their effect on the development of peripheral regions depends on the existence of other positive location factors in these regions. In fact, the removal of the distance barrier may lead to the development of untapped local resources, but also to the local market being flooded by the products of the more developed regions.

9.2.5. Labour market

Some co-ordination of national labour-market policies on the European level has become necessary by the increased integration of national economies, the greater geographical and occupational mobility within the Community, and the steep rise of unemployment rates in all European countries. To facilitate the structural adaptation that must go hand in hand with integration, measures have been taken to increase the employability of individuals made redundant. In the course of time, regional considerations have become increasingly important in European social policy. In fact, regional labour markets are developing in highly different ways and, as pointed out in Steinle's contribution, labour-market problems have accumulated in some regions. A large proportion of the European Social Fund is reserved to priority regions. However, the contribution of Community social policy to regional equilibrium seems to be trifling. One reason is that Community support does not add much to the effect of national measures: projects submitted by member states but not supported by the Community are often carried out anyway. (Only some innovative projects may be additional to current national measures.) A second reason is that various labour-market measures, both such direct ones as the programmes for young unemployed people, and indirect ones as early retirement schemes, seem to have been most successful in the most advanced regions.

In view of the regional cumulation and concentration of problem groups, regional labour-market policies should concentrate more on the problem regions. Regional policies and training policies, working on the supply side of the labour market, should be integrated with sectoral employment policies working on the demand side.

9.2.6. Trade

Trade is a policy area that has largely shifted from the competence of national governments to that of the EC. The objective of EC trade policy is to contribute, by a growing openness, to the world-wide specialisation of production, and hence to welfare. Possibly, that general objective can be reached only at the price of localised welfare losses, for instance if a regionally concentrated production is wiped out by international competition. On the other hand, some regions may be better equipped to improve their competitive position on external markets than others, and thus be more susceptible to economic growth. However, the effects of trade policy on the regions are much more intricate than is indicated by these two examples, as witness the chapter by Bröcker and Peschel. Indeed, they show that there is no evidence of trade having systematically favoured the richer regions. Hence, how to articulate regional policy to compensate for trade losses, is not obvious. Presumably, compensation measures will have to be taken outside the domain of trade policy.

9.2.7. Monetary policies

Macro-economic policies typically deal with national objectives, such as inflation, balance of payments, public budget deficit. They need to be co-ordinated on the European level in view of the high level of integration and interdependence among the national economies. The co-ordination of these policies has been stimulated by the establishment of the European Monetary System, pegging the exchange rates of national currencies.

The impact of monetary policies on the national economy is the average of their impacts on the regional economies. Brancati points out in his contribution that the regional response to monetary policies may differ because the value of the money multipliers and the degree of imperfection of the markets vary among regions.

On the other hand, regional imbalances may affect the national macroeconomic objectives, not so much because of the financial cost of explicit regional policies, as because of the high cost of other economic and social policies, which imply important regional transfers of public funds. Moreover, the achievement of national macro-economic objectives is affected by the characteristics of the supply side of national economies. Clearly, for a thorough analysis of the supply side a regional breakdown is necessary. The cost of the lack of regional equilibrium is difficult to establish, and for the EC as a whole the impacts are not yet very clear. As monetary integration progresses, the cost aspect certainly deserves much more attention than it has been given so far.

9.3. Method and results

9.3.1. Problems of the analysis of the impact of EC policies

To assess the regional impact of the various Community policies is no easy task, that much has become evident from the previous chapters. The researcher undertaking it faces four major difficulties.

The first is the variety of policies. In the present book we have refrained from criticising EC policies, taking them at their face value. However, any observer of the EC must be aware of the complexity of its policy-making machinery, due partly to the constant changes the EC goes through on its way to closer integration, and partly to compartmentalisation and sectoralisation. As a consequence, some EC policies are pursued with much more intensity than others. The importance attached to agriculture is reflected in the amount of money put into it, that of trade in the number of instruments the EC has available for it; that the EC is far less involved in macro and monetary matters can be deduced from the limited budget and the absence of instruments of any consequence.

The second problem is one of instruments. In policy fields where integration has not yet progressed much, the European Commission has only indirect instruments at its disposal, such as the co-ordination of national policies; it is then very difficult to dissociate the influence of national and EC policies. When directives for common action are adopted as a step towards further integration, the choice of instruments to attain the common objectives is still left to the member states, and the problems remain. Even at the next higher degree of integration, where common European laws (regulations) operate, the researcher finds himself at a loss owing to the poor specification of the policy instruments. Only where the EC operates its own financial instruments can one hope to reach solid ground, for the effects of investments have been analysed so often in national or regional frameworks that a transposition to the European level must be possible. Yet even this apparently solid ground may turn out to be quicksand, as many EC subsidies are given to member-state programmes which might have been carried out anyway, the EC money being used to relieve the exchequer in quite unrelated fields of government activity.

The researcher's life is not made any easier by his inadequate knowledge of the interaction among the economic systems of the Community, the countries and the regions, and of the way in which the policies he is studying influence (parts of) these systems; it is the third problem he faces. In point of fact, policy seem to have done no more than slightly bend the course which events would have taken anyway. And even when the course was policy-induced rather than autonomous, the effects remain very hard to trace correctly. Actors who are directly or indirectly influenced are ill defined; the micro aspects of their reactions are little known, etc. No wonder, then, that analysts of the impact of policies on regions tend to limit themselves to a simple top-down approach via the most obvious variables in the system, assuming certain reactions which have at best been estimated in a partial and macro setting.

A final complicating factor is the poor data situation. Admittedly, to complain about the lack of data is usual among those involved in empirical studies. Still we believe the complaint is warranted for the present study, which necessitates an extraordinary amount of data because of its wide scope (all European regions) and changing focus (on alternate aspects of the system), whereas the supply is scarcer than on the national level. National statistics (if available at all) can be used only in part and as second best, because they are only partly homogenised on the European level, many inconsistencies and insufficiencies persisting among them.

9.3.2. A wide diversity of methods

Surveying the chapters of this book, we observe a wide variety in methods applied, as well as in the extent to which they take account of direct and indirect effects. Let us briefly review the salient features of the methods used in the partial analyses.

The method used in the RICAP study described by Strijker and de Veer, to study the impact of support to agricultural prices, proceeds essentially through three stages: (1) calculating the difference between the price on the world market and the protected price on the EC market; (2) establishing the regional product mix as compared to the EC mix; (3) multiplying (1) and (2) to calculate the index of nominal protection. If the index is higher than the EC average, the region is said to have benefited more than others from the CAP; if the index is lower than the EC average, the region has experienced a relatively negative impact of the CAP. As far as the investments of the Guidance section of the Agricultural Fund are concerned, the impact analysis ends with the calculation of each region's share of the cake. No further comprehensive study has been made of the influence of either the price support or the investment support on the structure of regional activity in Europe.

The impact of industrial policy has been studied by many along the three stages generally used in shift-share analysis: (1) identification of the sectors of industry likely to experience a severe downturn (or upturn) in activity; (2) establishment of the present location patterns of these sectors; (3) calculation of the impact on total industrial activity in the various regional economies. Regions with a particularly negative combination of elements 1 and 2 are observed to experience a negative policy impact; others with a good combination are supposed to be positively influenced. The shift-share method is known to have considerable drawbacks. To circumvent some of them, Molle has proposed to use the FLEUR (Factors of Location in Europe) model, which takes interregional and interindustrial influences into account, and can be used for prospective purposes. Unfortunately, resource constraints have so far prevented the model's application to the impact of industrial policy.

A major objective of EC energy policy is to make the economy less vulnerable to supply disturbances. The appropriate instrument is to stimulate investment in flexible (infra)structures for energy provision. The most vulnerable regions have been identified with the help of simple indicators of dependence on imports. A second aspect of energy policy is the trend to let EC prices follow the world market. The effect of changes in the energy price on regions has been assessed by identifying the regions accommodating the marginal production units of the largest energy sub-sectors. The indirect effects of energy investments and disinvestments have not been analysed, although Bourgeois is aware of this and proposes a theoretically more satisfactory approach.

The analysis of the impact of transport and telecommunication policy comes up against the old problem that transport and communication are necessary but not sufficient conditions for regional development. From the results of national approaches, Gillespie and Fullerton have tried to deduce, without recourse to any rigourous methodology, what effect the restricted EC policy instruments could have on European regions.

The vague objectives of EC social policy and its close intertwining with national policy have led Steinle to the conclusion that its impact can hardly be measured and that attempts at any formal methodology are useless.

The analysis of the impact of <u>trade policy,</u> on the contrary, can benefit from a toolbox developed on the national level. Broecker and Peschel have tried out, for Germany and Scandinavia, an elaborate model measuring the static regional effects of integration (different trade patterns due to different tariff protection levels suggest that the distance protection for an activity at one location decreases less than that for the same activity elsewhere). Elaborate though it may be, the approach is limited to static effects and neglects the secondary interindustry and income effects.

<u>Macro and monetary policy</u> has not developed enough in the EC for its regional impact to be assessed. Nevertheless, Brancati, applying a model for credit rationing to Italy, shows that the influence of specific elements of monetary policy on regions can very well be estimated.

9.3.3. Review of regional effects

Efforts have been made, in the chapters of this book, to give evidence of the impact policy measures may have on the regions of Europe. In any single region, the impact can be positive for one policy area and negative for another. It would be interesting to aggregate the results of the analyses into one picture reproducing total effects of all policy measures. Unfortunately, the complexities described earlier make it difficult to detect common features in the way EC policies work out, and in particular in the way they influence the regional equilibrium. Nevertheless, in retrospect, the authors show a degree of consensus as to the need to take account of (1) the structural effects of policy in the regions, and (2) the multiplier effects of investments. So we may try to evaluate the effects on those two scores for sets of regions.

In 'structural' terms, all contributors tend to appreciate policy instruments directly by their success in enhancing the competitiveness of regional activities, and hence the sectoral level of activity in each region. That applies not only to infrastructural developments, such as transport and communication (differential cost reduction), but also to the training programmes of social policy, the decrease or increase of protection in trade policy, the security of energy provision, the availability of research centres, the subsidies for restructuring old sectors in industrial policy, and credit rationing in monetary policy. Even the income-support mechanisms of agricultural price guarantees can be judged in that way. After the appreciation of partial effects by sector-specific methods, the total effect of all the different policies in one specific region can in principle be established from the total change in that region's activity levels, with, for instance, value added or employment serving as numerator.

Some contributors have followed the second avenue of analysis, studying the effects of <u>investment outlay</u>. Total investment in the regions is easy to calculate (ECU serving as numerator) by attributing all investments to specific regions and adding them up. Similarly, the total effects of investments in different sectors (energy, transport) can be calculated by adding up the effects on all sectors.

Both the structural and the investment approach take only direct effects into account. Indirect (interindustrial and income) effects can in principle be calculated, by well known methods, once information is available on the interregional input-output relations of the system of European regions.

The chapters on EC policy areas provide only fairly aggregate indications of types of regions; none gives a full list of the effects in all European regions. Adding up effects is therefore not possible. Moreover, the groups of regions distinguished are not always identical.

We have nevertheless made an effort to distil some indication of the total regional effects of policy measures. To that end we have first made a division between the North and the South (N/S), in view of the general welfare difference in Europe, and next considered the effects of different policies in the usual four types of region: metropolitan, intermediate, agricultural/peripheral, and old industrialised. By putting scores of - negative, 0 neutral, or + positive influence against each of the policies investigated, the following table has been composed (not without some arbitrariness).

Table 9.1
Schematic view of impacts by policy area and type of region

Effect Policy area	Metro- politan N S		Inter- mediate N S		Agri/ periph. N S		Old in- dustrial N S	
Agriculture	0	0	+	0	0	-	0	0
Industry	-	0	+	+	0	0	-	-
Energy	0	-	0	-	-	-	0	0
Transport/Telecommunication	+	0	+	-	0	-	0	0
Social and Employment	?	?	?	?	?	?	?	?
Trade	0	0	0	0	0	0	0	0
Macro and Monetary	+	0	+	0	0	-	0	0

Two major conclusions are warranted.

First, that Community policies often have contradictory effects, and that the weights of the scores in each policy field should be carefully analysed before any generalisation is made.

Second, that the combination of scores tends to accumulate more positive (intermediate north or negative points for some regions than for others, negative points accruing in particular to the problem regions of long standing in Southern Europe. Thus, the urgency attached by the EC to the analysis of policy impacts on regional equilibrium seems warranted.

Given the limited character of the analysis, a word of caution and a plea for more insight seem to complete this section appropriately.

9.4. Regional policies and regional effects of other policies in the European Community

9.4.1. Three approaches

From the analyses presented in the various chapters of this book, the regional imbalances in Europe threaten to deteriorate unless other than regional policies are bent to regional objectives, or, should that be impossible, regions are compensated for the losses they incur for the whole EC to gather the welfare gains from progressive integration.

Chapter 1 indicated that the problem this book has taken up is only part of the much more complicated question of co-ordinating the objectives and instruments of policy.

Briefly reviewing the theoretical foundations of regional policy making, we have identified a neo-classical, a Keynesian (or redistributive) and an endogenous-growth approach. Taking up the arguments wielded by the 'Keynesian' and 'endog-enous-growth' schools, we shall see how the problem of policy co-ordination changes with the approach chosen. We will also consider a third approach, which seems typical of Europe in the course of integration, and which we will call the compensation approach. By our discussion, we hope to give some guidance to fu-ture efforts to co-ordinate European policies with regional objectives.

9.4.2. The redistributive approach

In a 'redistributive approach', the aim of regional policy, like that of social policy, is to achieve a more equal distribution of income and welfare among the regions. However, while social policies addressed themselves to specific disadvan-taged individuals or social groups, regional policies are meant to benefit the entire population of less developed regions, with a standard of living far below the nat-ional or Community average. Moreover, while social policies aim to redistribute public services and income transfers among the population, the main object of re-gional policies is to relocate production to redistribute the employment opportu-nities among the regions.

Regional policies may be based on the less developed regions' right to a more equitable income or employment distribution, or on feelings of solidarity on the part of the more developed regions, or again, be justified by the need to preserve social consensus among the regions and social groups within the nations and within the European Community. Actually, the motives behind the redistributive ap-proach to regional policy are political, since too wide regional disparities could endanger the political integrity of the individual countries and of the European Community. Regional policy measures may prevent local communities from sup-porting separatist movements within national states, and some countries from withdrawing from, or boycotting, the policies pursued by the European Commu-nity.

For a redistributive regional policy to be successfully conduced, indicators have to be specified by which to measure regional disparities. Likely indicators are: per capita income at current exchange rates, per capita income at purchasing-power parities, the unemployment rate, the migration rate, or some complex in-dicator representing the weighted sum of individual indicators. The measurement of regional disparities may vary a lot with the indicator used. Moreover, to iden-tify the regions eligible for intervention, policymakers have to set threshold levels for the indicators. Finally, the indicators should be used to establish a key for the redistribution of financial resources among the individual regions.

In a redistributive approach, the level and growth rate of national income is usually assumed fixed, the only aim of regional and social policies being to to change distribution in favour of the less prosperous regions and social groups. The problem becomes more complex when, on the supply side, the level of aggregate income is affected by the location of production. On the demand side, regional policy may moreover require increased public expenditure, a claim that may clash with such macro-economic objectives as the reduction of public deficits, or lower inflation rates, or lower balance-of-payment deficits. In such cases a conflict ari-ses between aggregate efficiency and distributive equity. Attempts to solve it by first concentrating production and then redistributing income to the less devel-oped region with the help of taxes and transfers are bound to fail, for such a two-stage procedure would only aggravate the differences among the regions. So, in practice, the procedure usually adopted in regional policy is the pragmatic one of working gradually towards a compromise, accepting some loss of economic growth and macroeconomic stability. The final result depends on the constantly changing view taken of regional disparities, and on the bargaining power of the regions.

9.4.3. Compensation approach

The 'compensation approach' provides a more rigorous economic foundation for a type of regional policy closely associated with the specific characteristics of an 'economic union', such as the European Community. By their very membership, all countries and all regions transfer of their autonomy to use instruments of economic policy to supranational institutions. Denied the free use of custom tariffs, exchange-rate policies or national export subsidies, regional and national governments find it harder to achieve certain objectives of economic policy. The national or local policy instruments lost should be compensated for by new ones which the European Community can operate in favour of less developed regions or countries.

The 'compensation approach', unlike the 'redistributive approach', starts from the assumption that the regional policy of European institutions can mobilise resources to compensate exactly the opportunity cost ensuing from the loss of policy instruments previously available. In other words, regions or countries should be compensated, by specific measures of regional policy, for what new policy measures of the Community cost them. By this approach, Community regional policy is a necessary condition for nations' participation in the Community and for their consensus on the adoption of new Community measures in various fields, such as agricultural, industrial, commercial or exchange-rate policy measures. The impact on regional economies should be evaluated, and measures of regional policy taken to grant compensation to regions or countries suffering losses.

The compensation approach is difficult and complicated to realise, the main problem being how to disentangle the effects of individual simultaneous measures of economic policy and separate them from other exogenous economic shocks. While in the 'redistributive approach' the resources to be allocated to regional policy could correspond to measurable disparities in standards of living, in the 'compensation approach' several forecasts have to be elaborated, subject to different hypotheses of policy intervention. In general, EC regional policy has sprung from the need to compensate the United Kingdom for potential losses on other scores. More specifically, the European regional programmes VALOREN, STRIDE, STAR, etc. discussed in the previous chapters, are all of them clearly inspired by the idea of compensation. Actually, the compensation is allotted to the very sector which has hatched the regional problem. For instance, if the energy situation has aggravated the regional problem, then a programme for energy is drawn up.

9.4.4. Endogenous-growth approach

A third approach to regional policy is the 'endogenous-growth approach', in which the objectives of regional policy are: (a) full employment of local resources, and (b) increase of their productivity. Regional resources, such as the labour force, local know-how, local sectoral specialisation, local social structure, urban and natural environment, are localised in space, and partly fixed. Regional policy-making consists in the selection of the most efficient allocation of these resources to different productive sectors, and the promotion of technological progress, increasing the competitiveness of regional production. Not the disparities in certain indicators of the standard of living are the main indicators of a 'problem region', but the 'disequilibrated' or 'unbalanced' use of local resources in the various regions. In that train of thought, regional differences in the unemployment rate and in the productivity of local resources can be explained from unflexible prices, preventing an equilibrium between factor supply and factor demand from establishing itself, and from obstacles to the interregional mobility of resources preventing the establishment of an equilibrium between their overall national supply and national demand. The disequilibrium in the allocation of regional resources indicates inefficiency and the waste of development potentials.

In the 'endogenous approach' to regional policy, measures promoting a greater interregional mobility of capital and other factors rate lower than measures promoting the efficient use of labour and other local resources. However, the two strategies are not contradictory and even to some extent complementary. In particular, the pace of development is the result not only of a region's locational advantages for new firms over other regions, but also of the local entrepreneurial capability to exploit these advantages. Mobile factors, such as capital, are not even crucial if they can easily be attracted by profitable initiatives developed in a region. Therefore, regional policy should try to influence not only the supply of productive factors but also their demand by firms and sectors, by dint of measures guiding the interregional flows.

How effective regional policy is, depends on the capacity to maximise regional product by increasing employment and raising productivity levels rather than on the levelling of disparities in the standard of living. While the 'redistributive approach' features a 'top-down' procedure to determine regional income, the 'endogenous growth approach' implies a 'bottom-up' procedure for the analysis of national product, taken as the sum of regional products.

9.4.5. Co-ordination of Community, national and regional policies

Obviously, regional growth may be adversely affected by specific national or Community policies, hence the 'compensation approach' to regional policy. A conflict may arise between them and regional policy. The 'endogenous approach' makes no clear distinction among the domains of these different policies; indeed, in this view regional policy should define the spatial framework for sectoral policies, or co-ordinate their implementation in particular regions. Regional policies take the specific characteristics of each regional economy into account, and may promote the synergy of decentralised sectoral policies.

A feature peculiar to the 'endogenous-growth' approach is that, unlike in the 'redistributive' and 'compensation' approaches, regional policy is formulated and carried not only by national and Community institutions but also by regional institutions. Regional policy-making is closely related to 'regionalism' and to regional decentralisation and autonomy. It should therefore concern not only a few 'problem regions' but all the regions of the member states and of the European Community. Regional programmes should be elaborated for all regions, and the measures to be carried out by regional, national and Community institutions made consistent and co-ordinated.

According to the idea of 'endogenous growth', there are two reasons why the European Community should issue measures of regional policy and supplement the efforts of regional and national institutions. In the first place, national and European economic growth depends on the efficient use of regional resources. To promote regional growth, Community intervention should be directed in particular to the more mobile production factors. A shortage of capital, technology and entrepreneurial ability could block a region's exploitation of its fixed local resources; by its policy, the Community can encourage the transfer of these factors from the more developed to the more backward regions, thus improving the latter's access to them. In the second place, regional economies are highly interdependent; regional and sectoral policies should be co-ordinated to prevent conflicting and inefficient implementation. From numerous studies, the economic growth of the less developed regions may be slowed down by cumulative processes, because they may be unable to sustain increased international competition, lose crucial factors to other regions, be excluded from new production prospects owing to the concentration of power, information, and service and research activities.

Each approach to regional policy emphasises a particular type of relation between regional and other national and Community policies. Figure 9.1, earlier presented in chapter 1, can be used to illustrate the differences in interdependence of objectives and instruments in the three approaches.

		Policy objectives	
		Community and national	Regional
Policy instruments	Community and national	A	B
	Regional	C	D

Figure 9.1
The interdependence of regional and Community policies

The 'redistributive' approach implies a clear separation between the objectives of national policies and those of regional policy. It also seems to suggest a clear separation between the instruments of regional policy and those of national and Community policies. Therefore, this approach only considers the cases A and D of the figure. Actually, from the redistributive standpoint, the instruments of national and Community policies, being 'Pareto-neutral' to distribution, have no appreciable effects on the objectives of regional policy (case B), nor do regional-policy instruments, which only aim to redistribute economic activities, affect the absolute level of economic activity or the objectives of national and Community policies (case D).

In a 'compensation approach' to regional policies, on the contrary, national and Community policy instruments may affect regional objectives (case B). It implies priority of national or Community objectives before those of regional policy, which only play the role of social buffer. It also seems to overlook the possibility of negative (or positive) feedback effects of regional policy to national and Community objectives (case C).

The 'endogenous-growth' approach to regional policy seems more general than the redistributive and compensation approaches, as it underlines the positive (or negative) relations between instruments of regional policy and national and Community objectives (case C), while the other two seem to recognise only a conflictual relationship between regional policy and national and Community policies. The 'endogenous-growth' approach requires an explicit analysis of all the regional, national and international factors which determine the process of regional growth, including the effects of national and Community policies on the objectives of regional policy (case B) and the constraints which these policies impose on the effectiveness of regional-policy instruments (case D).

9.5. Outlook

9.5.1. A new environment

The turn in the macroeconomic cycle which marks the second half of the 1980s and is supposed to last through the coming years in most western economies, may have profound implications for regional policies. The remarkable decrease of inflation rates, the recovery of industrial production and productivity, the drop in energy prices, the rising investment levels, the increase in world trade, the growing perception of the need for new policies to bring down the high rates of structural unemployment, the increased social consensus on measures of effective environmental protection, the progressive internationalisation of firms, the diffusion of new technological paradigms, call for a change in the objectives and instruments of macroeconomic and sectoral policies. The new scenario defines new opportunities for, and new constraints on, regional policy, and a changing need for co-ordination between policies.

Monetarist macroeconomic theories and policies cannot explain and remedy unemployment. On the other hand, Keynesian 'fine tuning' policies have proved unable to control the short-term evolution of macroeconomic variables, and stabler macroeconomic policies seem to be called for. Macroeconomic policies may represent only a necessary and not a sufficient condition for a positive evolution of the economy. In fact, a non-inflationary growth of production and employment seems to require not only expansionary macroeconomic policies, but also, and especially, an increase of productivity.

The finances of the <u>Common Agricultural Policy</u> have gone so clearly out of hand, and the negative results of this policy for third countries, consumers and tax payers have become so obvious, that a major change is now needed. It will not only undo some redistribution of wealth towards more developed regions, but may also negatively affect certain less developed areas. A major overhaul is needed to find a new way of compensating the less favoured regions, either through the CAP, or preferably through measures of regional policy.

The <u>industrial restructuring</u> of national economies, helped by industrial policy and a faster diffusion of innovations may play a crucial role. Product and process innovations are closely related, as new products require the development of new production techniques to insure a lasting competitive advantage. On the other hand, new products and the general conversion of local economies toward new sectors may be favoured by the recovery of world demand, and are extremely important because they stimulate job creation and make for lower unemployment levels. Regional policy may speed up the diffusion of modern technology. The adoption of innovations is negatively affected by specific local obstacles. The horizontal diffusion of new techniques indicates that the spatial contiguity of firms belonging to different sectors may lead to positive synergies. Drastic changes from traditional production may be necessary in some regions. Therefore, strategies of regional development should carefully combine measures supporting local firms with measures encouraging entrepreneurship external to the regions in question, to promote a better technological co-operation between local and external firms.

After the dismaying results of direct controls, indirect policies such as <u>infrastructure policy</u> seem to gain new support, inadequate public services representing a serious obstacle to new private initiatives. Clearly, the infrastructure needed for new kinds of production are rather different from traditional transport infrastructure. The development of service activities requires public investment in telecommunication. Investments in higher education and research centres are needed to increase the productivity of the labour force and to support the increase of technical know-how, a local resource that is even more important than capital stock.

Most new sectors require an urban location to profit from agglomeration economies. Greater emphasis should therefore be laid on the analysis of the changing nature of the <u>urban system,</u> and to the design of appropriate urban policies within regions. The concentration of important development projects in urban areas is justified not only because most of these areas have suffered from the diffusion of industrial production to rural areas, but also because they provide the modern services which are used by firms and population of the more peripheral areas.

The economic recovery of industrialised countries and the positive effects of lower oil prices on the balance of payments relieve the pressure toward protectionist measures and allow an expansion of world trade. Further integration of national economies depends on the progressive internationalisation of the activities of national forms, a process undoubtedly promoted by the remarkable progress in communications and the removal of other institutional barriers. This process heralds important changes in the international division of employment; on the other hand, its continuation calls for more co-ordination among national industrial policies to prevent overproduction in specific sectors. Appropriate measures should be designed to promote the conversion of sectors and regions adversely affected by the increasing international competition.

Regional policies within the European Community should favour the further diffusion of modern productions from the more developed to the less developed regions of the Community, to compensate the gradual decentralisation of traditional production from the latter regions to less developed countries. Instead of advocating new import controls, regional exports should be promoted by improving the quality of local productions and the marketing organisation of local firms on new foreign markets.

The economic crisis and the restrictive macroeconomic policies which characterised the 1970s have provoked the crisis of the 'welfare state', compelling national governments to cut down on the resources allotted to social policy as well as on financial transfers to local governments. In reverse, the economic recovery of the 1980s may allow new programmes to be drawn up, programmes to improve the quality of the natural and urban environment and protect the social groups suffering the negative effects of economic restructuring. More money invested in environmental protection may prevent natural calamities, improve the health of the population, attract new residents to certain areas, and permit the conversion of local economies to technologically advanced new productions.

One great problem of European policy makers how to construct the Monetary Union gradually without disturbing the regional equilibrium. Ways will have to be found to assist countries that can no longer have recourse to exchange-rate changes in their adjustment to the new circumstances, and to improve the efficiency of capital markets (and thus reduce the cost of capital for entrepreneurs in regions which up till now have remained in a backward situation).

9.5.2. Challenges for the future

The complex relations among regional and Community policies have changed in the last few decades with the evolution not only of regional policy, but also of the policy of European integration. Since the foundation of the Common Market, the European Community has tried, on the one hand, to regulate the markets of various products through commercial and industrial policies, and, on the other, to to safeguard macroeconomic stability through co-ordinated macroeconomic and exchange-rate policies. The principle aim of these policies is to remove obstacles standing in the way of the free international exchange of industrial and agricultural products. According to traditional neoclassical economic theory, greater commercial flows must in the long run lead to greater efficiency, more national income and greater prosperity among consumers. The final result of the abolition of custom tariffs, stable exchange rates and other co-ordinated macroeconomic and sectoral policy measures was evaluated on the national aggregate level, their regional impact being considered less important. In fact, regional problems used to be considered important only as far as they might slow down the realisation of the Common Market of agricultural and industrial goods.

In the last few decades, the policy spectrum of the European Community has gradually broadened, a tendency that is expected to continue in the near future. While previous policies were concerned only with the free international trade of goods, those recently adopted also promote the international mobility of services and production factors, such as capital, labour, technology and entrepreneurship. Thus, the traditional distinction between national and regional economies, based on the immobility of factors among national economies, has become blurred.

The transformation of the Common Market into an economic and political union, namely, the European Union, requires the adoption of policies that directly affect the allocation of economic resources and explicitly aim to foster economic growth. Such 'supply-side' policies are clearly different from the macroeconomic and commercial policies, which have only an indirect effect on the growth of the European economies. The European Monetary System and the close co-ordination on international monetary problems, the free movement of long-term capital, the development of structural funds for the agricultural, social and regional policies, the European programmes for the development of research in various areas, the increasing harmonisation of fiscal and legal regulations and education curricula, the development of an European environment policy, the reform of the European political institutions and the Community budget, the increasing co-ordination of defense and foreign policies, are all examples of the new type of European policy. Admittedly, the development of a European policy has been far from homogeneous. But the new policies are definitely changing the framework within which regional policies should be elaborated and implemented. Structural policies must be integrated with regional policies because their objective is the same: to make the European ecnomies more dynamic and more efficient.

During the 1970s, scarce economic resources and the need to promote a fast increase of productivity supported the diffusion of 'neo-conservative' ideologies and radical policy strategies, pleading both deregulation, or greater freedom for business, and the centralisation or abolishment of economic and social pro- grammes run by local governments. The new trends in the economy and the com- plexity of the problems may lead to a more pragmatic design of the institutional framework of economic policy. Administrative decentralisation and the existence of regional policital institutions may facilitate the relation between public institu- tions and private interests, and lighten the burden on national governments. Direct relations among all 'layers' of administration including those between the EC and local authorities, could help to get tasks done more efficiently.

The need for more efficient public programmes is certainly recognised more than it used to, but a clear division between public and private roles may not be the best solution. Private firms may contribute to important public projects in new fields on the urban and regional levels, where private investments may return adequate profits in the medium term. Moreover, the size of the investments re- quired may necessitate a close partnership between numerous private and public institutions. Major projects are so complex that they cannot be realised without the planning and entrepreneurship of regional governments.

In the past, the regional policy of the European Community has been severely hampered by the fact that it can only complement national measures of regional policy. The autonomous projects of the Community are negligible and mostly merely demonstrative. A more autonomous Community regional policy would give European institutions a distinct role in the execution of regional strategies agreed upon with national governments.

As the present book has pointed out, not only a constant monitoring of regional effects of other, non-regional policies is necessary to avoid new disparities occur- ring, but also an innovative regional policy, permitting to maintain the cohesion which the Community needs to achieve its first objective, which is to improve the living conditions of all European citizens.

9.6. <u>Notes</u>
1. R. Cappellin is primarily responsible for section 9.4, W. Molle for section 9.3.